PREFACE

THE essays in this volume have as their central figures Queen Elizabeth and Shakespeare. They are further linked in that they deal with movements or institutions which had their beginning in Tudor or early Stuart times, as these are reflected in the literature of the period, especially in the drama.

As Elizabeth was so enthusiastic a patron of the theatre it has seemed appropriate to trace her presentation in our drama from her own day to ours. This essay is a considerably expanded form of the Elizabeth Howland lecture commemorating the Queen's accession date, given in 1948 to the Streatham Antiquarian and Natural History and the Elizabethan Literary Societies. It is supplemented by an earlier Howland lecture in 1937 on the Queen and Edmund Tilney, buried at Streatham, who was Master of the Revels during the greatest period of Elizabethan drama.

The general outline of 'Shakespeare's Reading' was given at the Stratford-on-Avon Festival in August, 1948. A more specialised aspect of this, the dramatist's treatment of Classical Legend and History, was the subject of the Annual Shakespeare Lectures to the British Academy in 1943. Shakespeare was among the Elizabethan poets and playwrights whose debt to Ovid I discussed before the English Association and the London Branch of the Classical Association in 1947.

In commemorating in 1945 the 400th anniversary of Sir Thomas Bodley's birth before the Royal Society of Literature I pointed out how, by a paradoxical chance, his library has become one of the chief store-houses of the playbooks of which he thought so poorly. What a contrast is Lamb's enthusiasm for them, illustrated in a paper read to the Charles Lamb Society and printed in the English Association's *Essays and Studies*, vol. XXIX.

The scene shifts to wider and more active issues, as I traced the presentation of the soldier by playwrights through more than three centuries, in the Giff Edmonds lecture to the Royal Society of Literature (1942); and the reflection of American scenes in English

Literature from John Rastell to Mr. Churchill in my Presidential Address to the English Association (1944).

Queen Elizabeth in Drama and *Aspects of Shakespeare's Reading* have not previously been published. I have to make my acknowledgements to the Societies named above and to the Clarendon and Oxford University Presses for leave to reprint the other essays, with minor adjustments. I have also to thank Miss Clemence Dane for allowing me to make quotations from her *Will Shakespeare* and *The Lion and the Unicorn,* and Mr. Nevill Coghill from *The Masque of Hope.*

F.S.B.

CONTENTS

ONE

QUEEN ELIZABETH IN ELIZABETHAN AND LATER DRAMA

THIS essay deals with Elizabeth, Princess and Queen, as presented in Drama, old and new, but for a reason that will soon appear, I am beginning with a non-dramatic extract. It is part of the description by Edward Halle in his Chronicle of the christening of the infant princess Elizabeth on 10th September 1533 in the Church of the Greyfriars at Greenwich.

The old Duchess of Norfolk bore the child in a mantle of purple velvet with a long train furred with ermine. The Duke of Norfolk with his Marshal's rod went on the right hand of the said Duchess, and the Duke of Suffolk on the left hand. . . . . When the child was come to the Church door, the Bishop of London met it, with divers bishops and abbots mitred, and began the observances of the sacrament. The godfather was the Lord Archbishop of Canterbury; the godmothers were the old Duchess of Norfolk and the old Marchioness of Dorset, widows; and the child was named ELIZABETH. And after that all things were done at the Church door the child was brought to the font and christened, and this done, Garter, chief King of Arms, cried aloud: 'God of his infinite goodness send prosperous life and long to the high and mighty Princess of England, ELIZABETH.' And then the trumpets blew.

I have quoted this passage because in Holinshed's adaptation it was the source of the final scene of the play, *King Henry VIII*, in which the christening of Elizabeth is dramatically presented. The play was acted in 1613 and at one of the performances on 29th June of that year the Globe Theatre was burnt down. It was included in the Shakespeare first folio (1623), but internal metrical evidence has convinced most of its readers, including myself, that

9

Fletcher's hand is also found in it, and that the christening scene is to be assigned to him.

The elaborate stage-direction before the scene reproduces most of the details in the Chronicle, though the palace is substituted for the church and the Bishop of London is eliminated. The dialogue begins with Garter King-at-Arms re-echoing with minor variants the words quoted above from the Chronicle. Then the King enters and the Archbishop, kneeling before him, prays that

> All comfort, joy, in this most gracious lady
> Heaven ever laid up to make parents happy,
> May hourly fall upon ye.

To Henry's question, 'What is her name?' Cranmer answers 'Elizabeth'. Whereupon the King kisses her and cries:

> With this kiss take my blessing: God protect thee!
> Into whose hands I give thy life.

Then Cranmer, safely prophesying in 1613 after the fulfilment of his auguries, declares:

> This royal infant—Heaven still move about her!—
> Though in her cradle, yet now promises
> Upon this land a thousand thousand blessings,
> Which time shall bring to ripeness: she shall be—
> But few now living can behold that goodness—
> A pattern to all princes living with her,
> And all that shall succeed: . . . . .
>   truth shall nurse her
> Holy and heavenly thoughts still counsel her—
> She shall be loved and fear'd; her own shall bless her;
> Her foes shake like a field of beaten corn,
> And hang their heads with sorrow; good grows with her;
> In her days every man shall eat in safety
> Under his own vine what he plants; and sing
> The merry songs of peace to all his neighbours:
> God shall be truly known: and those about her
> From her shall read the perfect ways of honour,
> And by those claim their greatness, not by blood.

Of course, even in the golden days of Elizabeth's reign, all was not as sunny as in this picture, but the dramatist in 1613 was not thinking only of her but of her successor King James, whom he goes on to proclaim (very rashly, as we now know) a similar paragon:

Who from the sacred ashes of her honour
Shall star-like rise, as great in fame as she was.

After this *obligato* interlude (to be mocked by the event) in celebration of the reigning Stuart monarch, the Archbishop reverts to Elizabeth in her last years:

She shall be to the happiness of England
An aged princess; many days shall see her
And yet no day without a deed to crown it.
Would I had known no more; but she must die
She must, the Saints must have her; yet a virgin,
A most unspotted lily shall she pass
To the ground and all the world shall mourn her.

This famous scene from *Henry VIII* forms an appropriate introduction to my subject for it gives a bird's eye view of Elizabeth from her cradle to her grave, and beyond. The other dramas in which she appears, or in which there are allusions to her, deal with special phases or events of her career of seventy years. Of these the most detailed is the two Part play by Thomas Heywood, with the curious title *If You Know Not Me, You Know Nobody*. Heywood, born about 1574 and living till 1641, was during his long career one of the most versatile personages in a versatile age. Like Shakespeare he was both actor and dramatist, and in his dramatic canon are included historical and mythological, domestic and romantic plays. He also wrote extensively both in verse and prose.

Part I of *You Know Not Me* was published in 1605 by Nathaniel Butter, with the more informing sub-title, *The Troubles of Queen Elizabeth*. Even this is somewhat delusive for the 'troubles' are those not of Elizabeth as Queen, but as Princess before she came to the throne. Part I came into print in mangled form, for in an oft-quoted passage from a prologue to a revival of the play at the Cockpit, probably at a date between 1625 and 1632, Heywood complained that it had been taken down corruptly in shorthand during performance. He asserts that the play

> Did throng the Seates, the Boxes, and the Stage
> So much that some by Stenography drew
> The plot: put it in print (scarce one word trew):
> And in that lameness it hath limp't so long
> The Author now to vindicate that wrong
> Hath tooke the paines upright upon its feete
> To teach it walke, so please you sit, and see't.

At this revival therefore, Heywood appears to have had the play performed as he had written it. But the strange thing is that no less than six later editions of Part I appeared up to 1632 without any material alteration, followed by an arbitrarily revised last edition in 1639. I think that when he used the 'scarce one word trew', he was exaggerating, and in any case, whatever the deficiencies of the quarto version, it gives a graphic picture of Elizabeth in her troubles during her sister's reign.

The play opens when Mary has recently ascended the throne, when the conspiracy of Wyatt has been defeated, and when the arrival in England of Philip of Spain, to become the Queen's bridegroom is announced. At the instigation of Gardiner, Bishop of Winchester, whom Heywood portrays as Mary's evil genius, she suspects Elizabeth of having been a confederate with Wyatt, and sends Lords Thame and Chandos with a body of soldiers to bring her to London from Ashridge where she is lying ill. As an attendant gentleman declares,

> Her sleeps are all unquiet, and her head
> Beats and grows giddy with continual grief.

When Chandos insists on immediate admittance to the Princess, though it is during the night, there is the surprising stage-direction, 'Enter Elizabeth in her bed'. As J. P. Collier explains in his edition of the Two-Part play in 1851 for the Shakespeare Society, this means that 'the Princess, ill in her bed, was thrust out upon the stage, and the scene immediately supposed to be a bedroom'. She is attended by two doctors, and remonstrates with these unseasonable visitors.

We are not pleas'd with your intrusion, lords,
Is your haste such or your affairs so urgent
That suddenly, and at this time of night,
You press on me, and will not stay till morn?
Thame: Sorry we are, sweet lady, to behold you
   In this sad plight.
Eliz.:   And, I my lords, not glad.
   My heart oh how it beats!
Chan.:   Madam,
   Our message and our duty from our Queen
   We come to tender you. It is her pleasure
   That you, the seventh day of this month, appear
   At Westminster.
Eliz.: At Westminster? My lords, no soul more glad than I
   To do my duty to her Majesty:
   But I am sorry[1] at the heart—My heart!
   Good doctor, raise me. O my heart! I hope, my lords,
   Considering my extremity and weakness,
   You will dispense a little with your haste.

Thame and Chandos then ask the doctors if Elizabeth can be removed without danger to her life, and their answer is 'not without danger, lords, yet without death'.

Elizabeth than asks 'Well, must I go?' and Chandos answers 'So says the Queen', and the invalid acquiesces, 'Why, then it must be so.'

Thame: Tomorrow early, then you must prepare.
Eliz.: It is many a morrow since my feeble legs
   Felt this my body's weight—Oh I shall faint!
   And if I taste the rawness of the air,
   I am but dead; indeed I am but dead.

And then with truly royal consideration she gives orders for the comfort of her visitors, unwelcome as they are.

Conduct these lords into their chambers,
And cheer them well for they have journeyed far.

[1] sorry=ill.

Chandos then tells Elizabeth that the Queen has sent her litter for her:

Eliz.:   The Queen is kind, and we will strive with death
To tender her our life.
We are her subject, and obey her hest,
Good night; we wish you what we want[1]—good rest.

Meanwhile Mary and Phillip have become affianced and their wedding is fixed for 25th June. Philip, of whom Heywood gives a favourable representation, puts in a plea:

We want
One lady at this high solemnity:
We have a sister call'd Elizabeth
Whose virtues and endowments of the mind
Hath filled the ears of Spain.

Gardiner protests:

Great are the causes, now too long to say,
Why, she my sovereign, should be kept away.

Mary is told that Elizabeth has come but refuses her petition for an immediate interview. 'Let her attend[2]: we will find a time to hear her.' Again Philip puts in his plea:

But, royal Queen, yet for her virtues' sake
Deem her offences, if she have offended,
With all the lenity a sister can.

But Mary's only answer, even to her royal lover, is to appoint a commission, consisting of Gardiner, the Earl of Sussex, Lords Howard, Thame and Chandos, and the Constable of the Tower, to examine her of all supposed crimes—adding abruptly, 'So to our nuptials.'

When the Commissioners arrive and are seated, Elizabeth falls on her knees, but Sussex, who throughout is the most kindly disposed to her, will not have it:

Madam, although this place
Doth tie you to this reverence, it becomes not

---

[1] want=lack.
[2] attend=wait.

You, being a Princess, to deject your knee!
A chair there!

Eliz.:   My duty with my fortunes doth agree,
And to the Queen in you, I bend my knee.

Suss.:   You shall not kneel where Sussex sits in place.
The Chamber keeper! A chair there, for her Grace!

Gardiner begins the interrogation:

Madam,
I would you would submit unto her highness.

The Princess retorts indignantly:

Submit, my Lord of Winchester! tis fit
That none but base offenders should submit.
No, no, my Lord. I easily spy your drift:
Having nothing wherein you can accuse me,
Do seek to have myself myself betray:
So by myself my own blood should be spilt.
Confess submission, I confess a guilt.

Other Commissioners then question her concerning a connection with different rebels, Wyatt, Throgmorton, Carew, till she bursts out:

Ask the unborn infant: see what that will answer.
For that and I are both alike in guilt.
Let not by vigour innocent blood be spilt.

Gardiner sternly intervenes:

Come, Madam, answer briefly to these treasons.

Again, Elizabeth answers scornfully:

Treason, my Lord! It it be treason
To be the daughter to the eighth Henry,
Sister to Edward, and the next of blood
Unto my gracious sovereign, now the Queen,
I am a traitor; if not, I spit at treason.

The Constable of the Tower then speaks for the first time, in threatening tones:

The Queen must hear you sing another song,

Before you part with us.

Eliz.:   My God doth know
       I can no note but truth; that with heaven's King
       One day in choirs of angels I shall sing.

Gard.: Then, Madam, you will not submit?

Eliz.: My life, I will, but not as guilty.

The Commissioners go out to report to Mary and return with the grim announcement:

It is the pleasure of Her Majesty,
That you be straight committed to the Tower.

Elizabeth utters the anguished cry 'The Tower! for what?' Gardiner's only reply is to tell her that the Queen has discharged the Princess's household servants except a gentlewoman and her gentleman usher, Gage, and that she has appointed a hundred northern whitecoat soldiers to escort her next day to the Tower. Elizabeth cries beseechingly:

Oh God, my heart! a prisoner in the Tower!
Speak to the Queen, my lords, that some other place
May lodge her sister; that's too vile, too base.

And the kindly Sussex proposes that they should all join in a petition to the Queen that Elizabeth should be lodged elsewhere. But Gardiner declares that it would be in vain for the Queen's sentence is definite. Elizabeth again, as at Ashridge, has to bow to the inevitable.

Then to our chamber, comfortless and sad,
Tomorrow to the Tower—that fatal place,
Where I shall ne'er behold the sun's bright face.

Whatever may have been the deficiencies of the stenographer, I do not see how this scene between Elizabeth and the Commission could have been bettered. The proudly innocent bearing of the girl with her apt answers to her accusers, and the contrasted attitudes towards her of Gardiner and Sussex, are not below the level of some of Heywood's best work.

Elizabeth's persecutors do not spare her any humiliation. When the barge in which she is being ferried reaches the Tower she begs that she may not have to land at Traitor's Gate, and Sussex again pleads for her but in vain. In her perturbation she takes a false step and sets foot in the water, but it is all one to her.

No matter where I tread:
Would where I set my foot there lay my head.
Land traitor like? My foot's wet in the flood!
So shall my heart ere long be drenched in blood.

When she has landed Sussex calls for a chair for her but the Constable of the Tower sternly replies, 'Here's no chair for prisoners', and she has to sit on a cold stone in the rain, refusing the offer by Sussex of his cloak.

No, let it alone, see, gentlemen,
The piteous heavens weep tears into my bosom.

The Constable then coops her up in a cell without the privilege

Of any walk in garden, or to open
Her window's casements to receive the air.

He orders too that her meals shall be brought not by her servants but by soldiers whom her gentlemen usher dubs 'a company of base, untutor'd slaves'.[1]

But at the intercession of Sussex, backed in a dumbshow by Philip, the Queen releases her sister from the Tower, to be taken to Woodstock, the residence of the Lord of Thame, under the charge of Sir Henry Bedingfield, as harsh a guardian as the Constable. When on her journey he hears village bells being rung in her honour, he cries in fury:

Traitors & knaves! Ring bells!
When the Queen's enemy passeth through the town.
Go set the knaves by the heels!

But at long last Mary consents to receive her sister by night at Hampton Court, while Philip behind an arras listens to their conference. The Queen repeats Gardiner's question, 'Will you submit?' and Elizabeth answers as before:

[1] The Constable's latest successor in his office is Field Marshal Lord Wavell, who is also the President of the Royal Society of Literature. In moving a vote of thanks to him in that capacity, I expressed the hope that if any of the Council of the R.S.L. came under his jurisdiction as Constable he would deal more gently with them than his predecessor with Elizabeth.

My life, Madam, I will, but not as guilty.
                              Should I confess
Fault done by her that never did transgress?

*   *   *

Let your Grace
Exact all torture and imprisonment,
Whate'er my greatest enemies can devise,
And they all have done their worst, yet I
Will your true subject and true sister die.
Queen: You'll not submit, but end as you begin?
Eliz.:   Madam, to death I will, but not to sin.
Queen: You are not guilty then?
Eliz.:   I think I am not.
Queen: I am not of your mind.
Eliz.:   I would your highness were.

Then somewhat suddenly the Queen changes her tone.

Whate'er we think, arise and kiss our hand,
Say God hath raised you friends.

Philip steps from behind the arras with the cry:

And may the heavens applaud this unity!

Events then follow fast. Philip leaves for Spain. Gardiner and
Cardinal Pole die suddenly, and Mary herself is stricken with a
fatal illness. Sir Henry Carew is the first, riding post haste to
Hatfield, to salute the new sovereign, 'God save the Queen! God
save Elizabeth!' He is swiftly followed by others, both former
friends and foes. Finally comes the Lord Mayor, presenting from
the City of London a purse and Bible, for which Elizabeth expresses her gratitude with moving eloquence.

An English Bible. Thanks my good Lord Mayor.
You of our body and our soul have care,
This is the jewel that we still love best.
This was our solace when we were distressed.
This book that hath so long conceal'd itself,
So long shut up, so long hid, now lords, see

We here unclasp: for ever it is free.
Who looks for joy, let him this book adore:
This is true food for rich men and for poor.

Part II of the play followed a year after Part I, in 1606. It has as
sub-title, 'With the building of the Royal Exchange, and the
famous victorie of Queen Elizabeth in the year 1588.' Though it has
a longer and more accurate text than Part I it concerns us less for
during two thirds of the play the Queen does not appear, and the
central figure is the patriotic merchant, Sir Thomas Gresham, with
his scapegrace nephew John, and John's employer, the worthy
haberdasher, Old Hobson. Elizabeth makes her entrance when she
comes to open and name the great Burse erected in the City by
Gresham. There are present the imperial, French and Florentine
ambassadors whom she entertains and talks with, each in their
own language. As she is surveying the goodly frame of the Burse,
old Hobson runs in crying, 'God bless thy Grace, Queen Bess!'
The Queen asks, 'Friend, what are you?' and Hobson answers in
the words that give the play its title, 'Knowest thou not me,
Queen? Then thou knowest nobody.'

Bones a me, Queen; I am Hobson, and old Hobson.

In his humbler way he is as true a patriot as Gresham, whose
building Elizabeth now names with a trumpet call:

Proclaim through every high street of this City
This place to be no longer call'd a Burse
But since the building's stately, fair and strange,
Be it for ever call'd the Royal Exchange.

And she bids Gresham, kneeling before her, 'Arise Sir Thomas.'
   With the aid of a chorus the scene shifts to 1588, and to Tilbury
where Elizabeth is awaiting news of the progress of the sea-fight
with the Armada. One messenger follows another with successive
reports of victory. And last of all comes Drake with colours and
ensigns taken from the Spaniards. In the fourth edition of Part II
in 1633, this Armada episode was considerably expanded, but both
versions end with words applicable to this country's situation
to-day:

Towards London march we to a peaceful throne.
We wish no wars, yet we must guard our own.

Elizabeth had a special fascination for Heywood, for in another play, Part I of *The Fair Maid of the West,* he goes out of his way (so to speak) to glorify her. The Fair Maid is Bess Bridges, a tavern wench with whom Captain Spencer falls in love. When he is falsely reported killed in the island voyage to the Azores, she fits out a ship with a legacy he has left her, and goes in quest of his body. In the course of her adventures she comes to Fez where the King is captivated by her charms. When he hears that her name is Elizabeth he exclaims:

There's virtue in that name,
The virgin Queen so famous through the world,
The mighty empress of the maiden isle,
Whose predecessors have o'er run great France
Whose powerful hand doth still support the Dutch,
And keeps the potent King of Spain in awe,
Is not she titled so?
Bess: She is
King: Hath she herself a face so fair as yours?
Bess: You cast a blush upon my maiden cheek
To pattern me with her. Why England's Queen,
She is the only phoenix of her age,
The proudest glory of the Western Isles.

Finally, in 1631 Heywood wrote a prose account of *England's Elizabeth, from the Cradle to the Crown,* covering much of the same ground as Part I of *If you Know not Me.* It is remarkable that under James and Charles he should have been given so free a hand to extol the Queen who had signed the death warrant of their mother and grandmother, Mary, Queen of Scots.

One subject Heywood had left alone, Elizabeth's love or semi-love affairs. These could only be touched upon delicately under an allegorical veil. The relations between Elizabeth and Leicester are, I think, thus handled by John Lyly in two of his classical comedies, *Sapho and Phao* and *Endimion,* especially the latter. Cynthia was one of the names often poetically given to Elizabeth. Lyly reversing the classical story, represents Endimion as enamoured of

Cynthia, the moon goddess. For her he deserts his earthly mistress, Tellus, who in revenge has him charmed into a deep sleep from which he is awakened by a kiss from Cynthia. But he protests that this feeling for one so exalted cannot be called love.

Time was, Madam, is and ever shall be that I honoured your highness above all the world but to stretch it so far as to call it love, I never durst. There hath none pleased mine eye but Cynthia, none delighted mine ear but Cynthia, none possessed my heart but Cynthia. Such a difference hath the gods set between our states that all must be duty, loyalty and reverence, nothing (without it vouchsafe your highness) be termed love.

If Lyly under one mythological image pictured the bar that separated Elizabeth as queen from even the most highly favoured of her subjects, Shakespeare, as will be remembered, in another kindred image depicted her devotion, as a woman, to the virgin life. Oberon in *A Midsummer's Night's Dream* (II, 1.) tells Puck that he saw

Flying between the cold moon and the earth
Cupid all arm'd: a certain aim he took
At a fair vestal throned by the West,
And loosed his love-shaft smartly from his bow
As it should pierce a hundred thousand hearts.
But I might see young Cupid's fiery shaft
Quenched in the chaste beams of the watery moon,
And the imperial votaress passed on,
In maiden-meditation fancy free.

There is good reason to believe that *A Midsummer Night's Dream* was performed in honour of some great noble's wedding at which the Queen was present, and heard this tribute by Shakespeare. But if Shakespeare does not touch on any of Elizabeth's love affairs, he does in the Prologue to Act V of *King Henry V* mention the man, younger than Leicester, of whom it has been said that if she ever loved anyone it was he—the Earl of Essex. It was in 1599, and Essex was in Ireland in command against the Earl of Tyrone, and Shakespeare expected him to return home speedily amid popular acclaim.

Were now the general of our gracious Empress,
As in good time he may, from Ireland coming,
Bringing rebellion broached on his sword,
How many would the peaceful city quit,
To welcome him!

But Essex was unsuccessful and throwing up his command, returned home and fell into disgrace. With impulsive rashness in September 1599 he burst into the Queen's chamber in his riding habit, and found her with her hair about her face. In Ben Jonson's play, *Cynthia's Revels*, Cynthia, again representing Elizabeth, compares the punishment inflicted on Essex with that of Actæon who was torn by his hounds for looking upon Diana (Cynthia) unclothed. She claims that the punishment fitted the crime.

For so Actaem by presuming far
Did (to our grief) incur a fatal doom . . .
But are we therefore judged too extreme?
Seems it no crime to enter sacred bowers,
And hallowed places with impure aspect
Must lewdly to pollute?

The last lines seem to apply to Essex's escapade, to which the Oxford editors of Jonson would refer them, rather than to his abortive rising in the City in February, 1601, which was some months later than the play, and which led to his execution. If 'fatal doom' refers to this, the lines were added afterwards. However this may be, there is no doubt that Thomas Dekker in 1607 in his play *The Whore of Babylon*, where Elizabeth figures as Titania, is alluding to her reluctance to sign the Earl's doom when he puts into her mouth:

Must we then
Strike those whom we love? . . . .
Our hand was made to save, but not to kill. . . . .
How soon the blow is given!
Witness, so little we in blood delight,
That doing this work, we wish we could not write.

It is in this melting mood that we take leave of Elizabeth in contemporary drama. And it is a somewhat long leave, for it was not till 1681 that she made her reappearance on the English stage at Drury Lane in *The Unhappy Favourite, or The Earl of Essex* by *John Banks*. When the play opens Essex has returned against the Queen's orders from Ireland, and urged on by his enemies, Burleigh and Raleigh, she strips him of his offices and confines him to his house. When in desperation he heads the rising in the City, she condemns him to the Tower and to execution. But there is a constant conflict, expressed in a series of 'asides', between her duty as a sovereign and her love for the young Earl. Even to the last she trusts that he will send back her gift of a ring that will secure his pardon. But he has entrusted it to his discarded mistress, the Countess of Nottingham who keeps it back. When her treachery is revealed, Essex has already met his fate. As even Burleigh admits to the Queen.

At the block all hero he appeared,

*   *   *

Said little, but did bless your Majesty,
And died full of forgiveness to the world.

Banks, who had been a practitioner in heroic tragedy, carries much of the sentimentality and high-flown verbiage of that *genre* into this historical play. He sees in the fall of Essex a parallel to that of Sejanus and is prolific in classical allusions. He makes much of the feminine interest, in which Elizabeth has to compete with the vengeful Countess of Nottingham and the pathetic figure of the young wife whom Essex has secretly married. *The Unhappy Favourite* not only hit the taste of its own day but of many subsequent theatre-goers and readers. It was reissued thrice before 1700 and often afterwards till 1769, and was performed frequently between 1681 and 1752.

Banks was less successful in a later play in which Elizabeth again appeared, *The Island Queens or The Death of Mary, Queen of Scotland*. Completed in 1684 it was prohibited from performance by the Censor, whereupon Banks had it printed in self-defence. It was not however till March 1704 that through the good graces of Queen Anne it found its way to the boards of Dury Lane, in revised form, as *The Albion Queens*.

Its plot runs parallel in general outline to that of *The Unhappy Favourite*, Mary of Scotland being the counterpart of Essex in the earlier play. Elizabeth is torn between her feeling for her hapless 'sister' Queen and her duty to the State. With a reckless violation of historical truth Banks brings Mary to the English Court where Elizabeth transported by her charms embraces her, crying

> Throw thy lov'd arms as I do mine about thee,
> And never feel less joy than I do now. . . . .
> Witness ye Powers! take notice how I love her.

Mary responds in kind:

> O let me go!
> Give my wild joy some breath, some room to walk in;
> . . . . A thousand years of pain is not enough
> For this one moment of seraphic joy.

This is the flamboyant utterance of 'heroic tragedy' which finds voice also in the Duke of Norfolk's passionate love-speeches to Mary, for whose sake he goes to the block. But it is not till after the revelation of the Babington conspiracy, designed to kill Elizabeth and place Mary on the throne, that the Queen reacts against her rival. Even then it is only after Cecil and Davison have laid stress on the danger both to herself and her people that she bids Davison draw up the warrant for Mary's execution:

> Write, write, no matter how, if foul the better,
> Foul as the fact I am about to do.

And Restoration drama reaches a peak of sentimental extravagance in the stage-direction 'soft music ready with flutes' as Elizabeth signs the death-warrant.

A glorious chance was missed later in the eighteenth century. On 30th October 1779 Sheridan's *The Critic* was produced at Drury Lane. The enthusiastic Dangle and the cynical Sneer are watching the rehearsal of Puff's tragedy, *The Spanish Armada*. Dangle comments, 'I don't understand how you have contrived to introduce any love into it.'

Puff: Love! On nothing so easy: for it is a received point
           among poets that where history gives you a good

heroic outline for a play, you may fill up with a little love at your discretion; in doing which, nine times out of ten, you only make up a deficiency in the previous history of the times. Now I rather think that I have done this with some success.

Sneer: No scandal about Queen Elizabeth, I hope!

And what a comedy could the author of *The School for Scandal* have made out of the courtships of Queen Elizabeth! How well could we have spared for it such a tragedy as *Pizarro*. But Puff scouts the idea; 'O Lord! No. No. I only suppose the Governor of Tilbury Fort's daughter to be in love with the son of the Spanish admiral.'

Sneer: Is that all?
Dangle: Excellent i' faith! I see it at once. But won't that appear rather improbable?
Puff: To be sure it will, but what the plague! A play is not to show occurrences that happen every day, but things just **so** strange that though they never *did,* they *might* happen.

Almost a century was to pass before Puff's idea of filling up the historical outline with a little love was realized in a less fatuous way than in his tragedy. In May 1870, at the Queen's Theatre, Long Acre, was produced Tom Taylor's blank verse play, *Twixt Axe and Crown, or The Lady Elizabeth*. Suggested in part by a German drama it covers the same period and, broadly speaking, the same events as Part I of Heywood's play. But it differs from it in one radical aspect by introducing a sentimental theme, a love affair between the Princess and Edward Courtenay, Earl of Devonshire, who for her sake rejects the proffered hand of Queen Mary and becomes her champion. He even rides unbidden to Ashridge, and when Lords of the Council come there with a warrant for her arrest and conveyance to the Tower, he draws his sword in her defence. But Elizabeth shows herself a dutiful subject,

Render your weapon, Sir,
I need it not. As for the Council's warrant,

I charge my Lord of Devonshire to obey it
As I do. Look, my lords, I put myself
Upon your manhood to use needful kindness
To a sick woman. I will ride with you.

When the Princess and Courtenay are prisoners in the Tower, their enemies allow them to have a meeting in the hope that they will trap them into treasonable talk, but all they hear is an interchange of lovers' vows sealed by Elizabeth's gift of a ring.

Take thou this ring from me—'tis a pure opal
That changes with the faith of her that gives it.
If I thought I should change, I would not give thee
The tell-tale stone. But be true to thyself,
Fear not Elizabeth will be true to thee—
Aye, even to the scaffold.

And it is to the scaffold that her enemy Gardiner, incited further by Renard, the Spanish Ambassador, is bent on bringing her, if she remains in England. He offers her one chance of escape in marriage to the Duke of Savoy, and tells her, 'Tis the Queen's wish you entertain his suit.' The true voice of Elizabeth rings in her reply:

Say to the Queen: Imprisonment or freedom,
My life or death, I will take from her hand
Only *one* thing she shall not put on me—
That is a husband whom I have not chosen,
And a home out of England, that I'll none of.
Tell her I'd sooner hold six foot of England,
Though 'twere my grave, than a realm over sea.

And that wish for six foot of England is to be fulfilled that very night, if Gardiner has his way, for he returns with a warrant for her instant execution, signed by the Council but not by the Queen. But the Lieutenant of the Tower, differently conceived from the Constable in Heywood's play, refuses to obey a warrant which does not bear Mary's royal hand. That hand, however, is soon to be helpless. The last Act shows the Queen on her death bed, in deep distress because her husband, Philip, does not come to her, and roused for a moment to jealous fury when a letter from him bids her send the jewels,

> He left a gift with us, unto Elizabeth
> With words of brotherly greeting—brotherly!
> Cain's words were brotherly.

So she passes and Elizabeth wears the crown, but her day of joy is overshadowed by the news that Courtenay, who had been freed on condition that he went overseas, had died in Padua. It is only for her people that she now must live.

> What love is left to me now
> But their love? What to live for, but to make
> Them happier than their Queen can ever be?

It never rains but it pours, and only five years after *'Twixt Axe and Crown* appeared Tennyson's *Queen Mary* (1875). There is no evidence of his having known Taylor's play, and in the list of Elizabethan authorities consulted by him which is given in his son Hallam's memoir, there is no mention of Heywood. Unlike the dramas hitherto discussed, Mary, not Elizabeth, is here the central figure, and there is much in Tennyson's play with which we are not concerned. But like Taylor Tennyson deals with the relations between Elizabeth and Courtenay, though from a different angle. The love-making is all on the man's side.

> I love you,
> Lay my life in your hands . . . your ear;
> You shall be Queen . . .
> *Eliz.:* Stand further off or you may lose your head.
> *Court.:* I have a head to lose for your sweet sake.
> *Eliz.:* Have you my Lord? Best keep it for your own.
> Nay, part not, cousin.
> Not many friends are mine, except indeed
> Among the many, I believe you mine;
> And so you may continue mine, farewell!

The Queen overhears their whispering and orders her to retire to Ashridge. Lord William Howard warns her:

> This comes of parleying with my Lord of Devon,

Well, well you must obey . . . Your time will come.

And again we hear the true voice of Elizabeth:

> I think my time will come, Uncle,
> I am of sovereign nature that I know
> Not to be quell'd, and I have felt within me
> Stirrings of some great blow when God's just hour
> Peals.

Tennyson does not show Elizabeth in the Tower, but only voices her grim memories of it after she has been freed and sent to Woodstock.

> Those damp, black, dead
> Nights in the Tower; dead with the fear of death,
> Too dead ev'n for a death-watch. Toll of a bell,
> Stroke of a clock, the scurrying of a rat
> Affrighted me, and then delighted me,
> For there was life.

Her custodian Bedingfield delivers a missive from the Queen. 'It is the King's wish that you shall wed Prince Philibert of Savoy. You are to come to Court on the instant; and think of this in your coming. Mary, the Queen.'
Elizabeth left alone bursts forth:

> Think! I have many thoughts . . .
> I think the Queen may never bear a child.
> I think that I may be some time the Queen.
> Then Queen indeed: no foreign prince or priest
> Shall fill my throne, myself upon the steps.
> I think I will not marry anyone,
> Specially not this landless Philibert.

Even when Philip urges the match he has to confess:

> I talked with her in vain—says she will live
> And die true maid—a goodly creature too.
> Would *she* had been the Queen!

And when Mary, disappointed in her hope of an heir, is slowly dying, he sends Count de Feria to suggest an alliance between them.

> As to Philip and your Grace—consider,
> If such a one as you should match with Spain,
> What hinders but that Spain and England join'd
> Should make the mightiest empire earth has known.
> Spain would be England on her seas, and England
> Mistress of the Indies.
> *Eliz.:*   It may chance that England
> Will be the Mistress of the Indies yet,
> Without the help of Spain . . .
> Have you ought else to tell me?
> *Feria:*   Nothing Madam.
> Save that methought I gather'd from the Queen
> That she would see your Grace before she died.
> *Eliz.:*   God's death! and wherefore spake you not before?

She arrives in time at her sister's death-bed to be acknowledged by her as heir, and, when Mary has passed away, to receive homage from Cecil. But she has no joy in her exaltation, only firm resolve:

> Sir, I swear I have no heart
> To be your Queen . . . But with Cecil's aid
> And others, if our person be secured
> From traitor stabs, we will make England great.

Mention may here be also made of *Mary Tudor,* a copyright play by Wilfred Grantham, in which Mary was impersonated by Flora Robson, and 'Madam Elizabeth', before her accession, by Joyce Bland. It was produced at the Playhouse Theatre in December 1935, and published in 1936.

Into this survey hitherto except for Banks's ill-starred venture one cardinal event of Elizabeth's reign has not entered—the trial and execution of Mary Queen of Scots. That was not a subject on which any dramatist felt free to touch under the first James or Charles. But in 1905 it formed the main theme of Swinburne's play, *Mary Stuart,* the last of his trilogy on the Scottish Queen. The failure of the conspiracy of Anthony Babington and his confederates in the summer of 1586, designed to kill Elizabeth and set

Mary free from imprisonment, led directly to the arraignment of
Mary at Fotheringay before a special commission. She denied the
competence of the judges to try 'a princess free-born of all courts
on earth', and made a masterly defence. After her condemnation
the King of France sent an envoy to 'England's royal-souled
Elizabeth',

> To uphold Mary's cause who as queen
> Of Scotland, dowager queen of France,
> To none being subject, can be judged of none.

Elizabeth returns a mournfully defiant answer:

> I have read
> As deep I doubt me in as many books
> As any Queen or prince in Christendom,
> Yet never chanced on aught so strange and sad
> As this my State's calamity. Mine own life
> Is by mere nature precious to myself,
> And in mine own realm I can live not safe.
> I am a poor lone woman, girt about
> With secret enemies that perpetually
> Lay wait for me to kill me.

But a last letter from Mary herself, not pleading for life, but for
execution not in secret and for burial with Catholic rites, 'who
will then, as she hath lived, die her affectionate sister and prisoner',
so moves Elizabeth that she hesitates to sign the death warrant
which Davison has brought.

> I would it might not be,
> Or being so just were yet not necessary.
> Art thou not heartily sorry, would'st thou not,
> I say, be sad to see me sign it?
> Dav.:   Madam, I had rather guilt should bleed than innocence.

But Elizabeth still delays till Davison, fearing she might refuse to
sign, shows her an old letter of Mary, written but never sent,
accusing her of flagrant immorality. This turns the scale.

> Give me again
> The warrant I put by, being foolish . . .

Here in God's sight I set mine hand, who thought
Never to take this thing upon it, nor
Do God so bitter service. Take this hence,
And let me see no word nor hear of her
Till the sun see not such a soul alive.

Yet, as Clemence Dane presents her in the play *Will Shakespeare*, acted at the Shaftesbury Theatre in November 1921, Elizabeth was to feel envy of the woman whose fate she thus seals. The death of Marlowe has taken place in an affray between him and Shakespeare for the favours of Mary Fitton. Clemence Dane was writing shortly before Dr. Leslie Hotson had discovered the record of the inquest giving the official version of Kit's death. Elizabeth has summoned Shakespeare whom she has commissioned to write a new play, and to whom, in the highest sense her heir, she unburdens her soul.

Mid my state affairs . . .
Ever I heard the momentary clock
Ticking away my girlhood, as I reigned,
While she—while she—
Mary of Scotland, Mary of delight,
(I know her sweetheart names) Marybird, Mayflower,
The three times married honeysuckle queen,
She had her youth. Think you I'd not have changed,
Sat out for twenty years a prisoner,
Ridden her road from France to Fotheringay,
To have her story?

But in a spirit of majestic resignation she accepts her lot:

I know the flesh is sweetest, when all's said,
And summer's heyday and the love of men,
I know well what I lose. I'm head of the Church
And stoop my neck on Sunday—to what Christ?
The God of little children? I have none.
The God of love? What love has come to me?
The God upon his ass? I am not meek,
Nor is he meek, the stallion that I ride,
The great white horse of England. I'll not bow

To the gentle Jesus of the women, I,
But to the man who hung 'twixt earth and heaven
Six mortal hours, and knew the end (as strength
And custom was) three days away. Yet . . .
Spat out the anodyne and would not drink.
This was a god for kings and queens of pride,
And him I follow.

And to the royal rank she welcomes Shakespeare.

Take you the kingship on you.
Shakes.: A player king—
Eliz.:   As I a player queen! I play my part
          Not ill, not ill. Judge me, my English peer,
          And witness for me, that I play not ill
          My part . . . when I bear England in my breast,
          As God Almighty bears this universe,
          England moves in me, I for England speak.

How differently does Mr. Bernard Shaw bring the Queen and
the dramatist into contact in his *pièce d' occasion*, *The Dark Lady
of the Sonnets* (1910). Shakespeare has come by night to meet
Mary Fitton on the terrace of the Palace at Whitehall. A cloaked
Lady, whom he takes to be Mary, appears walking and talking in
her sleep like Lady Macbeth. He shakes her till she wakes, and
thinking her to be some lady of the Court compliments and offers
to kiss her. At this moment the Dark Lady comes behind them,
and with two cuffs knocks them asunder. As the cloaked Lady
uncovers crying 'High treason,' Mary shrieks 'Will, I am lost: I
have struck the Queen,' to which her lover retorts 'Woman: you
have struck William Shakespeare.'

In the dialogue that follows between Queen and player both
maintain a dignified part till Shakespeare is emboldened to beg 'a
boon of State'—'that you do endow a great playhouse, or . . .
a National theatre for the better instruction and gracing of your
Majesty's subjects.' Elizabeth asks, 'are there not theatres now on
the Bankside and in Blackfriars?' to which Will answers, 'there are
the adventures of needy and desperate men,' catering for the
sillier sort of people, while a State theatre would present only
what is best, independent of financial risk. Elizabeth thinks the

scheme impracticable in her own day but declares 'if I could speak across the ages to our descendants, I should heartily command them to fulfil your wish'. This is her prayer for posterity, which fitly evokes from Shakespeare the response, 'Goodnight, great Elizabeth. God save the Queen.' And with a Chancellor of the Exchequer now providing a million pounds for a playhouse on the Bankside there is a prospect of a National theatre being established with another Elizabeth as Queen Consort.

About a quarter of a century after her *Will Shakespeare*, Clemence Dane again drew Elizabeth in *The Lion and the Unicorn* (1945). Its main theme is the relation between the Queen and the Earl of Essex, from when he first appears at Court in his youthful beauty till the hour when he meets his doom after the rising in the City in February 1601. The fascination and the insolence of the Earl, at once attracting and enraging Elizabeth, are vividly drawn. So too are his rivalry with Raleigh, his hostility to the Cecils, his claim to lead the expedition to Ireland in 1598. The Queen's delight at first in his unexpected return, as she thinks victorious, and her anger, followed by his arrest, when she finds that he merely brings pledges from the rebel Tyrone, are truly characteristic. And so is her agonized hope, after his condemnation, that he will send her the ring which will enable her at the last moment to save him.

> Give me his life, O God! Give me his life!
> May I not save him? He is thirty-four,
> November child, the luckless month. . . . .
> The night ebbs out. No sign will ever come.
> Robin, your purpose was to rule my kingdom,
> My purpose is to make you rule yourself.
> God, if I swell against thee, pluck me down,
> If in my own conceit—give me his life!
> Give me his life, O God! Give me his life!

Even two years later when she is about to receive the Commons in the Council Chamber for the last time, he is still uppermost in her thoughts

> He saw me when he came from Ireland.
> Headlong and disobedient home he came,
> To the crooked carcass, tumbling out pell-mell

> The wrongs that I and all the world had done him.
> O my poor boy in his grave!

But as the Commons enter she stands to welcome them:

> Here is the ring with which you married me;
> So I must love you as a faithful wife
> The master of her youth, and hold this jewel
> Dearer than all my jewels—I mean your loves.

As the cry rises,

> God save your Majesty! Live long, live long,
> The Queen of England!

She catches it up:

> England! There continue!
> England is my delight and not the name
> Of king nor queen's authority.

And then from the lips of the almost dying woman comes the moving mingled utterance of pride and humility:

> For I am yours; and though of old you had,
> And may again have mightier princes sitting
> Where now I sit, yet had you never any,
> Nor shall have any prince that loves you better.
> If I should laud myself, a weakly woman,
> I were unworthy of God's life and mercies,
> And of the heart He put into my breast
> Incapable of fear, which never yet
> Faltered at foreign or home enemies—
> Give him the praise!

How gladly must she have welcomed from the Shades the tribute to her in the closing lines of the *Masque of Hope* with which Oxford greeted, in lines by Mr. Nevill Coghill, at University College on 25th May 1948, the Princess who (may the date be far distant!) is due by succession to be Elizabeth the Second. Clio, the Muse of History, speaks:

> Out of long memory, I could unfold

Many a tale of England etched in gold,
Many a glorious life and glorious death:
But I choose one—of Queen Elizabeth!
Beauty and genius robed her like a sun
And love of England. She made England one.
Under her rule this island was secure,
Her honour bright and her religion pure.
Under her rule the roving sailors pressed
To pearly Orient and golden West.
Under her rule *Learning* and *Art* arose
In Spenser's poetry and Bacon's prose.
What more is there to say in this recital?
This, she was *Shakespeare's Friend*. Her proudest title.

Then St. George enters on a white horse in full armour and repeats, with the change of 'infant' to 'Lady', and of 'cradle' to 'girlhood' the Archbishop's speech from *King Henry VIII*, with which this essay opened. Thus the wheel has come full circle.

And whatever differences of emphasis, of selection or modification of historical facts, may be found in these dramatic presentations of Elizabeth from the sixteenth to the twentieth centuries we cannot but be struck by the essential unity of the impression that is left. Whether viewed by playwrights of Tudor and Stuart, or of Victorian and Georgian days, she is still the same. They and we see her proudly confronting every threat and peril; loyal to her ideals of duty, first as subject, then as sovereign, even when in conflict with her womanly instincts; a virginal figure mated only to her England and its people; not without an alloy of ill-temper and passion, but in the fullest sense a patriot Princess and Queen.

TWO

QUEEN ELIZABETH, THE REVELS OFFICE AND EDMUND TILNEY

IT was in 1717 that Mrs. Elizabeth Howland bequeathed forty shillings to endow an annual discourse in commemoration of Queen Elizabeth on 17th November, the anniversary of her accession to the throne. The first Jacobite rebellion had been defeated two years previously, and Mrs. Howland may well have thought of Elizabeth not only as an upholder of Protestantism but as the representative of secure and settled government.

Not only have circumstances changed with the passing of the centuries, but notable additions have been made to our knowledge of Elizabeth's career and the events of her reign since the last of these discourses was delivered in St. Leonard's Church. Vast masses of documents in the Public Record Office, the British Museum, Hatfield House, and elsewhere have been abstracted and calendared in the great series of 'State Papers, Domestic and Foreign', which are invaluable to all students of the period. Another series of the highest importance is that of the Registers of the Privy Council for Elizabeth's reign, which have been printed from the manuscript. The archives of the City of London and of the County of Middlesex have yielded rich stores of new information. Many learned and religious societies have published Elizabethan records bearing on their special interests.

Some of this material was available to J. A. Froude for the later volumes of his *History of England from the Fall of Wolsey to the Defeat of the Spanish Armada* (1856-70). Froude was a literary artist, but he was a biased historian. His heroes were Elizabeth's father, Henry VIII, and her great minister, Lord Burghley. He held, as Mrs. Howland would have been scandalized to learn, that Elizabeth did much to check the vigorous Protestant policy of her ministers. Since Froude wrote there have been a number of more balanced surveys, including two recent notable volumes, Pro-

36

fessor J. E. Neale's *Queen Elizabeth* (1934) and Professor J. B. Black's *The Reign of Elizabeth* (1936). In these the results of research are set forth judicially and attractively.

In addition to these full-length portrayals of the Queen and her environment there has been a host of studies of leading figures or particular episodes of her reign. We have had (to give only a few instances) biographies of Sidney, Burghley, Walsingham, and Raleigh; Lytton Strachey's *Essex and Elizabeth;* Martin Hume's *The Courtships of Queen Elizabeth;* Mr. Gordon Smith's *The Babington Plot*. Every student of the period can readily add to the list.

And the strange thing is that the more we get to know about Elizabeth and her reign the more difficult is it to pronounce decisive verdicts on many points. As Professor Black has said:

A completely objective account of events in Elizabeth's reign, however desirable it may be in theory, cannot in actual fact be written. From time to time one treads on embers of controversies that still flicker with a baleful light as soon as they are disturbed. And there are questions on which historians will probably be divided to the end of time, for the simple reason that their points of view differ so greatly that the gulf between them is unbridgeable.

Among these questions are the character of Elizabeth, her attitude towards marriage and to her successive suitors, her relations with Mary Queen of Scots, the different phases of her foreign and her religious policy. I hope that some of these will be treated in later Elizabeth Howland lectures in a spirit removed as far as possible from partisanship. For myself I will only say that, after reading a good deal of what has been urged by advocates for the prosecution, I am still a believer in the spacious times of great Elizabeth.

I would emphasize the epithet 'great'. It may be fairly argued that Elizabeth was not always good, nor always wise. But to a woman who remained from youth to age the centre of so brilliant a galaxy of genius in many forms, and who won and retained the devotion of her stiff-necked people, the title of 'great' cannot, as I think, be refused.

And about one aspect of her reign there can be no controversy. It saw English music, English poetry, above all English drama rise to unsurpassed heights. It is with these that the Elizabethan Literary Society has been mainly concerned for over fifty years. And with these Streatham is fortunate in having a notable link through the burial in St. Leonard's Church of Edmund Tilney, Master of the Revels from 1579 to 1610. Could there be a more suitable subject for this inaugural Elizabeth Howland Lecture than the one that I have chosen?

A succession of stage-historians from the close of the eighteenth century onwards, including George Chalmers, J. P. Collier, Peter Cunningham, J. O. Halliwell-Phillipps, have collected and interpreted the surviving documents relating to the Revels Office. These earlier researches have been in the present century supplemented and largely superseded by the work of Professor A. Feuillerat and Sir Edmund Chambers. In 1908 Professor Feuillerat published a volume of *Documents relating to the Office of the Revels in the Time of Queen Elizabeth,* which was followed in 1914 by *Documents relating to the Office of the Revels in the Time of Edward VI and Mary.* Sir Edmund Chambers, who had printed in 1906 *Notes on the History of the Revels Office under the Tudors,* embodied the results of all previous investigations in his *The Elizabethan Stage* (1923), particularly volume I, chapter iii, and volume IV, appendix B.

The revels in the Tudor Courts, especially during the Christmas season, were at first under the direction of the Lord of Misrule, who held sway from All-Hallows Eve (31st Oct.) till after Candlemas Day (2nd Feb.). In the reign of Henry VIII he is mentioned for nearly every Christmas, with an annual fee of £6 13s. 4d. He continued to function through the next two reigns. But with the institution in 1545 of the permanent office of a Master of the Revels the Lord of Misrule became superfluous, and in Mary's reign he disappeared.

The Office of the Revels came into independent existence, though it was under the general jurisdiction of the Lord Chamberlain, when a John Farlyon was appointed by patent Yeoman of the Revels on 20th November 1534. In the patent he is described as 'Yeoman or Keeper of the King's vestures or apparel of masks, revels and disguisings, and of apparel and trappers of horses, for justes and turneys'. His wages were fixed at 6d. a day with one livery coat. A higher official was, however, needed to be head of a department of ever growing importance, and on 11th March 1545 Sir Thomas Cawarden of the King's Privy Chamber was appointed permanent Master of the Revels. In the patent he is called 'Magister Iocorum Revelorum Mascorum omnium et singularium nostrorum vulgariter nuncupatorum Revells and Masks', and the annual fee was £10. The Yeoman was of course under him, and, like most heads of departments then and now, he found at once that he needed additional subordinates, whom he got appointed, like himself, by patent: a Clerk Comptroller to act as check and prevent any loose dealings, and a Clerk to keep the books.

In 1547 Cawarden moved the staff belonging to the Revels from the royal mansion of Warwick Inn in the City to the dissolved Priory of Blackfriars, which now became the head-quarters of the office. He lived long enough to superintend the festivities at the coronation of Elizabeth. On his death on 29th August 1559 he was succeeded by Sir Thomas Benger, under whom the office was removed to the late Hospital of St. John of Jerusalem in Clerkenwell. Benger remained Master till his death in the summer of 1572. The detailed accounts of his last year of office, from Shrovetide 1571 to Shrovetide 1572, are preserved and amount to £1,558 17s. 5½d.

After his death there was an interregnum of seven years, during the greater part of which Thomas Blagrave, the Clerk, acted as chief officer. He was very anxious to be appointed Master, and so far as long service and experience are concerned he certainly had a strong claim. But his ambitions were finally disappointed when on 24th July 1579 a patent of appointment to the vacant post was granted to Edmund Tilney. His fee was to run from the previous Christmas, and he may have formally assumed his duties at that period. In any case his signature was attached with that of Blagrave and the other officers to the account for the period from 14th February 1578 to 31st October 1579.

Edmund Tilney was appointed to his office without any previous connexion with the Revels. He evidently owed his advancement to influence, and here the elaborate inscription on his monument in St. Leonard's Church gives light. It records that he was the only son of Philip Tilney, Usher of the Privy Chamber to Henry VIII, and Malin [Chambre] his wife. This Philip was younger son of Sir Philip Tilney, 'knight banerit', who was treasurer to the Scottish wars under the Duke of Norfolk, i.e. the Thomas Howard who as Earl of Surrey was in command at Flodden in 1513. This Duke married first Sir Philip Tilney's cousin Elizabeth after she had lost her first husband, Lord Barnes. After her death he married her cousin Agnes, Sir Philip's sister. Their son was the first Lord Howard of Effingham, and their grandson the second holder of that title, who in 1574 had become Lord Chamberlain and was later to be Lord High Admiral. The Revels Office, as has been said, was under the Lord Chamberlain, who took the opportunity of appointing a somewhat distant kinsman to be Master.

The aristocratic connexions proudly blazoned on Edmund Tilney's monument are confirmed in the most elaborate of the Tilney family pedigrees among the British Museum MSS., 19, 152, the Davy Suffolk Collections, lxxvi, ff. 26-43. As this manuscript is mentioned as an authority for the account of Tilney in the *Dictionary of National Biography*, vol. lvi (1898), it is all the more surprising to find the following statement: 'Edmund Tilney seems to have been the third son of Thomas Tilney of Shelly, Suffolk, by his wife, a daughter of Antony Swilland in the same county. Thomas Tilney, the father, was grandson of Sir Philip Tilney of Shelley.' Sir Sidney Lee here made the 'howler' of confusing the Master of the Revels with the much younger namesake who was a son of Thomas Tilney, himself the son of the Master's cousin Emery, of the Inner Temple, and great-grandson of Sir Philip Tilney.

It is curious that so serious a blunder should have gone so long uncorrected. Nor, so far as I am aware, has it been noticed in accounts of Edmund Tilney that, in spite of his powerful connexions, he had spent his early years under the shadow of dark family disgrace. His father, as the younger son, had received under Sir Philip Tilney's will, made on 4th December 1532 and proved on 8th October 1533, only £6 13s. 4d. in ready money and an annuity of 5 marks [£3 6s. 8d.], with 'a little standing cuppe gilte wth a rounde knopp' and wearing-apparel. As an Usher of the Privy Chamber he received a salary, and on 5th August 1536 he had confirmation of a previous grant of 'the room of a soldier of Calais, with wages of 8d. a day from 6th April last'.[1] In April 1539 he is still being paid 8d. a day (£12 5s. 4d.). Yet after his death, and his burial in St. Leonard's Church on 10th September 1541, his wife, Malin, lamented to the Duchess of Norfolk that he had died in debt, and she received a promise of help from the Duchess.[2]

Malin had been one of the household of her husband's kinswoman, Queen Catherine Howard, and was implicated in her tragic downfall. She was officially examined, and she was also asked by the Duchess of Norfolk, Catherine's grandmother, 'if she knew of the evil life of the Queen in her house and whether she should die'. Malin replied that she was 'commanded to make no answer therein'. She was one of the Queen's household who, on 22nd December 1541, was convicted of suspicion of treason and sentenced to perpetual imprisonment and loss of goods. This sentence was confirmed in the Bill of Attainder which received the royal assent on 11th February 1542. Two days later Catherine Howard and her confidante, Lady Rochford, were executed. Her lovers had already met their fate. The authorities then thought they could show clemency to the others involved, and Malin Tilney was among those who received a grant of pardon. The last mention that I have found of her is in July 1544, when the reversion of the manor of Leyham, Suffolk, then in her tenure, was granted for £254 10s. 3½d. to John Clerke of Hadley.[3] The inscription on her son's monument states that she was buried, besides her husband, at Streatham Parish Church, but there is no entry of this in the register, and the date of her death is unknown.

As Edmund Tilney lived till 1610, and as life was usually shorter then than now, he must have been a very young child when his father died in debt and his mother was convicted of treason. He was their only son, and apparently their only child. His unfortunate family circumstances may account for the fact that there is no evidence of his having received an education at a leading school,

[1] *Letters and Papers of Henry VIII*, vol. xi., p. 155, and *Addenda*, p. 480.
[2] Ibid., vol. xvi, p. 680.
[3] Ibid, vol. xix, pt. 1, p. 626.

at Oxford or Cambridge, or at one of the Inns of Court. The earliest mention of him that has been found is in the will of his uncle Thomas, who on 12th July 1559 made him, 'the onelye sonne of my brother Phillippe deceased', a contingent legatee of £40.

At the age of about 30 Tilney made a bid for literary reputation and for royal favour by issuing in 1568 a treatise in octavo entitled *A briefe and pleasaunt discourse of duties in Mariage*, and published by Henry Denham dwelling in Paternoster Row at the sign of the Star. Considering the association of his mother with the tragic fate of Queen Catherine Howard, which was so closely akin to that of Elizabeth's mother, Anne Boleyn, it was daring of Tilney to address an epistle dedicatory to 'the Noble and most Vertuous Princesse, Elizabeth, by the Grace of God, of Englande, Fraunce, and Irelande, Queene, defender of the Faith, &c.'

He confesses that when he weighed his sovereign's noble virtues, wisdom, and high dignity against the lowness of his own estate and his simple skill, he 'stoode as one dismayde, not daring to aduenture to put thys my base stile to the hearing eyther of your Maiesties reuerent eares, or to the iudgement of your skilfull eyes.' At last, however, he overcomes his scruples:

> Yet dailye perceyuing the clemencie of your highnesse most noble mind, conioyned with so high an Estate of Souereigntie, and noting your Princelye curtesie, and as it were a heauenly humilitie matched with the great knowledge graffed in the roote of your Maiesties royall hart, I was by this (though before discouraged) boldened to presume so farre, as humblye to offer this my simple Present vnto your Highnesse, expressing my good will.

He reminds her that the noble Alexander of Macedon and the Emperor Antoninus graciously accepted humble literary offerings, and he hopes that as she embodies their virtues and those of many other princes she will accept these few simple lines from him.

As the allusions to Alexander and Antoninus foreshadow, the work is plentifully sprinkled, after the fashion of the period, with examples and anecdotes from Greek and Roman history and legend, with marginal references to sources. But these references are very general, and there is not a single Latin quotation, to say nothing of Greek. It looks as if Tilney drew not from first-hand knowledge but from those compendia or handbooks which were so widely circulated during the Renaissance. The *D.N.B.* states that the *Discourse* 'shows considerable reading in Italian literature', but I can find no evidence of this except for one reminiscence of 'how *Boccace* and Countie *Baltizer* with others recounted many proper deuises, for exercise, both pleasaunt and profitable, which . . . were used in ye courts of Italie'. The *Decameron* seems to have suggested to Tilney the idea of a company of gentlemen and ladies passing the time in a garden with discourse, though this takes with him the form of a dialogue and not of tales. And it is singular, considering his family circumstances, that he should have chosen as his subject Duties in Marriage, and have written upon it with so much good sense, fine feeling, and moral insight.[1]

The *Discourse* has a short narrative introduction which has something of the easy grace of Tudor prose before the stylized elaboration of Euphuism or Arcadianism. On an early spring morning Tilney walked with a friend, Master *Pedro di luxan*, in the fields and groves till noon, when they sought refuge from the sun's heat at the house of a worthy Lady Julia. She was just sitting down to dinner with her company, including her daughter, the Lady Isabella, and a Lady Aloisa, 'with many other Ladyes and their lincked Mates, beside M. *Lodouic Viues,* and an olde Gentleman called M. *Erasmus*'. It is curious that Tilney should thus introduce into this imaginary company two persons named after the famous Renaissance Spanish and Dutch humanists. After dinner there was a discussion as to how they should spend the afternoon. 'Some liked well of carding and dicing, some of dancing, and other some of Chestes [chess]', but the majority thought that these were more suitable for Christmas. So they betook themselves to the garden, 'a place meruellous delectable', and seated themselves under an arbour. Then Master Pedro asked them if they would obey whomever he chose for their sovereign, and thereupon he crowned the Lady Julia with a garland of roses as the sovereign for the day.

---

[1] If Tilney's *Discourse* was directly based on a Continental original, this has not been traced. In my quotations the spelling of the octavo is kept, but the punctuation has sometimes been altered and a few abbreviations expanded.

He then suggested that they should discourse upon friendship, 'and because no friendship, or amitie, is or ought to be more deere, and surer, than the loue of man and wyfe, let thys treatise be thereof, wherein I would the duetie of the maried man to be discribed'. The Lady Julia then exercised her authority by commanding Master Pedro to give a discourse on this subject, which he entitled 'The Flower of Friendship'. He began by declaring the virtues of the matrimonial estate 'which (setting virginitie aside, as the purest estate) is both holy and most necessary'. Tilney evidently found it advisable in a work dedicated to Elizabeth, even though its theme was the married state, to introduce a commendation of virginity. Master Pedro, after citing the example of Adam and Eve in the blissful place of Paradise, then proceeds to expound the rites of divers nations in marrying, from the Babylonians and Chaldaeans to the French and Scots. When he mentions that Lycurgus ordained in Sparta that men should not marry before 37 and women at 18, Isabella, the daughter of the house, burst forth, 'I would neuer marry, rather than to take such old crustes, whose wyfes are more occupied in playstering than in enioying any good conuersation.' Master Pedro answered, 'You say truth . . . my opinion is that they differ not aboue foure or fiue yeres.'

He then describes with historical and other examples the perfect state of married love. One of the company, Master Gualter, interrupts from time to time with cynical jests, whereupon the Lady Aloisa cries out: 'This sawcie soole wulde be well beaten, and banished our company. For he is still pratling against women, and interrupteth oure pastime.' 'No, no,' quoth Master Pedro, 'he increaseth our sporte, and therefore we can not well want him.' Pedro passes on to speak of the poisoned weeds that will destroy 'the flower of friendshipp'. They are adultery, gaming, and drunkenness. Tilney writes very sensibly about gaming. 'I condemne not honest playing for recreation at times conuenient for some small matter, as the persons hability is. But what a monstrous thing is it, to consume whole dayes, yea, whole daies and nights, in gaming, swearing and forswearing.' On the other hand, there are delicate herbs which nourish the flower of friendship, such as discretion in speech, courtesy, secrecy, wisdom in counsel, diligence in providing for the household, absence of jealousy, care in the education of children. 'For much better were they vnborne than vntaught.' And the husband must above all things have the fear of God before his eyes.

The sun was now near setting, and Pedro made an end. But the Lady Julia declared that she would not be in quiet till she had 'heard the married woman prescribed in lyke sorte, as you have done the married man'. So it was arranged that they should all meet again the next day, when the Lady Julia set the garland upon the head of the Lady Aloisa and proclaimed her sovereign for the day. She at once commanded Julia to describe the office and duty of the married woman. In the light of some modern controversies and the looser code of morals in the Tudor age, it is remarkable to find Tilney, through the lips of the Lady Julia, insisting on the principle that marriage, come weal or woe, is for life.

For reason doth binde us to loue them, wyth whome we must eate and drinke, whome we must only accompany, of whose ioyes and sorrowes, welth and woe, we must be partakers, for whome also we forsake parents, friendes, and all, cleauing onely to them for no shorter time then during lyfe. And albeit they be cancred of nature, yll in conuersation, worse in condition, base of lynage, deformed of personage, and inaduised in worde and deede: yet being our chosen husbands, we may not, nor can we forgo them or chaunge with our neighbours, as did sometime the *Parthians,* but seeke gently to redresse them, indeuor to please them, and labour to loue them, to whome we haue wholy giuen oure bodies, our goodes, our lyues, and libertie.

The Lady Julia then illustrated her ideal of wifely devotion with a number of examples from Greek and Roman story. This precious Flower of Friendship must be steadfastly preserved by the woman in the marriage partnership. 'The greateste helpe whereto is shamefastnesse [modesty], which is of such power and vertue, that it sufficeth alone to defende it against all weathers.' This statement causes no discussion, but it is otherwise when Julia speaks of 'the goodly grace of obedience' to husbands. 'God commaundeth it, and we are bounde so to doe.' Hereupon her daughter, Isabella, retorts, 'I know not what we are bound to do, but as meete is it that the husband obey the wife, as the wife the husband, or at least that there be no superioritie betwene them. . . . For women haue soules as wel as men, they haue wit as wel as men. . . . What reason is it then that they should be bound, whom nature hath made free?'

This sounds a curiously modern note, and a debate follows in which Master Gualter, the Lady Aloisa, and Master Erasmus take part. But Julia reaffirms her position:

> This maryed woman, whom I haue taken upon me to discribe, must of dutie be vnto hir husband in all things obedient, and therefore, if he, sometimes moued, do chaunce to chide hir, she must forbeare. In doing whereof he shal neither eate ye more at his dinner, nor shee haue the lesse appetite to hir supper.

The married woman must also be very careful of her good name, 'which is so delicate a thing in a woman that she must not onely be good, but likewise must appeere so'. The chief means to this is for a woman to keep at home, which brings, among other advantages, 'expenses diminished and the greate excesse of apparell not required, wherein we are commonly so curious, that otherwise being naturally great sauers, onely therein are we as great wasters'. At home the wife is not to sit idle but to spend her time profitably, with her needle, her rock [distaff] or such 'otherlike'.

Then Julia sums up by declaring that to the wife her husband's face must be her daily looking-glass, 'wherein she ought to be alwaies prying, to see when he is merie, when sad, when content, and when discontent, whereto she must alwayes frame hir owne countenance'. This again is too much for Isabella, who bursts out, 'What if he be mad, or drunke, must we then shew the like countenance?' 'If you perceiue him in such case,' quoth the Lady Julia, 'speake him faire and flatter him, till you get him to bed, and there reprehende hym louingly.' Finally, the wife must put her trust in God, who will make the Flower of Friendship spring up in her abundantly.

The company then rose; the Lady Aloisa laid aside the sovreeignty with which she had been invested for the day, and all left the arbour for the garden, where they talked over the discourses that they had heard for the two days. Here Isabella, the daughter of the house, was Tilney's companion, and she asked him to put down in writing what had been said.

'For,' quoth she, 'your quiet silence both these dayes assureth mee that you haue well considered thereof,' and therewith the rest of the ladies ioyned with hir at whose importunate request, with the helpe of my friend Maister *Pedro,* and others, I haue aduentured to publishe this Discourse.

This is a neat ending to an attractive piece of writing, which was received with so much favour that it went through two further editions in 1571 and 1577 (of which single copies are in the Bodleian Library). It is curious that after this successful venture Tilney, so far as is known, never published anything further. Did the cares of office prevent him, like his greater contemporary, Thomas Sackville, from fulfilling in maturity the literary promise of his younger years?

It is something of a paradox that the man who, at the age of about 30, could write with so much eloquence and good sense about the highest ideals of matrimony waited for another fifteen years before entering himself into that estate. On 4th May 1583 a licence of marriage was issued from the Bishop of London's office between Edmund Tilney, of the City of London, esquire, and Dame Mary Braye.[1] She was the widow of Sir Edmund Braye, knight, whose fourth wife she had been, and she was the daughter of Sir Thomas Cotton of Oxenheath, co. Kent. The wedding presumably took place, but nothing is known of Tilney's married life. One would like to think that his wife was at his side when Queen Elizabeth visited him at Leatherhead early in August 1591, during one of her progresses. But in his will made in 1610 there is no mention of her or of any children. And it is beside his father, who died when he was a mere child, that he asks to be buried.

Between his appointment as Master of the Revels in July 1579 and his death in October 1610 he held his office for over thirty-one years. But it was not only for its long duration that his mastership was notable. It covered the most glorious period in the annals of the English stage. In 1576 the two first public playhouses, the Theater and the Curtain, had been built in Shoreditch, soon to be followed by others in Southwark and elsewhere. The impulse thus given to dramatic activities had speedy and significant results. In

[1] *London Marriage Licences,* ed. J. Foster, col. 1343.

the 1580's Thomas Kyd and Christopher Marlowe were drawing crowded audiences to *The Spanish Tragedy* and *Tamburlaine*. In their steps came William Shakespeare, whose career as a playwright, except for the few closing years, fell wholly within Tilney's mastership. So did the main achievement of Ben Jonson and the earlier work of Beaumont and Fletcher. Here indeed was God's plenty for a Master of the Revels.

Nor had Tilney been long in office before his powers were considerably extended by a patent issued to him on 24th December 1581. By this 'our welbeloved' Edmund Tilney was commissioned to take 'at competent wages . . . as many painters, inbroderers, taylors, cappers, haberdashers, joyners, carders, glasiers, armorers, basketmakers, skinners, sadlers, waggen makers, plaisterers fethermakers, as all other propertie makers and conninge artificers and laborers whatsoeuer' as he should think necessary for the service of the office of the Revels. He was also empowered 'to take at price reasonable . . . any kinde or kindes of stuffe, ware or marchandise, woode, or coale or other fewell, tymber, wainscott, boarde, lathe, nailes, brick, tile, leade, iron, wier and all other necessaries for our said workes of the said office of our Revelles'. And if any one was recalcitrant Tilney was given authority to arrest and imprison him.

Then the patent proceeded to confer upon Tilney other and even more important powers, It is decreed that

all and euery plaier or plaiers with their playmakers, either belonginge to any noble man or otherwise, bearinge the name or names of vsinge the facultie of playmakers or plaiers of Comedies, Tragedies, Enterludes or what other showes soever, from tyme to tyme and at all tymes to appeare before him with all such plaies, Tragedies, Comedies or showes as they shall haue in readines or meane to sett forth, and them to presente and recite before our said Serfant or his sufficient deputie, whom wee ordeyne appointe and auctorise by these presentes of all suche showes, plaies, plaiers and playmakers, together with their playing places, to order and reforme, auctorise and put downe, as shal be thought meete or vnmeete vnto himselfe or his said deputie in that behalfe.

Here again any offender was liable to arrest and imprisonment at Tilney's discretion.

There can seldom have been a more totalitarian authority in this country than was thus vested in Tilney over workmen and goods on the one hand and over actors, theatres, dramatists, and their plays on the other. The officers of the Revels had previously shared the responsibility of selecting and 'reforming' plays that were to be acted at Court before the sovereign. But by this patent Tilney was encouraged, as Sir Edmund Chambers points out, to treat it as his personal function. Moreover, his authority was so widely extended that he became theatrical censor for the whole country. And though there is no longer a Master of the Revels the function of censor is still exercised by the Lord Chamberlain, who was his departmental superior.

An illustration of how Tilney dealt with touring companies is furnished by an episode in the career of the Earl of Worcester's players. They obtained a licence from the Master of the Revels on 6th February 1583 by which they were 'bound to the orders prescribed by him', and which prescribed that 'no play is to be played, but such as is allowed by the sayd Edmund, & his hand at the latter end of the said booke they doe play'. Worcester's men left the licence in a box at an inn in Leicester, and it was found by some unlicensed players who tried to pass it off as their own before the Leicester corporation.

About a month after Tilney had issued his licence to Worcester's men a more unusual task fell to him. Owing to the illness of the Lord Chamberlain, the Secretary, Sir Francis Walsingham, sent for Tilney on 10th March 1583 to come to Court in order to choose out a company of players for the Queen. The Revels accounts record his travelling-charges of 20 shillings. Twelve of the best actors from existing companies, including the famous comedian Richard Tarleton, were chosen to be the Queen's servants and were also appointed to be Grooms of the Chamber.

This was a delicate business requiring tact on Tilney's part. He had to show his sterner side in November 1589. The theatrical companies in the City of London were presenting plays dealing with public questions, which he did 'utterly mislike'. He moved the Privy Council to write to the Lord Mayor, commanding him

to give orders for the 'stay' of all plays within the City. The Lord
Mayor summoned before him the Lord Admiral's and Lord
Strange's companies and forbade them to perform. The former
players very dutifully obeyed; the latter went to the Cross Keys
and played that afternoon, 5th November, with the result that
some of them were imprisoned. A week later the Privy Council
asked the Archbishop of Canterbury and the Lord Mayor each to
appoint a fit person to act with the Master of the Revels, to view
and consider all plays that were to be acted in and about the City of
London. Sir E. Chambers has found 'no later reference to these
assessors and it may be that before long the Master succeeded in
divesting himself of their assistance'.

In any case we have got the manuscript of one very important
play with which Tilney alone seems to have dealt as censor. It is
The Booke of Sir Thomas Moore, preserved in the British Museum.
This is a composite work in no less than six hands, one of which
has been identified by high authorities as that of Shakespeare. The
date of the play is conjectural.[1] It dealt with episodes in the life
of Sir Thomas More, including the anti-alien riots of the ill May-
day of 1517, which More as Sheriff quelled by his oratory. This
was not the sort of subject that Elizabeth's government wished
the players to meddle with. Hence in the margin of the opening
lines there is the following note:

Leaue out yᵉ insurrection wholy & yᵉ Cause ther off & begin
wᵗ Sʳ Tho: Moore att ye mayors sessions wᵗ a reportt afterwardes
off his good seruic, don being Shriue off Londō vppō a mutiny
Agaynst yᵉ Lubardes only by A shortt reportt & nott otherwise
att your own perrilles E Tyllney.

Against another passage he has written 'Mend this', and there are
further deletions and alterations. So drastic was Tilney's censorship
that Dr. Greg holds that the manuscript was laid aside and the play
never came on the boards.

But the Corporation of London would have liked Tilney to
exercise his powers more frequently and severely. In February and
March 1592 the Lord Mayor wrote to the Archbishop of Canter-

---

[1] For the latest summing up the evidence see R. C. Bald *The book of 'Sir Thomas More'
and its Problems* (Shakespere Survey, II, 1949).

bury asking him to use his influence with the Master of the Revels 'for the removing of this great inconuenience which groweth to this Citie by playes and players'. The Lord Mayor also proposed to the Merchant Taylors' Company that as an inducement they should pay Tilney 'one Anuytie', but the company replied that it would be a bad precedent. In any case Tilney had no need of such a bribe. He had his own property at Leatherhead, and his office as Master brought him in a regular revenue. Under his patent he had a fee of £10, but this was raised to £100 'for a better recompense'. He had also a proportion of the £40 paid annually as wages to the officers of the Revels. In 1598 his share was fixed at £21. He had an official residence, which from 1586 was part of the Revels premises of St. John's, Clerkenwell. Here he had thirteen chambers, with a parlour, hall, kitchen, stable and other appurtenances, and a convenient garden.

The Revels accounts of 1582–3, 1584–5, 1587–8 show that Tilney honestly earned his salary. Every officer had to attend for the 20 annual days of 'airing' or rehearsal, and for the actual nights, 16 in 1582–3, and 14 in '84–5 and '87–8, of the performances. In addition Tilney attended for 106, 117, and 116 days respectively, far more frequently than any of his subordinates. Moreover he had his fees for licences to companies and theatreowners. The entries in Henslowe's *Diary* between 1592 and 1597 show payments to him as Master of 7s. for each new play produced and fees for each week during which a theatre was open, rising by stages of 5s., 6s. 8d., 10s. and 15s. Acquittances were given for these by a number of men in Tilney's employment. Two for £3 each for a month's performances at the Fortune Theatre were given on 9th June and 29th August 1601 by Robert Hassard.[1] This is a name that we shall hear again.[2]

On 24th March 1603 Elizabeth's long reign ended. Tilney retained his office under James I, but he was now well on in the sixties and may already have been suffering from the sickness of which he speaks in his will. Early in the new reign, on 23rd June 1603, George Buck received a formal grant by patent of the reversion of the Mastership. 'On the same day was issued a new

[1] Henslowe's *Diary*, ed. W. W. Greg, i, pp. 160 and 132.
[2] See p. 54.

Commission for the office, similar to that of 1581, but in Buck's name instead of Tilney's from which it is to be inferred that he had become the acting Master. On 23rd July 1603 he was knighted.[1] For many years John Lyly, the author of *Euphues* and a successful dramatist, had hoped to get the reversion, but Buck's superior influence prevailed, as Tilney's had previously over Blagrave's.

The stage-historians state that he was Tilney's nephew, and the *D.N.B.* says that his mother was presumably Tilney's sister. But in no pedigree that I have seen is a sister mentioned. Edmund Tilney appears to have been both an only son and an only child. The one connexion that I have been able to find between the two families is that Frederick Tilney, Edmund's cousin, married Margaret Buck of Melford in Sussex. Presumably George Buck was her relation, perhaps a brother. After the death of Philip Tilney, a son of Frederick and Margaret, a commission was issued on 26th March 1602 for the administration of his goods by Emery and Thomas, his paternal uncles, 'sauing power to a codicil of deceased alleged on the part of George Buck to administer the goods &c of the deceased if he can first account for the truth of the said codicil'.

Though from June 1603 Buck appears to have been acting Master, Tilney continued to render the annual accounts of the office, including the full accounts for 1604–5, whose authenticity has been disputed but, as I think, successfully vindicated by Ernest Law, T. B. M. Wood, and Mr. E. A. Stamp. Among the performances at Court recorded between Hallowmas Day 1604 and Shrove Tuesday 1605 are those of seven plays: *Othello, The Merry Wives, Measure for Measure, Comedy of Errors, Love's Labour's Lost, Henry V,* and *The Merchant of Venice,* by 'Shaxberd', as the name is here uniformly spelt.

About 1606 the Master of the Revels acquired a new power, that of licensing plays for publication. Buck thus licensed Edward Sharpham's *The Fleire* on 21st November 1606, and Tilney the same dramatist's *Cupid's Whirligig* on 29th June 1607. He continued to render the accounts for 1607–8 and 1608–9, but he was a sick man in his house at Leatherhead.

On 1st July 1610 Tilney made his will, written with his own hand. He appointed as overseers of the will 'Mr. Rabbett, Parson

[1] Chambers, *Eliz. Stage,* i. 90.

of Streatham'[1] and 'Mr. Griffith Vaughan, Parson of Ashted', between whom all his books were to be divided, and each of whom was to have 'a greate siluer Bowlle wth the cover'. He directed that he should be buried in the Parish Church of Streatham 'neare vnto the Monument of my Father longe since buried there and that wth oute any Funerall pompe or charge other than a Sermon wth fortie shillings vnto the Preacher for his paynes', and another forty shillings to the Church. He further directed that a monument to him should be erected at the place agreed between himself and the Parson and churchwardens, and that this should be 'effected wthin six months next after my deceasse if my self in my lief tyme doe not finishe the same at twentye marks price [£13 6s. 8d.] as I have agreed wth the Stone Cutter neare vnto Charingcrosse for the makinge thereof'.

Then follows a surprising declaration from a Master of the Revels who had been so long concerned with the custody of costly and decorative garments: 'I bequeathe all my apparrell wherein I haue spent much monye verye vaynelie that might have bynne otherwise bettr ymployed, to be soulde at the best valewe thereof ... and ... the monye made thereof to be devided' between the poor inhabitants of the parishes of Leatherhead and Streatham. Apparently these included the thirteen poor old men and women of Leatherhead who 'were wonte to haue a weekely relief from me in Bread', to each of whom he left 'a Blacke frize gowne and Five shillings apeece'. Another benefaction of a different kind to Leatherhead was the bequest of one hundred pounds towards the reparation of the stone bridge, provided that with the help of other 'meanes and devotions' the bridge was finished within a year after his death. Otherwise the bequest was cancelled, as the rebuilding had already at the sessions of Kingston been laid upon the whole county.

Turning from public and charitable bequests to personal legacies, Tilney directs that fifty pounds should be paid to Margaret Cartwright, widow, upon the cancellation of a bond of £100 by which he was obliged to pay her quarterly a life annuity of ten pounds a year. If she did not survive him, the fifty pounds were to go to

[1] Nicholas Rabbet was Rector of Streatham from 5th April 1585 till his death in February 1631.

Anne Hassard, wife of his 'Cosynne' Robert Hassard junior, 'for the paines taken abut me in my sickness'. As Tilney died within a little more than three months afterwards, it is very unlikely that Anne Hassard got the fifty pounds, but there was another unconditional joint legacy to her and her husband of £100. In addition she was to keep 'the whole furniture of hir Chamber where shee ordinarilie lyeth for Beddinge and hanginge together wth such allowance of Brasse Pewter and Lynnen towardes theire howskeepinge as my Executors shall thinke convenient'. Tilney also left to their son Edmund, his godson, sixty pounds, and to their daughter Anne, twenty. These legacies to the Hassards raise some interesting questions. Though Edmund Tilney calls Robert Hassard his cousin, I have been unable to find this name in any of the Tilney family pedigrees. The word 'cousin' is therefore in all probability used, as often by the Elizabethans, to denote affectionate familiarity, not legal relationship. A Robert Hassard, it will be remembered, had twice in 1601 given acquittances on behalf of Tilney to Henslowe for payments for performances at the Fortune Theatre. He was either identical with the legatee of the will or may have been the father of this 'Robert Hassard junior'. In any case the terms in which Tilney speaks of his 'Cosynne', and his benefactions to him and his family, imply an unexpected degree of intimacy with a man who has hitherto been described merely as a servant of the Master of the Revels, or that servant's son.

Another godson, Frederick Tilney, the second son of his chief executor, Thomas Tilney, was to receive £200 to be employed 'vnto his vse' by his mother until he came of age. Every one of his old servants was to get a year's wages, and 'Rogers Chambers that wayteth on me in my Chamber five poundes'.

To discharge his legacies and pay his debts the executors and overseers were directed to sell his house at Leatherhead 'with the furniture thereof and the groundes therewith belonginge' at the best value.

The Remainder thereof . . . together wth what other legacies I shall give vppon my deathe bedd by worde of mouthe Witnessed by twoe sufficient wittnesses to be wholly vnto Thomas Tylney of Shelleye in the Countie of Suffolke Esquier wth all other my Plate and monye remayninge wth me at my deathe . . . whome I doe make . . . my executor.

As his assistant Tilney nominates Thomas Godman of Leatherhead, gentleman, who for his pains is to receive forty ounces of plate.

It must be assumed that Tilney's wife had predeceased him, as also any children of the marriage, if such there were. As the testament of a widower without an heir, the detailed provisions of the will place him, as I think, in a very attractive light. All public and private obligations are scrupulously fulfilled. He shows gratitude for services rendered to him, and he specially provides for his poor neighbours and his personal attendants. I think that we may see in it something of the same spirit that had made Tilney so attentive in earlier days to his duties as Master of the Revels, and had led him to write about the duties rather than the joys of matrimony.

His executor, Thomas Tilney, was the son of his cousin Emery. He became High Sheriff of Suffolk in 1612. Besides carrying out, as we may assume, the provisions of Edmund's will, he had to act for him in an official capacity by rendering the Revels accounts for 1609–10, made up to 31st October, some weeks after Edmund's death. The *D.N.B.* states, without giving any authority, that this took place on 10th August. But this must be wrong, for, though the exact date is not known, there is the entry of his burial in the St. Leonard's Church register on 6th October 1610. In the next year on Hallowmas Eve 'Shaxberd's' *The Tempest* was acted at Court, and through Prospero's lips it furnishes an epitaph for Edmund Tilney and all who have held his office:

Our revels now are ended. . . .
        . . . We are such stuff
As dreams are made on, and our little life
Is rounded with a sleep.

THREE

ASPECTS OF SHAKESPEARE'S READING

IN 1875 W. Carew Hazlitt published in six volumes what he called *Shakespeare's Library*, containing what he considered the sources of his plays. Much of what he included was valuable, but some of the supposed sources were either doubtful or partly irrelevant. In 1904 H. E. D. Anders published *Shakespeare's Books*, a more up-to-date collection. This article aims at giving a general outline of the subject.

Our primary evidence of Shakespeare's reading lies in the plays, poems, novels, biographies, chronicles and so forth which can be identified as the bases of his dramas. And here it must be remembered that the Elizabethan ideas of plagiarism were entirely different from ours to-day. Literary copyright, so far as authors was concerned, (as distinguished from publishers) scarcely existed. But what Shakespeare borrowed, he always, except in occasional details, turned to higher uses.

In addition to source-materials we can gain some further light from occasional allusions in the plays. But how helpful it would have been had he mentioned some of his books in his will, in addition to the second-best bed; or had, like Ben Jonson, left a number of them with his autograph evidence of their ownership. Claims have been made for Shakespeare's signature in copies of the 1502 *Ovid's Metamorphoses*, and of the 1603 Florio's translation of Montaigne's essays, but they are disputable. And there is still a conflict of opinion about Shakespeare's classical knowledge, as to which Jonson declared that he had 'small Latin and less Greek'. Grammar School teaching had in his day mainly a Latin basis. At his school in Stratford-on-Avon he would be drilled in the grammar of that language, and such an elementary phrase book as *Sententiæ Pueriles*. There are echoes of such lessons in *The Merry Wives of Windsor*, where Sir Hugh Evans, the curate, puts little Will Page through his accidence, and warns him if he forgets his 'quis, quaes, and quods' he must be 'preeches'. From the same

Grammar School sources Holofernes, the schoolmaster, in *Love's Laaour's Lost*, draws some of his Latin phrases. But Miss Frances Yates in her study of the play (1936) has shown that the dialogue between him and Sir Nathaniel is also indebted to John Eliot's *Ortho-Epia Gallica* (1593), a skit on the popular manuals for teaching foreign languages. Another source, as an American scholar, D. T. Starnes, has pointed out, is Sir Thomas Elyot's *Bibliotheca* enlarged by Thomas Cooper (1552 and 1559). Ovid was certainly Shakespeare's favourite among the classical poet Holofernes was, I think, speaking for him in the words: 'For the elegance, facility, and golden cadence of poetry . . . Ovidius Naso was the man.'

But, in my opinion, Ovid was known mainly to Shakespeare in translation. A few lines in the original Latin are found in *Titus Andronicus* and *The Taming of the Shrew*, but these are probably not entirely by Shakespeare. A couplet from the *Amores* is on the title page of *Venus ana Adonis*. The only Latin line in an entirely Shakespearean play is not from Ovid but from the popular Renaissance poet, Mantuanus, whose eclogues were favourite school reading. It is the first line in them, 'Fauste, precor, gelida quando pecus omne sub umbra' *L.L.L.* IV. ii, 95.

But whatever Shakespeare's small Latin amounted to it was from Arthur Golding's translation of *The Metamorphoses* (Books I-iv, 1565; V-XV 1567) that he was chiefly indebted to Ovid. In Shakespeare's 'first heir' of his 'invention' *Venus and Adonis*, the description by Venus of the boar which Adonis wants to hunt (11. 619-30) is like Golding's version of the story in *Metamorphoses* Book X. And quite unmistakable is his adaptation in one of his latest plays, *The Tempest* of Golding's rendering of the lines in which the sorceress Medea appeals for aid to the elemental powers. For the relation between Medea's speech and Prospero's abjuration of his 'rough magic', and for an echo of Golding in *Much Ado About Nothing*, I would refer readers to the essay on *Ovid and the Elizabethans*, pp. 108-10. Of Greek authors in the original Shakespeare probably knew nothing. He was interested in the Pythagorean theory of transmigration of souls. Plato he does not mention. And it is a first-class anachronism when in *Troilus and Cressida* he makes Hector speak of

Young men, whom Aristotle thought
Unfit to hear moral philosophy.

For the tragic love-story of Troilus and Cressida, and other
romantic elements, he may have been indebted in part to Chaucer's
Troilus and Criseyde, or Raoul de Fèvre's *Receuil des Histoires de
Troye*, translated by Caxton. For the unfavourable light in which
the great Greek heroes, Achilles and Ajax, are represented, the
most likely theory, in my opinion, is that Shakespeare had been
reading and was retorting to George Chapman's translation of the
first seven books of *The Iliad* (1599). I hold to the view that
Shakespeare was referring to this translation in fourteen syllable
metre when in sonnet 86 he complained to William Herbert, or
whoever else he was addressing, of the rival poet, with

The proud full sail of his great verse
Bound for the prize of all too precious you.

This is all the more probable because a later edition of the translation contains a dedicatory sonnet to Herbert. Nor was this the
only work of Chapman which Shakespeare seems to have read.
Sonnet 86 goes on:

Neither he, nor his compeers by night,
Giving him aid, my verse astonished.
He nor that affable familiar ghost,
Which nightly gulls him with intelligence.

These singular lines refer to a poem of Chapman, *The Shadow of
the Night*, and to the dedication in which he speaks of skill in
poetry being sought by its true devotees 'with invocation, fasting,
watching, yet not without having drops of their soul like a
heavenly familiar'. In the phrase 'the school of Night' in *Love's
Labour's Lost* he had already probably tilted against these esoteric
productions of Chapman and his compeers.

It was Chapman who completed Marlowe's unfinished poem
Hero and Leander, one of the most lovely products of the Renaissance enthusiasm for classical legend, and a finer piece of art than
either of Shakespeare's youthful poems. That Shakespeare read and
remembered Marlowe's poem is shown by his quotation of a line

from it in *As you Like It*, III, v. 83. Rosalind is bidding Phebe, whom she calls shepherdess, love Silvius and not herself, whereupon Phebe cries:

> Dead Shepherd, now I find thy saw of might
> 'Who ever loved that loved not at first sight?'

This is the closing line of the couplet in *Hero and Leander*, I. 175-76.

> Where both deliberate, the love is slight
> Who ever lov'd that lov'd not at first sight?

The passage is generally quoted as an affectionate tribute of Shakespeare to Marlowe, but would he have put this into the mouth of the fickle Phebe?

For the story of a much later pair of star-crossed lovers than Hero and Leander, Shakespeare had recourse chiefly to a poem far inferior to Marlowe's two Sestiads, but with considerable merit in its own style, Arthur Broke's *Romeus and Juliet* (1562). The story had been known in different forms for about a century but it was Broke's long narrative poem in couplets, of which the first line is six feet and the second is seven, that had been read by Shakespeare and which inspired him. It was Broke who first gave prominence to the character of the Nurse. Here are some of the words in which she consoles Juliet after Tybalt's death and Romeo's banishment:

> With patience arme thyselfe, for though that Fortune's cryme,
> Without your falt, to both your greefes, depart[1] you for a time,
> I dare say, for amendes of all your present payne,
> She will restore your owne to you, within a month or twayne,
> With such contented ease, as never erst you had,
> Wherefore rejoyce a while in hope, and be no more so sad.

She advised the girl to hie to Frier Lawrence's cell and it is Broke who invented the scene of Romeo's despairing outburst there.

Shakespeare also made use of the prose version of the story translated from the French of Pierre Boisteau by William Painter and included in his collection of novels, *The Palace of Pleasure*,

[1] depart=separate.

1567, where it is the 25th in the series. Thus we pass from poems original or translated which Shakespeare read to novels and romances.

Boisteau's tale was itself a version of one by the Italian novelist, Bandello. Another novel by Bandello, in a French translation by Belleforest in his *Histories Tragiques*, may have given Shakespeare the basis of the stratagem by which Claudio is led to think Hero unfaithful in *Much Ado About Nothing*. No English version of this is known, but Sir J. Harington in his translation of Ariosto's *Orlando Furioso* (1598) treated a similar episode. Nor is any English translation known of the tale by the Italian Cinthio, 'The Story of a Moorish Captain' in his *Hecatommithi*, which provided material for *Othello*.

The Spanish pastoral romance *Diana* by Montemayor was translated by Bartholomew Yonge, but not printed before 1598, too late for Shakespeare to have used the story of Felismena in it as the basis for *Two Gentlemen of Verona*. In the *Palace of Pleasure*, Shakespeare found a translation of Boccaccio's novel, *Giglietta di Nerbona*, source of *All's Well*.

But Shakespeare's reading of novels was not confined to those of foreign origin. That he was well acquainted with John Lyly's *Euphues* is plain from Falstaff's parody of the peculiarities of its style when in a mock impersonation of King Henry IV, he is reproving Prince Hal. These peculiarities include an artificial balance of clauses in a sentence through antithesis and transverse alliteration; and the introduction, especially in the form of similes, of an almost entirely fictitious natural history. Here is part of Falstaff's speech, I *Henry IV*, Act II, Sc. iv:

> Harry, I do not only marvel where thou spendest thy time, but also how thou art accompanied; for though the camomile, the more it is trodden on, the faster it grows, yet youth, the more it is wasted, the sooner it wears . . . pitch, as ancient writers do report, doth defile; so doth the company thou keepest: for Harry, now I do not speak to thee in drink, but in tears, not in pleasure, but in passion; not in words only, but in woes also.

How plain are the Euphuistic stigmata there! But if Shakespeare, with his keen sense of any extravagance or absurdity, could thus caricature the weaker points of Euphuism, he was also not without a debt to it. The besetting temptation of much of Elizabethan prose was a loose, broken-backed redundancy, and the clear-cut, taut prose dialogue of *Much Ado* and *As You Like It* owes something to Lyly's structural technique.

Indeed *As You Like It* has its source in a tale directly inspired by Lyly's didactic novel. Thomas Lodge during a voyage to the islands of Tercera and the Canaries diverted himself by writing a romance which he called *Rosalynde: Euphues Golden Legacie* which he represented that Euphues had bequeathed to the sons of his friend, Philautus. In the tale Rosader is wronged by his elder brother Saladin, corresponding to Orlando and Oliver. And the two Dukes in the play, the usurper and his dispossessed brother, correspond to Torismond and Gerismond, the lawful King of France. Rosalind keeps her name in both novel and play and her cousin Alinda becomes Celia. In the last words of Sir John of Bordeaux to his sons we can hear the Euphuistic echoes:

> Women are wantons, and yet man cannot want one; and therefore, if you love, choose her that hath eyes of adamant, that will turn only to one point; her heart of a diamond, that will receive but one form; her tongue of a silken leaf, that never wags but with a southeast wind; and yet, my sons, if she have all these qualities, to be chaste, obedient and silent, yet for that she is a woman, shalt thou find in her sufficient vanities to counteract her virtues.

But even such warnings avail nothing against the charms of Rosalynde, the paragon of all earthly perfections. In describing her Lodge heaps up, in another fashion of speech borrowed from Euphuism, mythological similes:

> The blush that gloried Luna, when she kissed the shepherd on the hills of Latmos, was not tainted with such a pleasant dye as the vermilion flourished on the silver hue of Rosalynde's countenance . . . [her eyes] courteous and yet coy as if in them Venus had placed all her amorets and Diana all her chastity . . . the tresses that fold in the brows of Apollo were not half so rich to the sight, for in her hair it seems love had laid herself in ambush.

For such ornate phraseology Shakespeare substituted the magical freshness of his own forest of Arden, while Jaques and Touchstone are entirely his own creations. But had there been no *Rosalynde: Euphues Golden Legacie*, there would have been no *As You Like It*.

So too had not Shakespeare read and adapted Greene's novel *Pandosto*, or *Dorastus and Fawnia*, as it was afterwards called, there would have been no *Winter's Tale*. Like *Rosalynde*, Greene's tale combines Euphuistic mannerisms with a pastoral element. Shakespeare, however, departs more freely from his source than he did in *As You Like It*. Bellaria (Hermione) dies as the result of her jealous husband's treatment, instead of living in concealment to be restored after many years to his arms. Hence the main part of Greene's tale is concerned with the fortunes of Fawnia, Shakespeare's Perdita.

It is more difficult to say what Shakespeare read before writing *Twelfth Night*. The main love-plot with its complications he may have found in Barnabe Riche's story of *Apollonius and Silla* or in Forde's *Parisumus*, which introduces the names Olivia and Violetta. But the play has striking resemblances to an Italian comedy, *Gl' Ingannati* (the Deceived) and to the Cambridge Latin play, *Laelia*.

For the under plot of Gloucester and his sons in *King Lear*, Shakespeare appears to have been indebted to the story of the blind King of Paphlagonia in Sidney's *Arcadia*. Whether he had read the old play of *King Leir*, as well as Holinsted's chronicle, before writing the main plot is doubtful, in any case he changed to tragedy what they both had made a happy ending, with Lear reinstated and Cordelia surviving to succeed him.

With the mention of the old *King Leir* we may turn from novels read by Shakespeare to plays which he either used as sources or to which he made incidental allusion. And here we must remember that some of these source plays have not survived. There are two specially notable instances in connexion with *The Merchant of Venice* and *Hamlet*. The two plots in *The Merchant* of the Jew usurer and the pound of flesh, and of the choice of the caskets, could have been found separately by Shakespeare in various forms. But Stephen Gosson in his *Schole of Abuse* (1579) alludes favourably to a play '*The Jew*, shown at the Bull, representing the greediness of worldly chusers and the bloody minds of usurers'. For Gosson to speak well of a play it must have had considerable merit, and his phrases imply a combination of the caskets and the pound of flesh episodes, which seems likely to have given the suggestion to Shakespeare.

But there remains the sub-plot of Jessica and her Christian lover, and here Shakespeare must have been remembering Abigail, the daughter of Barabas in Marlowe's *Jew of Malta*. When Shylock exclaims, 'My daughter and my ducats,' is he not echoing the cry of Barabas, as Abigail throws money-bags into his arms, 'O girl, O gold, O beauty, O my bliss!'

So with *Hamlet*. It is true that the story appeared in French prose in Belleforest's *Histoires Tragiques* (1570) but the earliest known English version is *The Historie of Hamblet*, 1608. On the other hand Nashe in his preface to Greene's novel, *Menaphon*, about 1589, speaks of 'shifting companions who will give you whole Hamlets, I should say handfuls of tragical speeches.' Lodge in his *Wit's Miserie*, 1598, alludes to 'the visard of the ghost which cried so miserably at the Theater "Hamlet revenge".' There was thus an earlier Hamlet play, almost certainly by Kyd, whose *Spanish Tragedy* deals with a father's procrastinating revenge for the murder of his son, as *Hamlet* with a son's procrastinating revenge for the murder of his father. There can be little doubt that Shakespeare took this play as his basis, and it is possible that the first quarto represents something of the transition stage between the two.

In these cases there is necessarily room for speculation, but in others we can point directly to plays that Shakespeare must have read and used. The *Taming of a Shrew* supplied the basis of *The Shrew* including the Christopher Sly background. I disbelieve in the recent attempt to make out that *A Shrew* is a bad quarto of *The Shrew*. Similarly unacceptable is the theory that the two part *Troublesome Raigne of King John* is a bad quarto of *King John*, of which it is really the source. But Shakespeare drew closely together what was prolix in the older play and omitted some unseemly monastery scenes. In *Richard II* there are such close echoes of a play, recently edited by Mr. Rossiter from MS. as *Woodstock*, that it looks as if Shakespeare knew this play dealing with the conflict between the favourites Bushy, Bagot and Greene and the good Protector, Richard's uncle, 'plain Thomas'. From *The Famous Victories of Henry V* he drew some material for Prince Hal's youthful escapades, and the name Oldcastle, as Falstaff was originally called. On the other hand *The First Part of the Contention* and *The True Tragedy of Richard, Duke of York,* have now been generally accepted as bad quartos of Parts II and III of *King Henry VI.*

Apart from sources we get some interesting light on Shakespeare's reading from incidental references to other plays. Thus the phrase 'Basiliso' used by Faulconbridge in *King John,* I, 1–244, is a reference to a character in the anonymous *Soliman and Perseda,* which also forms the plot of the play within the play in Kyd's *Spanish Tragedy.* In the same scene in I *Henry IV,* II, iv. in which Falstaff impersonates the King, affecting Euphuistic style, he also declares that he will speak 'in passion, in King Cambyses vein', an allusion to the notorious melodramatic play, by Richard Preston. And Pistol's quotation in II *Henry IV,* II, iv.

> Ye pampered jades of Asia,
> Which cannot go but 30 miles a day

is a garbled version of the speech in which Marlowe's Tamburlaine spurs on the conquered Kings yoked to his triumphal car. But, so far as I know, Shakespeare shows no sign of having read Marlowe's most characteristic play, *Doctor Faustus.* No two magicians could be more different than Faustus and Prospero.

Other incidental allusions cast some light on what I may call Shakespeare's miscellaneous prose reading. Beatrice accuses Benedick of getting his witticisms out of *The Hundred Merry Tales.* The devils, whose names Edgar in *King Lear* rattles off when he assumes the disguise of a Tom of Bedlam, are lifted from a controversial treatise by Samuel Harsnett, *The Declaration of Popish Impostures,* (1603). For the framework of *The Tempest,* Shakespeare must have gone to Sylvester Jourdain's *A Discovery of th Bermudas, otherwise called the Isle of Divels* (1610). Jourdan had been a member of the expedition which set out across the Atlantic in 1609 under the command of Sir George Somers. The Admiral-ship had been separated in a storm from the other vessels and driven on

the Bermuda coast. The crew, of whom Jourdan was one, escaped
and having built two boats of cedar set sail for Virginia where
they re-embarked for England. The Bermudas appear in *The
Tempest* as the 'still-vext Bermoothes'; and the Isle of Devils is
echoed in Shephano's exclamation when he first sees Caliban,
'Have we devils here?' And Jourdain's narrative gave Shakespeare
his hint for the separation at the beginning of *The Tempest* of the
King's ship from its companion vessels and the miraculous preservation of the shipwrecked mariners.

Shakespeare before he wrote *The Tempest* must also have been
reading Florio's translation of Montaigne's *Essays* (1603), which
contains the following passage:

> It is a nation that hath no kind of traffic, no knowledge of letters,
> no intelligence of numbers, no name of magistrate, nor of
> politic superiority, no use of service, of riches or of poverty, no
> contracts, no successions, no partitions, no occupation but idle;
> no respect of kindred but common; no apparel but natural, no
> manuring of lands, no use of wine, corn or metal.

Gonzalo is evidently echoing this when he declares what he
would do if he were King of the isle:

> I' the commonwealth I would by contraries
> Execute all things; for no kind of traffic
> Would I admit; no name of magistrate:
> Letters should not be known, riches, poverty,
> And use of service none; contract, succession,
> Bourn, bound of land, tilth, vineyard, none.
> No use of metal, corn, or wine, or oil;
> No occupation; all men idle, all;
> And women too, but innocent and pure.
> No sovereignty.

Whereupon Sebastian bursts out, 'Yet he would be King on't'
and Antonio truly comments, 'The latter end of his commonwealth
forgets the beginning.'

But if Shakespeare could in his later days make incidental mock
of the idea of a Utopian commonwealth, he had for many years
lingered over the story of his own country as related by the

chroniclers, especially Raphael Holinshed. His *Chronicles of England, Scotland and Ireland* had appeared in 1577 in two folio volumes. This was followed by a new edition in January, 1586–7, in three volumes, and it was this that Shakespeare used.

It has to be remembered that it was not only for what we now class as the historical plays that Shakespeare went to Holinshed, and in a minor degree to Halle and Stow. *King Lear, Macbeth* and in part *Cymbeline* are drawn from Holinshed as well as the Henrys and the Richards. Shakespeare like the earlier dramatists who put *Gorbodue* and *The Misfortunes of Arthur* upon the lawyers' stage did not recognize the cleavage between the legendary regal figures and the Plantaganets which scientific history has taught us to draw. Nor would it occur to him to ask whether Macbeth was in reality the tyrant whom he found depicted in the chronicle, or was in truth a reputable King. He took what he found and gave it the triumphant impress of his genius. He altered however occasionally when it was necessary for his dramatic perspective. To give one striking example, Harry Percy, Hotspur, was considerably senior to Prince Hal, but to point the contrast between them Shakespeare gives the impression that they are about the same age.

And the very fact that Holinshed and his contemporaries were chroniclers, not in the full sense historians, made them all the more adapted to Shakespeare's purposes. They did not deal with economic and social problems but gave prominence to personal characteristics and the more striking and highly coloured aspects of events. They thus provided the very stuff out of which drama could be wrought.

This is even more true of another of Shakespeare's favourite books, Sir Thomas North's translation (1579) of Amyot's French version of *Plutarch's Lives of Illustrious Greeks and Romans*. The late Greek writer Plutarch was not, like Holinshed, primarily an annalist but, as the title of his work shows, a biographer. He sought as he tells 'the distinctive marks of the soul, in the smallest facts, in witty answers and lively off-hand remarks which often show a man's character more clearly than murderous combats, or great battles, or the taking of towns'. His is a psychological interpretation of history and with this he combined remarkable artistic quality, which did not suffer in Sir Thomas North's brilliant translation. And that Shakespeare instinctively recognized this is evident from the surprising fidelity with which he followed North's wording while yet raising the dialogue to a still higher level. This is true of all the three Roman history plays, *Julius Cæsar, Antony and Cleopatra,* and *Coriolanus,* and in part of *Timen of Athens.* And it reaches its climax in *Antony and Cleopatra* where Plutarch's Life of Antony, itself a half-oriental glowing romance, provided subject material of which Shakespeare made equally superb use.

Lastly in Shakespeare's reading we must of course include the Bible. Mr. Richmond Noble in his Shakespeare's *Biblical Knowledge* (1935) has reckoned that he made identifiable quotations from, or allusions to, at least 42 books of the Bible, 18 each from the Old and New Testaments, and 6 from the Apocrypha. Of the different versions available in Elizabeth's reign, he thinks that he used the Geneva Bible (1560) for the Old Testament, together with Laurence Tomson's revised version of the New Testament which was often bound up with it. He also used the Bishops' Bible (1568) and the Book of Common Prayer.

The following are some selected examples from the plays with the corresponding Biblical passages illustrating the medley of uses, serious and humorous, to which Shakespeare turned his scriptural knowledge:

THE MERCHANT OF VENICE.

Shylock (I, iii):
When Jacob graz'd his Uncle Laban's sheep . . .
Mark what Jacob did.
When Laban and himself were compromised
That all the eanlings which were streaked and pied
Should fall as Jacob's hire . . .
The skilful shepherd peel'd me certain wands
And, in the doing of the deed of kind,
He stuck them up before the fulsome ewes,
Who then conceiving did in eaning time
Fall parti-coloured lambs, and those were Jacob's.

Based on *Genesis* Chap. XXX, 32–41.

Gratiano (I, i):
    I do know of these, that therefore only are reputed wise
    For saying nothing, when I am very sure,
    If they should speak, would almost damn those ears
    Whick hearing them would call their brothers fools.

Matthew V, 22:
    Whosoever shall say unto his brother 'Raca' shall be in
    danger of the council, but whosoever shall say 'thou fool'
    shall be in danger of hell fire.

Portia (IV, i):
    The quality of mercy is not strained,
    It droppeth as the gentle rain from heaven
    Upon the place beneath.

Eccles. XXXV, 19:
    O how fair a thing is mercy in the face of argument and
    trouble; it is like a cloud of rain that cometh in the time of
    drought.

KING JOHN.

Constance (III, i):
    Nay rather turn this day out of the week.

Job III, 6:
    Let it not be joined unto the days of the year.

Faulconbridge (V, vi):
    Withold thine indignation, mighty heaven,
    And tempt us not to bear above our power.

I *Cor.* X, 13:
    But God is faithful, which shall not suffer you to be tempted
    above that you are able.

HAMLET.

Hamlet (I, iv):
    Angels and ministers of grace defend us!

Hebrews I, 7:
    He maketh his angels spirits and his ministers a flame of fire.

Hamlet (III, ii):
    By these pickers and stealers.

The Catechism:
Thy hands from picking and stealing.

Hamlet (V, ii):
There is special providence in the fall of a sparrow.
Matthew X, 29:
Are not two sparrows sold for a farthing, and one of them shall not fall on the ground without your Father.

TROILUS & CRESSIDA.
Hector (II, ii):
Have ears more deaf than adders to the voice.
Psalm LVIII, 4–5:
They are like the deaf adder that stoppeth her ears; which refuseth to hear the voice of the charmer.

Pandarus (III, i):
. . . is love a generation of vipers?
Luke III, 7:
Oh, generation of vipers.

Troilus (IV, iv):
A kind of godly jealousy.
II *Cor.* XI, 2:
For I am jealous over you with godly jealousy.

THE TAMING OF THE SHREW.
Petruchio (III, ii):
She is my goods, my chattels, she is my house,
My horse, my household stuff, my field, my barn,
My ox, my ass, my anything.
The 10*th Commandment:*
Thou shalt not covet thy neighbour's house,
Thou shalt not covet thy neighbour's wife,
Nor his servant, nor his maid, nor his ox,
Nor his ass, nor anything that is his.

THE WINTER'S TALE.
Leontes (I, ii):
My heart dances but not for joy.

Psalm XXVII, 8:
Therefore my heart danceth for joy.

OTHELLO.
Iago (III, iii):
Good name in man or woman . . .
Is the immediate jewel of their souls.
Prov. XXII, 1:
A good name is more to be desired
than great riches.

Othello (IV, ii):
Had it pleas'd Heaven
To try me with affliction, had he raised
All kinds of sores and shames on my bare head,
Steep'd me in poverty to the very lips.
A remembrance of the trials of Job.

MIDSUMMER NIGHT'S DREAM.
Bottom (IV, i):
The eye of man hath not heard, the ear of man hath not seen,
man's hand is not able to taste, his tongue to conceive, nor
his heart to report what my dream was.
I *Cor.* II, 9:
The eye hath not seen, and the ear hath not heard, neither
have entered into the heart of man the things which God hath
prepared for them that love him.

I. HENRY IV.
The Prince (I, ii):
Wisdom cries out in the streets and no man regards it.
Proverbs I, 20–24:
Wisdom crieth without: she uttereth her voice in the streets.

Falstaff (II, iv):
If to be fat be to be hated, than Pharaoh's lean kine are to be
loved.
Gen. XLI, 3–4:
Pharaoh's dream.

Shakespeare was thus what the libraries would now call a 'general reader'. But I would prefer to say that he had the catholicity of taste, the boundless curiosity typical of the Elizabethan age. With all the calls upon him as an actor, a playwright, and a man of business with interests both in London and Stratford, he found time to read widely. All was fish, poetry, novels, plays, pamphlets that came to his net. His mind has been compared to a sensitive photographic plate that retained every impression upon it.

He was not a learned man, and all the fantastic theories based upon the assumption that the plays could only have been written by such a one may be given short shrift. His knowledge of the glories of Israel, Greece and Rome in the past, and Italy and France of his own day, was gained at secondhand through translations and cyclopaedias, but it was not second-rate. By the instinct of supreme genius he transformed, enriched and raised to transcendent heights what he had read and memorised, and Shakespeare's reading has thus left to the world in his plays an imperishable legacy.

FOUR

ASPECTS OF CLASSICAL LEGEND
AND HISTORY IN SHAKESPEARE

I NOTICED that in a recent volume on Marlowe my study of the classical influences on his work appeared to have roused interest. I have therefore thought that it might not be inopportune to discuss once more some features of the old but ever fresh theme of Shakespeare's 'small Latin and less Greek'. I wish to make it clear at once that I shall not be primarily concerned with the Roman history plays, but with the stream of classical allusions that runs through the Shakespearian canon.

Recent investigation has thrown new light on some probable sources of Shakespeare's humanist outfit. Its basis was of course laid at Stratford-on-Avon Grammar School, where he was drilled in William Lily's Latin grammar and in such an elementary phrase-book as *Sententiae Pueriles*. There is an echo of this grounding in the scene in *The Merry Wives* where Sir Hugh Evans puts Will Page through his *qui*'s, *quae*'s, *and quod*'s. It furnished phrases for the talk between Holofernes and Sir Nathaniel in *Love's Labour's Lost*. But in her able study of that play (1936) Miss Frances Yates indicated that the dialogue was also indebted to John Eliot's *Ortho-epia Gallica* (1593), which was an elaborate skit on the popular manuals for teaching foreign languages, including not only Florio's Anglo-Italian *First Fruits* and *Second Fruits* and Hollyband's *The French Schoolmaster* but also J. L. Vives's Anglo-Latin colloquies. An American scholar, Mr. D. T. Starnes, has also recently drawn attention[1] to the material in Renaissance dictionaries, especially Sir Thomas Elyot's *Bibliotheca,* twice revised and enlarged by Thomas Cooper in 1552 and 1595. This was in the first place a dictionary in which Latin words and phrases were rendered by a number of English synonyms. Thus *coelum* (in addition to other meanings) is 'heaven, the firmament, the air', and *terra* (also

[1] 'Literary Features of Renaissance Dictionaries', in *Studies in Philology* (Jan. 1940).

with additions) is 'earth, land, ground'. Is not Holofernes copying this method, when he talks of 'the ear of *coelo*—the sky, the welkin, the heaven', and 'the face of *terra*—the soil, the land, the earth' (*L.L.L.* IV. ii. 5–7)? But the *Bibliotheca* was also a cyclopaedia giving *inter alia* accounts of classical worthies, legendary or historical, though not always with a sense of proportion. Thus Hercules has a column and a half, while Dido is merely 'a lady that builded Carthage'. Cicero has a generous allowance, but Julius Caesar is simply listed under his 'noble house' as the first emperor of Rome. Such compilations were very popular and they may well have supplemented for the dramatist North's *Plutarch* and Golding's version of Ovid's *Metamorphoses*. Turberville's translation of the *Heroides* and Marlowe's of the *Amores* were also available. The couplet from the *Amores* prefixed to *Venus and Adonis, 'Vilia miretur vulgus'*, &c., and that quoted from the *Heroides* in *T. of Sh.* III. i. 28–9, '*Hic ibat Simois*', &c., might seem to prove that Shakespeare was acquainted with these poems in the original. But even what I may call the tempered orthodoxy of Sir Edmund Chambers, to which I adhere, regards the underplot in *T. of Sh.* as probably not from his hand; and the publisher may have been responsible for the quotation at the head of *Venus and Adonis*. The only Latin verse in a play that is indisputably Shakespeare's is the neo-classic first line of the *Eclogues* of Mantuanus declaimed by Holofernes in *L.L.L.* IV. ii. 95. Other Latin verse quotations (as distinguished from schoolbook words and phrases) from Ennius, Horace, Virgil, Seneca, and Ovid are found in early plays and are, in my opinion, *pro tanto* evidence against Shakespeare's sole authorship. The more that I am convinced of the dramatist's absorbing interest in classical lore, the less can I trace signs of intimate first-hand familiarity with the Roman masters of poetry and prose.

One other source of Shakespeare's classical outfit should not be overlooked. It must have been from personal observation that he describes pictures and tapestries depicting old-world scenes. There are the paintings of the siege of Troy in the chamber of Lucrece and of the mythological subjects offered to the tinker Sly. The shaven Hercules in 'the smircht wormeaten tapestry' (*Much Ado*, III. iii. 133–4) contrasts with the tapestry of silk and silver which adorns

Imogen's chamber, depicting the meeting of Antony and Cleopatra on the river Cydnus (*Cymb*. II. iv. 69 ff.), while the chimney-piece was carved to represent chaste Diana bathing.

With such equipment how did Shakespeare envisage the gods, heroes, and mortals of antiquity?

Of the Olympian deities Jupiter was seen by him chiefly under two aspects. He is the all-powerful god, the thunderer. As Dr. R. K. Root has observed in his valuable monograph, *Classical Mythology in Shakespeare* (1903), the conception here is at times Hebraic rather than classical. He is the 'thunder-bearer', 'the thunder-darter'. The Duke of Exeter in *Hen. V*, II. iv. 99-100, warns the French king that

> in fierce tempest is he coming,
> In thunder and in earthquake, like a Jove.

In *Cor*. IV. v. 109-11 the idea of Jupiter as a god of elemental power is combined with that of him as the embodiment of absolute truth:

> If Jupiter
> Should from yond cloud speak divine things,
> And say ' tis true'.

Here again the conception has something of a Hebraic note. But, strangely enough, the most majestic image of the chief Olympian's creative power is to be found in Nestor's splendid tribute to Hector in his militant glory (*Tr. and Cress*, IV. v. 191):

> Lo, Jupiter is yonder, dealing life.

In singular contrast is the other aspect in which the god most frequently figures in the plays, as a lover, pursuing the daughters of men in animal disguise. Of his amours, that which caught Shakespeare's fancy most vividly was his wooing of Europa in the shape of a bull. When Poins in *2 Hen. IV*, II. ii. 186 ff. proposes to the Prince that they should disguise themselves as drawers to wait upon Falstaff and Doll Tearsheet, Henry exclaims, 'From a god to a bull? a heavy descension! it was Jove's case'. Falstaff himself in *M.W.W*. V. v. 3, while waiting for Mistress Ford in the forest, calls out, 'Remember, Jove, thou wast a bull for thy Europa; love set on thy horns'. And he reminds the god of another of his amorous transformations: 'You were also, Jupiter, a swan for the love of Leda'. In *Much Ado* V. iv. 45 ff., Claudio makes a punning allusion when rallying Benedick:

> All Europa shall rejoice at thee,
> As once Europa did at lusty Jove,
> When he would play the noble beast in love.

When Benedick answers,

> Bull Jove, sir, had an amiable low,

there is apparently a reminiscence of Golding who says of the metamorphosed god that he 'goes gently lowing up and down'. Florizel in *W.T.* IV. iv. 25 ff., in excusing to Perdita his disguise for her sake as a shepherd swain, declares:

> The gods themselves,
> Humbling their deities to love, have taken
> The shapes of beasts upon them: Jupiter
> Became a bull, and bellow'd.

The rape of Io, though the god is not mentioned by name, is one of the realistic pictures offered to Sly for his entertainment in the Induction to *T. of Sh.* ii. 56–8.

> We'll show thee Io as she was a maid,
> And how she was beguiled and surprised,
> As lively painted as the deed was done.

The pure-minded Juliet can scarcely have known such stories, yet it is she who reminds Romeo (*R. and J.* II. ii. 92–3),

> at lovers' perjuries,
> They say, Jove laughs.

Another of Jupiter's transformations, for less questionable purposes, which caught Shakespeare's imagination was his lodging in the shape of a servant with the rustic couple Philemon and Baucis. The story is told by Ovid in *Metamorphoses*, viii. 630 ff. and is introduced enigmatically into the ball-room dialogue between Hero and Don Pedro, both masked, in *Much Ado*, II. i. 90 ff.

When the former tells the latter that she does not like his 'favour' or appearance, Don Pedro replies, 'My visor is Philemon's roof; within the house is Jove'; whereupon Hero retorts, 'Why, then, your visor should be thatched'. Here again the reference is to Golding's description of the cottage, 'The roofe thereof was thatched all with straw and fennish reede'. A more oblique allusion to the same episode comes somewhat more aptly from the cynical lips of Jaques in *A.Y.L.* III. iii. 10–12. When Touchstone has told Audrey, 'I am here with thee and thy goats, as the most capricious poet, honest Ovid, was among the Goths', Jaques comments, 'O knowledge ill-inhabited—worse than Jove in a thatched house!' The audience in the Globe or the Blackfriars must have been remarkably 'quick in the uptake' to seize the allusion here.

Three other gods are associated with Jupiter in Hamlet's description of his father—Hyperion, Mars, and Mercury. Hyperion chiefly denotes the Sun-god in his flaming intensity, while Phoebus figures mainly as driving his chariot. Thus the play-scene in *Hamlet* begins,

> Full thirty times hath Phoebus' cart gone round
> Neptune's salt wash and Tellus' orbed ground.

Juliet, eagerly expectant of the night that will bring Romeo to her arms, not only urges the sun's horses to their utmost speed but prays for Phaethon to bring day to a premature end by repeating his disastrous attempt to drive them (*R. and J.* III. ii.. 1–4):

> Gallop apace, you fiery-footed steeds,
> Towards Phoebus' lodging: such a waggoner
> As Phaethon would whip you to the west,
> And bring in cloudy night immediately.

It is Shakespeare's only mention of the Phaethon legend, but it is exquisitely felicitous on Juliet's lips.

Mars for the most part appears in his conventional roles of the war-god and the lover of Venus, but there are two compressed references in *Tr. and Cress.* (III. iii. 188–90) and *Cymb.* (V. iv. 30 ff.) to the singular episode, deriving ultimately from the *Iliad*, v. 864, where he interfered in the battle, was wounded, and was rebuked by Jupiter.

Mercury, like Jupiter, has a curiously double character as the herald of the gods, 'new lighted on a heaven-kissing hill', and as the patron of crafty traders and even of rogues. Thus Feste can pray him to endue Olivia with 'leasing' or lying; and Autolycus boasts himself as 'littered under Mercury' and therefore 'a snapper up of unconsidered trifles'. It is of the god in this ungracious aspect that Armado is thinking when at the end of *L.L.L.* he declares 'The words of Mercury are harsh after the songs of Apollo'. Shakespeare thus regards Apollo pre-eminently as the divinity of music and the arts. When Sly is offered entertainment (*T. of Sh.* Ind. ii) he is asked,

Wilt thou have music? hark! Apollo plays.

Berowne describes Love (*L.L.L.* IV. iii. 342–3)

>   as sweet and musical
> As bright Apollo's lute, strung with his hair.

Even to Thersites in *Tr. and Cress.* (III. iii) he is 'the fiddler Apollo'. But like Jupiter he also figures as an amourist. One of the pictures suggested to Sly is of the god's pursuit of the ill-fated Daphne through a thorny wood, while with Helena and Demetrius the parts are reversed (*M.N.D.* II. i. 231):

Apollo flies, and Daphne holds the chase.

Another episode of rape, that of Proserpina, by the divinity of the underworld, Pluto or Dis, suggests some of the loveliest lines in two of Shakespeare's latest plays. The supposedly rustic Perdita must have been reading Golding's version of the story of the seizure of the maid in a garden, and the flowers slipping from her lap, in Book V of the *Metamorphoses*, when she makes her appeal:

>   O Proserpina,
> For the flowers now that, frighted, thou lett'st fall
> From Dis's waggon! daffodils
> That come before the swallow dares, and take
> The winds of March with beauty.

In *The Tempest* masque Ceres tells Iris that since Venus and Cupid

did plot
The means that dusky Dis my daughter got,
Her and her blind boy's scandal'd company
I have forsworn.

Here and elsewhere, without any apparent classical authority, Shakespeare represents Cupid as blind. Thus Helena, bewailing the dotage of Demetrius on Hermia, exclaims (*M.N.D.* I. i. 234–7)

Love looks not with the eyes, but with the mind,
And therefore is wing'd Cupid painted blind:
Nor hath Love's mind of any judgement taste;
Wings, and no eyes, figure unheedy haste.

Hence Cupid in the plays personifies love not so much in its sensuous as in its capricious, mischief-making aspects. It is characteristic of this tricksy boy-god that he can at will unloose either a golden or a leaden-headed arrow, of which the one causes love and the other arrests it. Here again Golding is the source when Hermia swears

by Cupid's strongest bow,
By his best arrow with the golden head,

that she will meet Lysander.

But for once Cupid used this golden shaft in vain when (*M.N.D.* II. i. 157 ff.)

a certain aim he took
At a fair vestal throned by the west,
And loosed his love-shaft smartly from his bow,
As it should pierce a hundred thousand hearts;
But I might see young Cupid's fiery shaft
Quench'd in the chaste beams of the watery moon,
And the imperial votaress passed on,
In maiden meditaion, fancy-free.

Again Shakespeare does not trouble about consistency, nor ask how a blind archer could take a certain aim. But we forget this in the beauty and historical interest of Oberon's description. Venus, in contrast with her son, is the embodiment of sensual love. This is elaborated in 'the first heir of his invention', *Venus and Adonis*, and is touched upon in references to her intrigue with Mars whereby her sooty husband Vulcan is made a cuckold. But there comes a refreshing breath from the allusions to the doves which bear her through the air, as in the lovely description by Iris in *The Tempest* (IV. i. 92–4):

> I met her deity
> Cutting the clouds towards Paphos, and her son
> Dove-drawn with her.

Opposed to Venus is Diana, the type of chastity. Claudio, crying out against the 'seeming' of Hero, whom he believes false, exclaims bitterly,

> You seem to me as Dian in her orb.

Here there is also the conception of her as the moon-goddess. Thus Lorenzo in the gardens of Belmont bids the musicians wake Diana with a hymn. This image of her is combined with that ot the virgin huntress in Falstaff's exhortation to Prince Hal (1 *Hen. IV*, I. ii. 28 ff.): 'Let us be Diana's foresters, gentlemen of the shade, minions of the moon.'

'Great Juno comes; I know her by her gait', cries Ceres in *The Tempest* masque. She may fitly here close the procession of deities in Shakespeare. She too has a double role. She is for the most part an Olympian virago. Volumnia speaks of herself (*Cor.* IV. ii. 52) as lamenting 'in anger, Juno-like', and Coriolanus invokes 'the jealous queen of heaven' (V. iii. 46). But she appears in more gracious guise when at the close of *The Tempest* masque she pronounces the benediction,

> Honour, riches, marriage-blessing,
> Long continuance, and increasing.

But it is doubtful if any of the Olympians left so deep an impression on Shakespeare as the semi-divine hero, Hercules, or Alcides, son of Jupiter and Alcmena. He is to him the incarnation of bravery and strength. From first to last his exploits seem to have hovered before Shakespeare, if not always in accurate recollection. Thus in *L.L.L.* IV. iii. 340–1 Berowne cries,

> For valour, is not Love a Hercules,
> Still climbing trees in the Hesperides?

and Menenius Agrippa (*Cor.* IV. vi. 99–100) alludes to Hercules shaking down mellow fruit. The Hesperides were, of course, the guardians of the fruit, and it was gathered not by the hero himself but by Atlas for him. In the show of the Nine Worthies in *L.L.L.* he is paradoxically personated by Moth, the page, though Armado protests that 'he is not so big as the end of his club'. Holofernes answers that he represents him 'in his minority'.

> Great Hercules is presented by this imp,
>   Whose club kill'd Cerberus, that three-headed canis,
> And when he was a babe, a child, a shrimp,
>   Thus did he strangle serpents in his manus.

It is true that Hercules, according to Ovid, in his infancy strangled serpents, but though he brought Cerberus to the upper world he did not kill him. Some of the other labours are frequently but vaguely mentioned, the Nemean lion and the Hydra. But the most explicit and vivid description of the hero is Portia's curiously exotic comparison of him in his deliverance of Hesione to Bassanio when he makes his choice of the caskets (*M. of V.* III. ii. 53 ff.):

> Now he goes,
> With no less presence, but with much more love,
> Than young Alcides, when he did redeem
> The virgin tribute paid by howling Troy
> To the sea-monster: I stand for sacrifice;
> The rest aloof are the Dardanian wives,
> With bleared visages, come forth to view
> The issue of th' exploit. Go, Hercules!
> Live thou, I live.

A less lurid aspect of the hero's exploits is remembered by Hippolyta (*M.N.D.* IV. i. 116 ff.):

> I was with Hercules and Cadmus once,
> When in a wood of Crete they bay'd the bear
> With hounds of Sparta. . . . I never heard
> So musical a discord, such sweet thunder.

Yet even this man of might can be vanquished and humiliated by a woman's wiles. Benedick must have had his subjection by Omphale in mind, when he declaims against Beatrice (*Much Ado*, II. i. 260–2): 'She would have made Hercules have turned spit, yea and have cleft his club to make the fire too.' More unexpected is Morocco's comparison of himself and his rivals in the choice of the caskets (*M. of V.* II. i. 32 ff.) to the hero and his page:

> If Hercules and Lichas play at dice
> Which is the better man, the greater throw
> May turn by fortune from the weaker hand:
> So is Alcides beaten by his page.

In more tragic mood Antony, infuriated by Cleopatra's betrayal of him in the sea-fight, wishes to emulate Hercules' treatment of Lichas in his death-agony (*A. and C.* IV. xii. 43–5):

> The shirt of Nessus is upon me:—teach me,
> Alcides, thou mine ancestor, thy rage:
> Let me lodge Lichas on the horns o' the moon.

Hercules was the traditional ancestor of the Antonii, and it is an omen of the Roman's coming doom when music underground betokens that his protector is leaving him (*A. and C.* IV. iii. 16).

It must have helped to keep Hercules prominently before Shakespeare's imagination that the sign of the Globe Theatre was the hero bearing up the world. This explains the punning answer of Rosencrantz to Hamlet's question (II. ii. 377), 'Do the boys carry it away?' 'Ay, that they do, my lord; Hercules and his load too'. But it was left to Ben Jonson to endow the hero with an academic title. In *The New Inn* (IV. iii), after Lovel has delivered an oration on true valour, Lady Frampul cries,

> most manly utter'd all,
> As if Achilles had the chair in valour,
> And Hercules were but a lecturer.

Another of the semi-divine figures, Prometheus, was known to Shakespeare as the bearer of the creative fire. It is mentioned in two strangely diverse connexions. Berowne declares (*L.L.L.* IV. iii. 348) that women's eyes 'sparkle still the right Promethean fire'.

F

Othello, in another of Shakespeare's most exquisite of classical adaptations, thus murmurs over the light beside Desdemona's bed (V. ii. 7 ff.):

> Put out the light, and then put out the light:
> If I quench thee, thou flaming minister,
> I can again thy former light restore,
> Should I repent me; but once put out thy light,
> Thou cunning'st pattern of excelling nature,
> I know not where is that Promethean heat
> That can thy light relume.

The only reference to his punishment by Jove is when Aaron speaks (*Tit. And.* II. i) of Tamora being faster bound to his eyes 'than is Prometheus tied to Caucasus'. Here Shakespeare's hand is doubtful.

Other legends are drawn upon readily to serve varied purposes. Bassanio compares Portia's sunny locks to a golden fleece (*M. of V.* I. i. 171 ff.),

> Which makes her seat of Belmont Colchos' strand,
> And many Jasons come in quest of her,

and Gratiano later cries exultingly, 'We are the Jasons, we have won the fleece'. There is a more recondite allusion to the Argonauts when the restoration of Jason's father to youth by their leader's sorceress wife is visualized by Jessica in her moonlight duet with Lorenzo (*M. of V.* V. i. 12 ff.):

> In such a night
> Medea gathered the enchanted herbs
> That did renew old Æson.

In the same scene of moonlight enchantment Jessica, inspired by Golding, tells how

> In such a night
> Did Thisbe fearfully o'ertrip the dew,
> And saw the lion's shadow ere himself,
> And ran dismay'd away.

Yet at almost the same time Shakespeare did not hesitate to turn the Pyramus and Thisbe story in *M.N.D.* into an immortal burlesque. Bottom, too, can incidentally parody a still greater love tale when he assures Thisbe, 'Like Limander, am I trusty still'; and later Benedick can instance 'Leander, the good swimmer' as one of those 'whose names yet run smoothly in the even road of a blank verse' (*Much Ado,* V. ii. 33–4). Rosalind gives Leander's swimming exploits a yet more satirical twist when she tells Orlando (*A.Y.L.* IV. i. 100 ff.) that on a hot midsummer night 'he went but forth to wash him in the Hellespont, and being taken with the cramp was drowned; and the foolish chroniclers of that age found it was—Hero of Sestos'. Yet in the same play he quotes from Marlowe's *Hero and Leander* the line, 'Who ever loved that loved not at first sight?', and the dramatist of *Romeo and Juliet* must have been thrilled by the poignant beauty of the dead shepherd's unfinished version of this tragic tale of love.

Perhaps the most singular of all Shakespeare's surprising applications of a classical story is to be found in 2 *Hen. IV,* II. ii. 93, where the page cries to the red-faced Bardolph, 'Away, you rascally Althaea's dream, away'. Well may the prince intervene, 'Instruct us, boy; what dream, boy?' whereupon the page explains, 'Marry, my lord, Althaea dreamed she was delivered of a firebrand, and therefore I call him her dream'. But the boy has not verified his references, for Althaea was in truth not merely in a dream delivered of a firebrand, like Hecuba before the birth of Paris. She was warned that her son Meleager would die if a log on the hearth was consumed. There is a more accurate allusion by Shakespeare or another in 2 *Hen. VI,* I i. 235–6 to

> the fatal brand Althaea burn'd
> Unto the prince's heart of Calydon.

But o'ertopping all other old-world legends in sustained interest for Shakespeare were the related sagas of Troy and Carthage. The episodes in the ten years' siege that seem to have chiefly captured his imagination were not primarily the feats of arms but the eloquence of the veteran Nestor, the treachery of Sinon which led to the entry of the wooden horse, the pitiful death of Priam and Hecuba's frantic grief, and the flight of Aeneas bearing his father Anchises. In the well-painted piece portraying the siege hanging in the chamber of Lucrece the three former elements are prominent. Remarkably vivid, after brief sketches of Ajax, and Ulysses, is the picture of grave Nestor surrounded by 'a press of gaping faces', swallowing up his 'golden words'. To Berowne (*L.L.L.* IV. iii. 169) one of the extreme examples of the incongruous is to see 'Nestor play at push-pin [a childish game] with the boys'; and Salarino (*M. of V.* I. i. 54–6) is scornful of the fellows of vulgar aspect who will

> not show their teeth in way of smile,
> Though Nestor swear the jest be laughable.

In 3 *Hen. VI*, III. ii. 188–90, Richard, Duke of Gloucester, planning how to catch the English crown, declares,

> I'll play the orator as well as Nestor,
> Deceive more slily than Ulysses could,
> And, like a Sinon, take another Troy.

In the description of the picture of Troy in Lucrece's chamber no less than ten stanzas are devoted to perjured Sinon and Lucrece's lmpassioned comparison of his hypocrisy with that of her ravisher, Tarquin. In the last scene of *Tit. And.* V. iii. 85–7, Marcus bids Lucius

> Tell us what Sinon hath bewitch'd our ears,
> Or who hath brought the fatal engine in
> That gives our Troy, our Rome, the civil wound.

There are other incidental allusions in *Pericles* and *Cymbeline*.

Of all the tragic consequences of the entry of the 'fatal engine' into Troy Shakespeare seems to have been most deeply stirred by the fate of 'credulous old Priam'. One of the most poignant, though unexpected and classically unsupported, allusions to the catastrophe is Northumberland's outburst in 2 *Hen. IV*, I. i. 70 ff. to Morton who brings him news of the fatal outcome of the battle of Shrewsbury.

> Even such a man, so faint, so spiritless,
> So dull, so dead in look, so woe-begone,
> Drew Priam's curtain in the dead of night,

And would have told him half his Troy was burnt;
But Priam found the fire ere he his tongue.

This does not derive from Virgil, nor does the first player's recital
(*Hamlet* II. ii) of Aeneas' tale to Dido. As I have attempted to show
elsewhere, the *Aeneid*, Book II, gives no authority for a long-
drawn, horrific account of the slaying of the aged king by
Pyrrhus. It is Marlowe in *Dido, Queen of Carthage*, who elaborates
the episode, adding grisly details, and telling how Pyrrhus

>   whisk'd his sword about
> And with the wind thereof the king fell down;
> Then from the navel to the throat at once
> He ripp'd old Priam.

Shakespeare must have had these lines in mind when he wrote:

> Pyrrhus at Priam drives; in rage strikes wide,
> But with the whiff and wind of his fell sword
> The unnerved father falls.

And when the player tells of 'the mobled queen', Hecuba,

> When she saw Pyrrhus make malicious sport
> In mincing with his sword her husband's limbs,
> The instant burst of clamour that she made—
> Unless things mortal move them not at all—
> Would have made milch the burning eyes of heaven,
> And passion in the gods,

there is a more far-off echo of Marlowe's description of the
'frantic queen', leaping upon Pyrrhus, while

>   the soldiers pull'd her by the heels
> And swung her howling in the empty air,
> Which sent an echo to the wounded king,
> Whereat he lifted up his bed-rid limbs,
> And would have grappled with Achilles' son.

But even in burlesque Shakespeare is not over-troubled to be
consistent, and such lines as

> Would have made milch the burning eyes of heaven,
> And passion in the gods

have the ring of the true grand manner, and make us feel it natural that the player should turn his colour and have tears in his eyes.

The flight of Aeneas from the burning city bearing his father was of special significance to the Elizabethans because he was the link between Troy, Carthage, Rome, and, according to medieval and Renaissance belief, Britain. Shakespeare may not have penned young Clifford's comparison when carrying from the battle-field his father's body (2 *Hen. VI,* V. ii. 62 ff.):

> As did Aeneas old Anchises bear,
> So bear I thee upon my manly shoulders.

But to him we certainly owe the similar parallel by Cassius after he had rescued Caesar from drowning (*Jul. Caes.* I. ii. 112 ff.):

> I, as Aeneas, our great ancestor,
> Did from the flames of Troy upon his shoulder
> The old Anchises bear, so from the waves of Tiber
> Did I the tired Caesar.

The reception of Aeneas by Dido, his recital of the fall of Troy, and their short-lived amour have frequent echoes in the early plays of the Folio, though here again Shakespeare's own hand is doubtful. Queen Margaret cries to her husband (2 *Hen. VI,* III. ii. 116) that she has tempted Suffolk

> To sit and witch me, as Ascanius did
> When he to madding Dido would unfold
> His father's acts commenced in burning Troy.

Tamora (*Tit. And.* II. iii. 21) invites Aaron to

> conflict such as was supposed
> The wandering prince and Dido once enjoy'd,
> When with a happy storm they were surprised,
> And curtain'd with a counsel-keeping cave.

Shakespeare too may probably be acquitted of the singularly inappropriate allusion to Dido's loving intimacy with her sister in *T. of Sh.* I. i. 158–9, when Lucentio asks counsel from his servant Tranio,

That art to me as secret and as dear
As Anna to the Queen of Carthage was.

Yet scarcely less far-fetched is the pledge of Hermia to Lysander
(*M.N.D.* I. i. 173–4),

> By that fire which burn'd the Carthage queen,
> When the false Troyan under sail was seen,

that she will keep tryst with him.

These references, whatever their immediate source, derive
ultimately from Virgil, but there is nothing in the *Aeneid* to
suggest the magical loveliness of Lorenzo's picture (*M. of V.* V. i.
9 ff.):

> In such a night
> Stood Dido with a willow in her hand
> Upon the wild sea-banks and waft her love
> To come again to Carthage.

And nothing could bear the more authentic seal of Shakespeare's
imagination at its transcendent height than Antony's cry to
Cleopatra (*A. and C.* IV. xiv. 51 ff.):

> Stay for me:
> Where souls do couch on flowers, we'll hand in hand,
> And with our sprightly port make the ghosts gaze:
> Dido and her Aenas shall want troops,
> And all the haunt be ours.

From this radiant vision of Dido and Aeneas in the Elysian fields
with their admiring 'troops' it is a disconcerting descent to
Shakespeare's last allusion to them in *The Tempest*, II. i. 74 ff.
When Adrian remarks that 'Tunis was never graced before with
such a paragon to their queen' as Claribel, Gonzalo interjects,
'Not since widow Dido's time'.

Ant.: Widow! a pox o' that! How came that widow in?
    Widow Dido!

Seb.: What if he had said, 'widower Aeneas' too? Good Lord,
    how you take it!

Adr.: Widow Dido, said you? you make me study of that: she
          was of Carthage, not of Tunis.
Gon.: This Tunis, sir, was Carthage.

What unforeseen significance had these last words in 1943 when
Tunis was the symbol in all eyes of even more tremendous issues
than was Carthage in the ancient world!

In *Troilus and Cressida*, as has been too little noted, Aeneas
figures in a very different role from that of the faithless lover of
the Carthaginian queen. He is the intermediary between the two
camps; the urbane master of the ceremonies. Detailed discussion
of the problems raised by *Troilus and Cressida* lies outside my
purpose, for alike in the love-story and in the secondary plot
introducing the Greek and Trojan leaders, it is not of classical but
medieval origin. Not Homer nor Virgil but Dares Phrygius,
Benoit de Saint-More, Guido Colonna, Boccaccio, Chaucer, and
Raoul le Fèvre's *Recueil des histoires de Troie*, translated by Caxton,
built up stage by stage this sentimental, pseudo-chivalrous romance, which depicted not only the delirious passion of Priam's
youngest son, Troilus, for Cressida, but an amour between Achilles
and Priam's daughter Polyxena, together with challenges and
interchange of visits between the opposing warriors after the
approved feudal fashion. It is true that this distinction did not
mean as much to Shakespeare as to us, but in any case his humanist
enthusiasm was never felt by him to be inconsistent with a read-
iness to make game of classical legends. His attitude reminds me
of G. K. Chesterton's saying that no one was sufficiently at home
with his religion till he could make fun of it. The show of the
Worthies in *L.L.L.*, the tragical mirth of Pyramus and Thisbe in
M.N.D., Rosalind's raillery of the Leander story in *A.Y.L.*, the
first player's recital in *Hamlet*, are in their different ways illustrations. They should be borne in mind if we are to get Shakespeare's attitude in *Troilus and Cressida* into the right perspective.
But of course the ridicule there is far more embittered and may
have been in part a *riposte* to the publication in 1598 of eight books
of the *Iliad* translated by Chapman, at whose *The Shadow of Night*
he had already tilted in *L.L.L.* (See page 58.)

A recent critic of *Troilus and Cressida*, Professor O. J. Campbell

of Columbia University,[1] has, I think, given help in our approach
to what is perhaps the most difficult of all the problems connected
with the play, and the only one to which I will briefly draw
attention—the character of Thersites. Here there is little question
of medieval influence. Chapman's lines, in his translation of Book
II of the *Iliad*,

> He the filthiest fellow was of all that had deserts
> In Troy's brave siege; he was squint-ey'd and lame of either foot,

seem to have given the hint for the full-length figure compact of
ribaldry and slime to whom 'all the argument is a cuckold and a
whore'. Professor Campbell classes the play as 'a comical satire',
in line with Jonson's *Every Man out of his Humour* and *Cynthia's
Revels*. He lays stress on what I confess that I had insufficiently
appreciated, the professional status of Thersites. He sees him performing 'all the various offices of the railer and the buffoon in the
new satiric comedy', and compares him to Carlo Buffone in
Every Man out of his Humour. But I would add that even if we do
not go outside the Shakespeare canon his professional position is
akin to that of Feste 'the avowed fool' and of the 'all-licensed fool'
in *Lear*. He is at first attendant on Ajax, his 'sodden-witted lord',
'the elephant Ajax' who returns railing for railing and adds blows.
Achilles, though he too is his butt, appreciates his status, and
inveigles him from Ajax. When Patroclus interrupts him, Achilles
reminds his minion that Thersites is 'a privileged man', and bids
him proceed with his catalogue of all fools (II. iii. 63 ff.).

> *Ther.:* Agamemnon is a fool to offer to command Achilles;
> Achilles is a fool to be commanded of Agamemnon;
> Thersites is a fool to serve such a fool; and Patroclus is a
> fool positive.
> *Patr.:* Why am I a fool?
> *Ther.:* Make that demand to the Creator. It suffices me thou art.

It is an unanswerable retort. The amazingly nimble wit of
Thersites and his unsurpassable command of Elizabethan Billings-
gate extort an aesthetic admiration of his most outrageous out-
bursts. But, though he is a privileged man, he stretches beyond

[1] *Comicall Satyre and Shakespeare's 'Troilus and Cressida'* (1938).

even the widest endurable limit Feste's dictum, 'There is no slander in an avowed fool though he do nothing but rail'. By a strange development the Homeric demagogue, transformed into a wearer of the motley, became a mouthpiece of that acute phase of Shakespeare's disillusionment, due perhaps, as Sir Edmund Chambers has suggested, to mental and physical strain, which had its climax in *Timon of Athens*.

In the most glaring of Shakespeare's anachronisms (*Tr. and Cress.* II. ii. 166–7), Hector likens his brothers to

> young men, whom Aristotle thought
> Unfit to hear moral philosophy.

How far Aristotle really took this view, attributed to him also by Erasmus and Bacon, I leave you to infer from a detailed discussion by Sir Sidney Lee.[1] Among the other Greek philosophers, Pythagoras, with his theory of transmigration, is known to Gratiano, Rosalind, and Feste. Epicurus and Socrates, as the husband of Xanthippe, are mentioned, but the great name of Plato is not found in the Shakespearian canon. I must ask Professor Dover Wilson and Miss Yates to make their account with this stark fact in their recent ingenious attempts to show that Shakespeare's cosmology is predominantly Platonic rather than Aristotelian.[2] However this may be, I can find no trace in his conception of sexual relations of the doctrine of so-called Platonic love which was to influence strongly Jacobean and Caroline drama.

Similarly with the great Athenian soldiers and statesmen. Miltiades and Themistocles are unknown to the First Folio. The only Pericles with whom Shakespeare is concerned is the Prince of Tyre, and the Alcibiades in *Timon of Athens* has nothing but his name in common with his historical prototype. The single authentic Greek man of action to whom Shakespeare refers is Alexander the Great. He appears in the show of the Nine Worthies in *L.L.L.* as 'the world's commander', impersonating whom Sir Nathaniel the curate is 'a little o'er-parted'. Henry V before Harfleur, with an unexpectedly 'highbrow' flourish, exhorts his soldiers to prove worthy of their fathers who, like so many Alexanders, had shown their prowess in the fields of France. To

[1] *Life of William Shakespeare*, 653–4, n. 2.
[2] See *University of Edinburgh Jornal*, Summer and Autumn Nos., 1942.

Fluellen it is the king himself who is to be compared with 'Alexander the Pig' (IV. vii. 47 ff.), 'As Alexander killed his friend Cleitus, being in his ales and his cups; so also Harry Monmouth, being in his right wits and his good judgements, turned away the fat knight, with the great-belly doublet'. Was not George Steevens, when he suggested that Shakespeare was here ridiculing Plutarch's method in his *Parallel Lives,* considering too curiously? That is Horatio's criticism of Hamlet when in the graveyard he lets 'imagination trace the noble dust of Alexander till he find it stopping a bung-hole'. But the Prince expatiates further on this grim theme, and with Alexander he couples imperious Caesar in such a sordid anti-climax to their living greatness. Let us with Hamlet pass from Greece to Rome.

Just as Lear and Cymbeline were to Shakespeare probably little less real than the Henrys and Richards of the chronicle-plays, so the legendary figures of early Rome were not as sharply differentiated by him as by us to-day from the personages of the later republic. He had an instinctive conception of the integrity, the 'gravitas', and 'pietas' of the typical Roman character. Hamlet's staunch friend Horatio speaks of himself as

More an antique Roman than a Dane.

Bassanio pays the highest tribute to his dearest friend Antonio when he describes him to Portia as (*M. of V.* III. ii. 297–9)

> one in whom
> The ancient Roman honour more appears
> Than any that draws breath in Italy.

It is the glory of Brutus in the hour of his defeat and death that his own singleness of soul has met a full response (*Jul. Caes.* V. v. 33–5):

> Countrymen,
> My heart doth joy that yet, in all my life,
> I found no man but he was true to me.

It is the same quality that inspires Shakespeare's Roman women. Lucrece is a model of loyalty to her husband Collatinus, and when she has become the victim of Tarquin's outrage she must die by her own hand. Volumnia incarnates the very spirit of Roman patriotism. Perhaps I may be allowed to repeat words which I have already written about her last interview with her son:

> 'The voice of Volumnia pleading with austerely majestic elo-
> quence on behalf of her country, is not so much the voice of the
> human mother as the voice of Rome speaking through her lips.
> All personal feeling is annihilated in the absolute self-surrender
> to the welfare of the State. The Roman who can wound Rome
> is to Volumnia an alien, though he be born of her own body.'
>   Come, let us go:
> This fellow had a Volscian to his mother;
> His wife is in Corioli, and his child
> Like him by chance.

It is significant that the heroine of *The Merchant of Venice* bears the honoured Roman name of Portia. As Bassanio declares, she is (I. i. 165–6),

>   nothing undervalued
> To Cato's daughter, Brutus' Portia.

Thus Shakespeare had felt the magnetism of this classical Portia long before he drew the picture of her in *Julius Caesar* as her husband's perfect helpmeet who after the ruin of his fortunes swallowed fire.

It is curious that Shakespeare's interest in Roman history should apparently have been concentrated on two widely separated epochs. One includes the last days of the monarchy and the beginnings of the republic. The figures of Tarquin and Lucrece had bitten deep into his consciousness. Apart from the poem devoted to them Petruchio declares of Kate (*T. of Sh.* II. i. 297–8):

> For patience she will prove a second Grissel,
> And Roman Lucrece for her chastity.

The characteristic seal of Olivia in *Twelfth Night* is a Lucrece. To Macbeth's heated imagination murder (II. i. 25–6)

> With Tarquin's ravishing strides towards his design
> Moves like a ghost.

The Constable of France warns the Dauphin who has spoken scornfully of King Henry V (II. iv. 36–8):

> You shall find his vanities forespent
> Were but the outside of the Roman Brutus,
> Covering discretion with a coat of folly.

The reference here is of course to the Lucius Junius Brutus, the nephew of Tarquin, who, after the murder of his elder brother, assumed a lunatic pose till the expulsion of the tyrant when, with Lucrece's husband as his colleague, he became one of the first two Consuls.

The action of *Coriolanus* is also laid in the early period when a revolted general, in league with a hostile State, could threaten the life of the young Republic. Then follows a long blank. There is no allusion by Shakespeare to the story of Appius and Virginia, in which Webster was to find a theme. More surprising is it that his preoccupation with Carthage seems to have ended with the flight of Aeneas and the death of Dido. He has not a word about the struggle for the mastery of the Mediterranean world between the African city and Rome. The Shakespeare Concordance does not include the Scipios. Armado appearing as Hector in the show of the Nine Worthies refers almost slightingly to the hero of Carthage,

> This Hector far surmounted Hannibal.

Nothing is said of Sulla or Marius, whose rivalry was the theme of Lodge in *The Wounds of Civil War*.

Shakespeare's eye seems to have glided over the centuries till it became fixed on the figures of Gnaeus Pompeius and Julius Caesar. Pompey, like Alexander, makes a burlesque entrance in the show of the Nine Worthies, impersonated by the clown Costard,

> Pompey, surnamed the Great,
> That oft in field, with targe and shield, did make my foe to sweat.

In *Meas. for Meas.* (II. i. 262 ff.) Escalus makes derisively coarse play with this surname to Pompey, the bawd's servant, and threatens, 'I shall beat you to your tent, and prove a shrewd

Caesar to you; in plain dealing, Pompey, I shall have you whipt'.
But to the shrewd and valiant, if quaint-spoken, soldier Fluellen,
Pompey stands for the model of true military discipline (*Hen. V*,
IV. i. 68 ff.):

> 'If you would take the pains but to examine the wars of Pompey
> the Great, you shall find, I warrant you, that there is no tiddle-
> taddle nor pibble-pabble in Pompey's camp; I warrant you, you
> shall find the ceremonies of the wars, and the cares of it, and the
> forms of it, and the sobriety of it, and the modesty of it, to be
> otherwise.'

What exactly is Fluellen's authority for this tribute I do not know,
but according to him Pompey anticipated the military authorities
of to-day in warning the rank and file against talk that would help
the enemy. There is more historical guarantee for the picture
drawn by the tribune when he reproaches the fickle populace for
welcoming Pompey's victor (*Jul. Caes.* I. i. 42 ff.):

> Knew you not Pompey? Many a time and oft
> Have you climb'd up to walls and battlements, ...
> To see great Pompey pass the streets of Rome:
> And when you saw his chariot but appear,
> Have you not made an universal shout? ...
> And do you now strew flowers in his way
> That comes in triumph over Pompey's blood?

Shakespeare's dramatic instinct can interpret the tribune's indignant feelings, but his own sympathy would have been with the
welcoming crowds. For in the eyes of Shakespeare what Jove was
among the Olympians and Hercules among the half-divine heroes,
Julius Caesar was among mortal men. His presence seems to have
haunted him from his earliest to his latest days of play-making.
Some of the first references are to his connexion, real or legendary,
with Britain. Lord Say, appealing to the men of Kent to save him
during Cade's insurrection (2 *Hen. VI*, IV. vii), declares:

> Kent, in the Commentaries Caesar writ,
> Is term'd the civil'st place of all this isle.

This, the sole reference in the Folio to Caesar merely as an author, is questionably Shakespeare's, but we hear his voice when the young Prince of Wales in *Richard III* (III. i. 69) asks whether Caesar built the Tower of London, and gives a precocious summing-up of his carer:

> That Julius Caesar was a famous man;
> With what his valour did enrich his wit,
> His wit set down to make his valour live:
> Death makes no conquest of this conqueror.

For Shakespeare Caesar sets the standard of all military achievement. When Lord Bardolph brings a report, later proved false, of a victory by Hotspur at Shrewsbury, he ends exultingly (2 *Hen. IV*, I. i. 20–3),

> O! such a day,
> So fought, so follow'd, and so fairly won,
> Came not till now to dignify the times
> Since Caesar's fortunes.

Iago describes Cassio as a soldier fit to stand by Caesar—the highest tribute that could be paid. In *All's Well*, III. vi, a French lord speaks of a disaster of war that Caesar himself could not have prevented, if he had been there to command. And in one of the latest plays, *Cymbeline* (III. i. 2–4), the Roman general, Caius Lucius, speaks reverently of

> Julius Caesar—whose remembrance yet
> Lives in men's eyes, and will to ears and tongues
> Be theme and hearing ever.

Only in one respect did the idol seem to expose feet of clay— in his boast after defeating Pharnaces at Zela, *Veni, vidi, vici*. No less than four times does Shakespeare make game of this. Don Armado plays characteristically upon it in his love-letter to Jaquenetta; Rosalind declares that there was never anything so sudden as the love between Oliver and Celia, but Caesar's thrasonical brag of 'I came, saw, and overcame'. Falstaff, after taking prisoner Sir John Coleville (2 *Hen. IV*, IV. iii), exclaims, 'I may justly say with the hook-nosed fellow of Rome, I came, saw, and overcame'. Cymbeline's queen, parleying with the Roman general, declares (III. i. 22–4):

> A kind of conquest
> Caesar made here, but made not here his brag
> Of 'came, and saw, and overcame'.

Yet it is the telegraphic brevity of this report that serves as the model for the dispatches of generals in the field in modern war.

Shakespeare seems to have had Caesar especially in his thoughts while he was writing *Hamlet*. The appearance of the Ghost, portending 'fierce events', recalls to Horatio how

> In the most high and palmy state of Rome,
> A little ere the mightiest Julius fell,
> The graves stood tenantless and the sheeted dead
> Did squeak and gibber in the Roman streets.

Everyone remembers how in *Jul. Caes.* I. iii, in the dialogue of Casca with Cicero and afterwards with Cassius, the fantastic terrors of that 'dreadful night, that thunders, lightens, opens graves', are portrayed.

Is it not almost a case of Moth representing Hercules that Polonius in a university play should have enacted Julius Caesar? 'I was kill'd i' the Capitol; Brutus killed me', which provokes Hamlet's cynical punning retort, 'It was a brute part of him to kill so capital a calf there'. In more serious mood is the Prince's sardonic meditation in the graveyard on the base uses to which the noblest of mortals may return after death,

> Imperious Caesar, dead and turn'd to clay,
> Might stop a hole to keep the wind away.

'The mightiest Julius', 'imperious Caesar'! Yet when we turn to the play that bears his name the impression is at first scarcely less paradoxical than that made by *Troilus and Cressida*. His infirmities physical and mental are emphasized. He is deaf of one ear and subject to the falling sickness. He is superstitious, vacillating, arrogant. He is killed in Act III. i. Hence on the stage he is overshadowed, in their different ways, by Brutus, Cassius, and Antony, who are the star parts. But though the man Julius is struck down, the spirit of Caesar triumphs. It is embodied in the ghost that appears in his tent at Sardis and on the field of Philippi to Brutus, who, as he looks on the body of Cassius, cries (V. iii. 94–6):

> O Julius Caesar! thou art mighty yet!
> Thy spirit walks abroad, and turns our swords
> In our own proper entrails.

This is echoed in the pregnant phrase in *A. and C.* II. vi. 12–13, recalling how 'Julius Caesar . . . at Philippi the good Brutus ghosted'. And the spirit of Caesar lingers over this later play. It even intrudes into the transcendent love tragedy of the Roman general and the Egyptian queen, for four times, twice by Cleopatra herself, we are reminded that Caesar had been her earlier paramour, and twice mention is made of their son Caesarion. But the play is not merely Shakespeare's most consummate delineation of amorous passion. It depicts the struggle for the mastery of the Roman world. Here Octavius overcomes in turn his two fellow triumvirs, Lepidus and Antony, as well as Sextus Pompeius, who for a time revives on the sea his father's dignities and fame. Thus Octavius succeeds to the role of Julius, of whom Shakespeare, to emphasize their kinship, makes him not the nephew but the son. And the fact that throughout the play he is called simply Caesar indicates that the name has already been transformed into a title, and that (as was historically true) the imperial spirit, which the daggers of the republican conspirators could not reach, was re-embodied in this astute younger scion of the Julian house.

Such an interpretation is, I believe, legitimate. But I cannot go farther and find, as some would do, a political philosophy implicit in these two linked tragedies. Thus recently an American critic, Dr. J. E. Philipps, in a stimulating volume, *The State in Shakespeare's Greek and Roman Plays* (1940), has written:

> The defeat of the conspirators and the discrediting of the aristocratic principle which they represent suggest that Shakespeare saw the inevitability as well as the necessity of rule by one man. The action of *Julius Caesar* demonstrates primarily this necessity of monarchy; the culmination in the slight but positive action of *Antony and Cleopatra* demonstrates its inevitability.

I do not think that Shakespeare's mind moved along such lines of abstract reasoning.

Nor is this the end. 'Westward the course of empire takes its way', and it draws Shakespeare from Cleopatra's Egypt to the Britain of Cymbeline. There when the king's uncle, Cassibelan, was ruler, Julius Caesar had made 'a kind of conquest', though according to Holinshed and Cymbeline's queen (III. i. 26 ff.) his shipping had been wrecked on our terrible seas and 'he was carried From off our coast, twice beaten'. Yet in the end Cassibelan promised a yearly tribute to Rome of three thousand pounds, which Cymbeline had left unpaid. It is demanded in the name of the emperor, now after his long period of settled rule known not as Octavius but Augustus. The queen anticipates her husband in a blunt refusal, and is backed up in characteristically clownish terms by her son Cloten,

> Britain is
> A world by itself; and we will nothing pay
> For wearing our own noses.

The Roman general thereupon formally proclaims Augustus Caesar enemy of the British king, and war follows, affecting not only national fortunes but those of the chief figures in the romantic plots interwoven with the legendary historical action. In the end Britain wins the field, but Cymbeline follows the precedent of Cassibelan (V. v. 460 ff.):

> Although the victor, we submit to Ceesar,
> And to the Roman empire, promising
> To pay our wonted tribute. . . .
> > Publish we this peace
> To all our subjects. Set we forward: let
> A Roman and a British ensign wave
> Friendly together; so through Lud's town march:
> And in the temple of great Jupiter
> Our peace we'll ratify.

Was not the spirit of mighty Caesar potent yet, when the patriot William Shakespeare could present a British king, though undefeated, submitting to the claims of imperial Rome, and confirming this early treaty of London, as we may call it, in the shrine of the chief of the classical gods?

Thus we have come the full circle, for it was with Jupiter that I began this survey. And as I look back on it I feel impelled to urge that Shakespeare's case refutes Pope's dictum that 'a little learning is a dangerous thing'. The evidence shows that the dramatist's classical lore was for the most part gained at second hand. It was also curiously partial, both in its concentration and in its omissions. The gods and heroes of Greece were known to him only under their Latin names. He drew no line between the original old-world legends and the medieval accretions. Every schoolboy is familiar with the anachronisms in the Roman history plays.

None the less, Shakespeare's classical knowledge, though second-hand, was not second-rate and should not be branded as superficial. It was emphatically not on the surface. On the contrary, I would apply to it an epithet unknown in his day, subliminal. It had seeped into his subconscious self, and thence, as he wrote, it welled forth at any moment on to his manuscript. The results, as I have tried to show, were not always equally fortunate. We can point to inconsistencies and incongruities and what seem to modern taste adventitious frills. But for the most part how rich and varied were Shakespeare's gains from the ancient treasure-house! To Marlowe the pagan world stood pre-eminently for beauty, personified in Helen. For Shakespeare too it meant beauty but also wisdom, as embodied in Nestor and Ulysses, and above all power, as exemplified by Jupiter among the gods, Hercules among the heroes, Alexander and Caesar among men. And here again I would submit that the acid test of the quality of Shakespeare's humanism is to be found not in the Roman history plays or *Troilus and Cressida* but in the galaxy of allusions scattered throughout the canon. A Bernard Shaw may, when it suits him, make dramatic sport with Caesar and Cleopatra, or Androcles and the Lion, but we should, I fancy, search his other plays in vain for classical references.

What did the audiences in the Globe and the Blackfriars make of it all? This is to me a constant enigma. The young gallants of the Inns of Court who, like Ovid in Jonson's *Poetaster,* were devotees of poetry instead of law, may have appreciated such echoes of their humanist studies. But how about the citizens and 'prentices, the groundlings? What was Hecuba 'and all that' to them, or they to Hecuba?

Nor is this a matter of merely antiquarian interest. In Shakespeare's time Latin had established itself as the basis of all higher education, and that position it maintained till recently when its ascendancy (and with it the less assured position of Greek) has been challenged from various angles. In his striking presidential address to the Classical Association in April 1942 Mr. T. S. Eliot claimed that the 'maintenance of classical education is essential to the maintenance of the continuity of English literature'. With the wider implications of that thesis I am not here concerned. But it has a direct bearing upon the appreciation and understanding of Shakespeare's work. He was a Warwickshire man, born and bred in the very heart of Elizabethan England; his professional life was spent in its capital city. Yet like so many of his Renaissance contemporaries he had also if not a spiritual, an imaginative, home on the old-world, muse-haunted, Mediterranean shore. If under a new order of education there should arise generations ignorant of classical literature and lore, they will doubtless read and stage the plays, but they will be the poorer through having lost the key to much that is of richest worth in the vast Shakespearian treasure-house.

FIVE

OVID AND THE ELIZABETHANS

I WOULD like this essay to be considered in part a tribute to the memory of two distinguished men, to whom Classical and English literatures were equally dear—Dr. J. W. Mackail and my brother-in-law, Dr. S. G. Owen. Dr. Mackail's eminent services to the classical cause have been eloquently commemorated by Sir Frank Fletcher in his 1946 presidential address to the Classical Association, and all who knew him would echo the words that his 'character was permeated with the beauty of the poetry which he studied and interpreted'. I first knew him when I was a freshman at Balliol, and he was one of a brilliant group of senior men who rose to eminence in letters and public life, in the Church and the law. In later life our chief contact was in the Elizabethan Literary Society, of which he was to the last a devoted member. It was he also who enlisted me in the ranks of the Classical Association, with the luring words that the subscription was only five shillings. His masterpiece in little on Latin literature has been my treasured possession since its appearance in 1895. He is one of the select few who have been Presidents of both the Classical and the English Associations, which jointly rejoiced when he received the Order of Merit.

Dr. S. G. Owen was, like Mackail, a Balliol undergraduate, but after a short period as lecturer at Manchester he returned to Oxford as a senior student and classical tutor of Christ Church, of which he became a loyal adopted son. His special field was the Roman Augustan period, particularly Juvenal and Ovid, but the width of his interests was shown by his labours for a number of years as editor of *The Year's Work in Classical Studies*. In English literature his somewhat austere taste found its favourite reading in the eighteenth century. Was there not a sign of austerity too when, as a comparatively young man, he chose among Ovid's works the *Tristia* in 1889 for intensive editorial labours. In 1915 he contributed it with *Ibis* and the *Pontic Epistles* to the Oxford Classical

Texts, and in 1924 he published the Second Book with a translation
and commentary. Meanwhile, in 1912, he contributed an attractive
essay on 'Ovid and Romance' to the volume *English Literature
and the Classics*, edited by G. S. Gordon, afterwards President of
Magdalen.

We have thus been brought to the threshold of our subject this
afternoon. Will the learned classicists present bear with me while
for the sake of any who on this particular occasion may be among
the weaker brethren I summarize briefly Ovid's career. Publius
Ovidius Naso was born on 20th March, 45 B.C., at Sulmo, about
ninety miles east of Rome. His family were of equestrian rank,
and he was destined by his father for a legal and public career.
He did attain to some minor offices, but his training in rhetoric
and literature was soon diverted to other than forensic ends.
Like Pope he 'lisped in numbers, for the numbers came'. He himself tells that he was giving recitations of his youthful poem, the
Amores, when his beard had been cut but once or twice. The
immediate popularity won by this poem, together with his con-
versational and other gifts, at once secured for Ovid a distinguished
place in Roman literary and social circles. He was married three
times, the first two unions being short. The third, though childless,
was one of mutual devotion.

The exact chronology of his writings is obscure. But the *Amores*
was followed by the *Heroides*, a series of love-letters from legendary
ladies of renown. Then came, about 1 B.C., the eventful *Ars
Amatoria*, 'a systematic treatise', as it has been described, 'in
voluptuous pleasure'. As an antidote to the scandal that it aroused
it was succeeded by the *Remedia Amoris*. In the second period of his
literary career Ovid turned away from the erotic field in which
he had so signally triumphed. In the *Metamorphoses* he achieved
equal success in poetic narrative, which embodied a mass of
mythological stories whose only connecting link was that they
involved the transformation of human beings into some other
shape. Of his major works *Metamorphoses* alone was written not in
the elegiac metre but in hexameters. His other chief narrative work,
the *Fasti*, based on the calendar of the months, and 'a storehouse
of religious and antiquarian lore', was less successful and was never
published in complete form.

Then suddenly in A.D. 8 came a bolt from the blue. Augustus ordered the poet's banishment to Tomis, a small town in a desolate and bitterly cold region, about sixty-five miles south-west of the nearest mouth of the Danube. The cause of Ovid's 'relegatio', technically the milder form of the penalty, has never been fully solved. He himself attributed it to a 'carmen' (poem) and an 'error'. It is generally agreed that the 'carmen' was the *Ars Amatoria* which the Emperor considered an obstacle to his plans for moral reformation in Rome. As to the 'error' it was at one time thought that it had some relation to the profligacy of the Emperor's granddaughter, Julia, who was banished in the same year as Ovid. But it is now usually believed to have been not of a domestic but of a political nature. In any case Augustus, and after him Tiberius, was obdurate to the confessions of guilt and the pleas for mercy which poured from the desolate exile in his last group of poems, the *Tristia* and *Epistulae ex Ponto*. He had to linger on, heart-broken, till his death in A.D. 16 or 17.

But however tragic the close of his fortunes, Ovid's confidence that his fame would survive has been fully justified. Of his general European popularity in the Middle Ages this is not the occasion to speak. But in fourteenth-century England both Chaucer and Gower show his influence. Their respective debt to the *Metamorphoses* in their treatment of the Pyramus and Thisbe story in *The Legend of Good Women* and the *Confessio Amantis* has been recently discussed by Mr. Norman Callan in *R.E.S.,* October 1946, as also other contrasted borrowings. The eagle that bears Chaucer to the House of Fame even calls the *Metamorphoses* 'thyne owne book', but an unlearned reader would not grasp the allusion.

The first attempt, so far as I know, to make any part of Ovid intelligible to the English laity in the vernacular was Wynkyn de Worde's publication in 1513 of *The flores of Ovide de arte amandi with theyr englysshe afore them*. This may have been something in the nature of a school-book like Nicholas Udall's *Floures for Latine spekyinge selected and gathered out of Terence* (1533), phrases from three plays of Terence with their English equivalents. Except, however, for Wynkyn de Worde's venture it was not Ovid who had the distinction of leading the way among the Latin poets in the great outburst of Tudor translation from the Classics. As all know, the priority fell to Virgil, when the ill fated Henry Howard, Earl of Surrey, rendered Books II and IV of the *Aeneid* into the then unfamiliar metre which we now know as blank verse. The translation was published by Tottel in 1557 but probably dates not long before Surrey's execution early in 1548. Gawin Douglas's version of the whole poem in Scottish vernacular, though finished in 1513, was published in 1553. In 1558 there came from Thomas Phaer his rendering of the first seven Books of the *Aeneid* in fourteeners, followed in 1562 by the first nine Books.

Between these two publications Ovid had made his first appearance in England in Elizabeth's reign. In 1560 appeared *The fable of Ovid tretting of Narcissus, translated out of Latin into English metre, with a moral thereunto, very pleasaunte to rede,* by T.H. He was Thomas Howell, secretary successively to the Earl of Shrewsbury and the Countess of Pembroke, and a minor poet. His work was, in part, a rendering of ll. 342–510 of Book III of the *Metamorphoses,* telling the story of Narcissus, hopelessly beloved by the nymph Echo, and himself consumed by an equally hopeless passion for his own image reflected in a pool. Howell's version is in couplets of which the first line has six feet and the second has seven. Here is his translation of Narcissus's farewell words with Echo's repetition ('v' replacing 'u' and punctuation modified):

> Thus lokyng in the well, the last he spake was thys:
> Alas! thou ladde to much in vayne beloved of me a mys!
> Whych selfe same wordes agayne this Ecco streight dyd yell,
> And as Narcissus toke hys leve, she bad hym eke fayre well.

But the translation of about 170 Latin lines is made by Howell the occasion of, almost the excuse for, his own moralization of Ovid's fable of Narcissus in 127 rhyme-royal stanzas of seven lines each. After asking pardon for his youthful lack of skill Howell declares:

> I meane to shewe, according to my wytte,
> That Ovyd by this tale no follye mente.

and he adds this warning,

> Whiche Ovid now, this Poete sure devine,
> Doth collour in so wonderfull a sorte

That such as twyse refuse to reade a lyne
Wyth good advice, to make there wytte resorte
To reasons schole, their Lessons to reporte,
Shall never gather Ovids meanyng straunge
That wysdome hydeth with some pleasaunt chaunge.

He then proceeds to expatiate on the fate of Narcissus as the result of overweening pride, and in characteristic Renaissance fashion cites other Biblical and Classical examples, beginning with Lucifer and ending with Cleopatra.

And he goes on improving the occasion till he finally asserts that by the metamorphosis of Narcissus into a flower Ovid intended to signify

That youth and bewghte come and soone be paste
Even as the flower that wetherithe fall fast.

Two other versions of selected stories from the *Metamorphoses* followed in the same decade. In 1565 Thomas Peend of the Middle Temple produced *The pleasant fable of Hermaphroditus and Salmacis* (Book IV) of which the only copies are in the Bodleian and the Rylands library. In 1569 there came from the pen of William Hubbard, with a different appeal in the title, *The tragicall and lamentable historie of Ceyx, Kynge of Trachine and Alcione his wife* (Book XI). Of this the Bodleian has the only copy. In the same year Thomas Underdown published a translation of Ovid's *Invective against Ibis*.

The piecemeal excerpts from the *Metamorphoses* in the vernacular were eclipsed by the comprehensive undertaking of Arthur Golding, who in 1565 issued his translation of the first four Books of the poem, and in 1567 completed the version of all the fifteen Books. Like Howell he gave an enticing assurance that it was 'a woorke very pleasant and delectable', accompanied by a warning:

With skill, heede, and judgment thys woorke must be red,
For els too the reader it stands in small stead.

Golding was born about 1536, and was connected by marriage with John de Vere, sixteenth Earl of Oxford. He wrote a 'Discourse' upon the earthquake of 6th April 1580 but otherwise confined himself almost entirely to translations, in which he was prolific and versatile. They included, *inter alia,* various works of Calvin, Beza's tragedy, *Abraham's Sacrifice,* Seneca's *Benefits,* Caesar's *Gallic War,* and the completion of Sir P. Sidney's version of de Mornay's *History of Christianity.* But it is on the *Metamorphoses* that his fame and influence chiefly rest. Its popularity is attested by the call for successive editions in 1575, 1587, 1603 and 1612. The modern reader who may find it difficult to cope with the closely printed black-letter text of the original publication has had his way smoothed by Dr. W. H. D. Rouse in his handsome and scholarly edition issued by the De La More Press in 1904.

In the 1565 translation of the first four Books, Golding prefixed a prose dedication to the Earl of Leicester asking him to accept it as a New Year's gift. In the 1567 publication he substituted a long verse epistle to the Earl, declaring

> The woork is brought t'o end by which the author did account
> (And rightly) with eternal fame above the starres too mount,
> For whatsoever hath been writ of auncient tyme in greeke
> By sundry men dispersedly, and in the latin eke,
> Of this same dark Philosophie of turned shapes, the same
> Hath Ovid into one whole masse in this booke brought to fame.

Golding proceeds to summarize the stories in each of the Books, adding a moral interpretation of each, and then turns to forestall possible objectors.

> If any man will say theis things may better lerned bee
> Out of divine philosophie or scripture, I agree
> That nothing may in worthinesse with holy writ compare.
> Howbeit so farre foorth as things no whit impeachment are
> Too vertue and too godlynesse but furtherers of the same,
> I trust we may them saufly use without desert of blame.

So far, so good, but Golding's further appeal falls, at any rate to-day, on less responsive ears.

> What man is he but would suppose the author of this booke
> The first foundation of his woorke from Moyses wryghtings
>   tooke?
> Not only in effect he dooth with Genesis agree,

But also in the order of creation, save that hee
Makes no distinction of the dayes.

Golding then goes on to harmonize the Scriptural accounts of
the Creation, Paradise and the Flood with what he takes to be their
equivalents in the *Metamorphoses*. The Epistle to Leicester is
followed by 'the Preface to the Reader', in somewhat similar
defensive and moralizing vein. And now that he has finished his
labours, Golding claims that he has made of Ovid an English
poet:

And now I have him made so well acquainted with our toong,
As that he may in English verse as in our own be soong,
Wherein although for pleasant style I cannot make account
Too match myne author, who in that all other dooth surmount,
Yit (gentle Reader) I doo trust my travell in this cace
May purchace favour in thy sight my dooings to embrace.

You will have noticed that my quoataions from Golding's Epistle
to Leicester and from the Preface to the Reader have been in the
long fourteen-syllable line, and this is the metre that Golding uses
to represent the Latin hexameter of the original from beginning
to end. I think that something less than full justice is done in Charles
Whibley's comment in Chapter I of Vol. IV. of the *The Cambridge History of English Literature*.

'The chief characteristic of the translation is its evenness. It
never falls below or rises above a certain level. The craftsmanship
is neither slovenly nor distinguished. The narrative flows through
its easy channel without the smallest shock of interruption. In
other words, the style is rapid, fluent and monotonous. The author
is never a poet, and never a shirk.'

I will quote in illustration of Golding's style two passages, both
of which have an association interest. The first is part of Medea's
appeal to the elemental powers to aid her when she is about to
restore the youth of Jason's father. The lines are from Book VII,
197–206, beginning:

Auraeque et venti, montesque, amnesque, lucusque,
Dique omnes nemorum, dique omnes noctis adeste.

Golding's rendering is:

> Ye Ayres and windes: ye Elves of Hilles, of Brookes, of Woods
> alone,
> Of standing Lakes, and of the Night approche ye everychone.
> Throughe helpe of whom (the crooked bankes much wondring
> at the thing)
> I have compelled streames to run cleane backward to their
> spring.
> By charmes I make the calme Seas rough, and make the rough
> Seas plaine,
> And cover all the Skie with Cloudes and chase them thence
> againe.
> By charmes I rayse and lay the windes and burst the Vipers jaw,
> And from the bowels of the Earth both stones and trees doe
> drawe.
> Whole woods and Forestes I remove; I make the Mountaines
> shake,
> And even the Earth itselfe to grone and fearfully to quake.
> I call up dead men from their graves.

Compare with this the following:

> Ye elves of hills, brookes, standing lakes, and groves . . .
>   by whose aid—
> Weak masters though ye be—I have bedimm'd
> The noontide sun, call'd forth the mutinous winds,
> And 'twixt the green sea and the azured vault
> Set roaring war; to the dread-rattling thunder
> Have I given fire and rifted Jove's stout oak
> With his own bolt; the strong-based promontory
> Have I made shake; and by the spurs pluck'd up
> The pine and cedar; graves at my command
> Have wak'd their sleepers, ped, and let men forth
> By my so potent art.

Everyone will recognize that this is part of Prospero's speech before abjuring his 'rough magic'. That it was inspired by Golding's rendering of Medea's incantation is plain not only from the unmistakable verbal echoes but from the whole conception of magic being employed in both instances to reverse the natural order, even of life and death. Of course in the *Tempest* passage there are the added touches of Shakespearian imagination and melody.

My second excerpt is from the account in Book VIII of the visit of two of the gods to Philemon and Baucis in the Phrygian hill-country, beginning at l. 626,

> Juppiter huc specie mortali cumque parente
> Venit Atlantiades positis caducifer alis.

Here is Golding's version:

> The mightie *Jove* and *Mercurie* his sonne in shape of men
> Resorted thither on a tyme. A thousand houses when
> For roome too lodge in they had sought, a thousand houses bard
> Theyr doores against them. Neretheless one Cotage afterward
> Receyved them, and that was but a pelting one indeede.
> The roof thereof was thatched all with straw and fennish reede,
> Howbeet two honest auncient folke of whom she *Baucis* hight
> And he *Philemon,* in that Cote theyr fayth in youth had plight,
> And in that Cote had spent theyr age.

Now turn to *Much Ado about Nothing,* II, i, and the talk between Don Pedro and Hero at the masked ball:

> *D. Pedro:* Lady, will you walk about with your friend?
> *Hero:* So you walk softly, and look sweetly, and say nothing, I am yours for the walk; and especially when I walk away.
> *D. Pedro:* With me in your company?
> *Hero:* I may say so, when I please.
> *D. Pedro:* And when please you to say so?
> *Hero:* When I like your favour; for God defend the lute should be like the case!
> *D. Pedro:* My visor is Philemon's roof; within the house is Jove.
> *Hero:* Why, then, your visor should be thatch'd.
> *D. Pedro:* Speak low, if you speak love.

Here, very unexpectedly, there is brought in a reference to Philemon's thatched roof, which the gallants and the groundlings in the Globe Theatre must have been remarkably 'quick in the uptake' to appreciate. And Shakespeare's equally unlooked-for insertion into a long prose scene of a fourteener rhyming couplet is evidently in imitation of Golding.

There is another unexpected reference to the same episode at the beginning of Act III, ii, of *As You Like It*. When Touchstone condescendingly tells Audrey, 'I am here with thee and thy goats, as the most capricious [fantastic] poet, honest Ovid, was among the Goths', Jaques exclaims, 'O knowledge ill-inhabited, worse than Jove in a thatched house!'

The mention of Ovid among the Goths shows that Shakespeare knew about the *Tristia* or at any rate about the conditions in which that poem was written. A couplet from the *Heroides* I, 35–6, beginning 'Hac ibat Simois' is found in *The Taming of the Shrew*, III, i, 28 and another line II, 66 'Di faciant, laudis summa sit ista tuae' in *III Henry VI*, I, iii, 48. The second half of *Metamorphoses* I, 150, 'Terras Astraea reliquit' comes in *Titus Andronicus*, IV, iii, 4. But even if one is not a 'disintegrator', one may have doubts about the completely Shakespearian authorship of these plays. On the title page of *Venus and Adonis* there is a couplet from *Amores* I, XV, 35–6.

> Vilia miretur vulgus; mihi flavus Apollo
> Pocula Castalia plena ministret aqua.

But this may have been affixed by the publisher, and the description of the boar in the poem, ll. 619 ff., as Dr. Rouse has pointed out, recalls a passage in Golding's version, viii. 376. My own view, set forth in my 1943 Shakespeare Lecture to the British Academy, is that the dramatist's knowledge of the Classics in the original was very limited. However this may be, when Shakespeare puts into the mouth of Holofernes in *Love's Labour's Lost*, IV, ii, the punning eulogy, 'Ovidius Naso was the man; and why indeed, Naso, but for smelling out the odoriferous flowers of fancy, the jerks of invention?' it was not the Ovid of the Classical Association, but the Ovid of Arthur Golding that was mainly in his mind.

In the same year, 1567, that Golding's complete *Metamorphoses* appeared there was issued a translation of the *Heroides* by George Turbervile with the title, *Heroycall Epistles*. Turbervile, born about 1540, was educated at Winchester and New College, Oxford. He

was the author of a small book of peoms, but like Golding he
made his mark as a versatile translator. Among his English versions
were the *Eclogues* of Mantuanus and *Tragical Tales* from Boccaccio
and Bandello. But the *Heroycall Epistles* is his chief achievement.
Though he speaks of it as a 'trifling toye', it was a really formidable
undertaking, for the twenty-one Epistles contain almost 4000
elegiac lines which are nearly doubled in Turbervile's English. This
is not mainly due to freedom in translation but to Turbervile's use
mainly of comparatively short lines. Unlike Golding he varies his
metre. His favourite form is a four-line stanza, of which the first,
second and fourth lines contain three feet and the third has four.
He uses less frequently the more familiar four-line stanza with
alternate four and three feet. And six of the Epistles are rendered,
as Surrey had done with two Books of the *Aeneid,* into blank
verse. Let me give an illustration of Turbervile's use of each of
these three metres. In Epistle XIX, 9–16 beginning:

> Vos modo venando, modo rus geniale colendo,
>> Ponitis in varia tempora longa mora,

Hero contrasts her lonely state with Leander's varied choice of
occupations. Here is Turbervile's version:

> You men contrive the time
>> And loathsome tide away:
> Sometime in tillage of your soyles,
>> Sometime you hunt the day.
> Sometime at open barre
>> You pleade a clients case:
> To tennis now, and then with horse
>> You runne a lusty race.
> Sometime you pitch for foule,
>> For fish you lay your line;
> And when the day is spent and gone,
>> You fall to quaffing wine.
> Now I can none of these,
>> Though lesser were my flame;
> Thy Hero can do nothing els
>> But cleape her lovers name.

In Epistle V, ll. 13 ff., beginning:

> Saepe greges inter requievimus arbore tecti,
>   Mixtaque cum foliis praebuit herba forum,

Oenone reminds Paris of their former rural joys. Turbervile thus translates:

> How oft have we in shaddow layne
>   Whilst hungry flocks have fed?
> How oft have we of grasse and groaves
>   Prepard a homely bed?
> How oft on simple stacks of straw
>   And bennet did we rest?
> I sundry times have helpe to pitch
>   Thy toyles for want of ayde,
> And prest thy houndes to climbe the hills
>   That gladly would have stay'd.
> The boysteous Beech Oenons name
>   In outward barke doth beare;
> And with thy carving knife is cut
>   Oenon every where.

In Epistle XII, ll. 31–36, beginning:

> Tunc ego te vidi, tunc coepi scire quis esses,
>   Illa fuit mentis prima ruina meae,

Medea reminds Jason of how she first became enamoured of him. This is Turbervile's blank-verse reading:

> Then saw I thee and perisht eke inflamed
> With fire unknowne, and fried with straungie gleade,
> As fore the Aultars burnes the torch of Pyne.
> Both featurde well thou were and fates me drew;
> Thine eyes my dazeled lights did ravish quite
> Which quickly thou discridste. For who may well
> Keep love in mewe, that no man it discerne?
> Ay flame it selfe, by casting light, bewrayes.

These are, I think, favourable examples of Turbervile's style in his different metres. He is at his best when, as in my two first quotations, he is turning Ovid's concrete details, with some elaboration, into racy, picturesque English. In quest of this Turbervile employs a diversified and sometimes outlandish vocabulary, e.g., in the above extracts, 'cleape' =call,'bennet'=grass-stalk, 'boysteous'=rough, 'gleade'=flame. He is less happy when, as often, he uses words that are colloquial or have undignified association, e.g. 'fist' for hand, 'brat' for child, 'smack' for kiss. And partly owing to the discrepancies between synthetic Latin and analytical English he often fails to reproduce Ovid's deliberate and pointed balance. That he himself realized the difficulties of his task is plain from the confession in his Epilogue.

> He shall find he hath a Crow to pull
> That undertakes with well agreeing File
> Of English verse to rub the Romans stile.

All the more therefore

> it is a worke of prayse to cause
> A Romane borne to speake with English jawes.

That Turbervile's contemporaries found it a 'worke of prayse' is evident from the fact that after 1567 four later editions were called for of which the last was in 1600. If one cannot point to any link between the *Heroycall Epistles* and an Elizabethan literary figure as definite as that between Golding's *Metamorphoses* and Shakespeare, yet its influence in making the heroines of Greek legend and their lovers generally familiar must have been far-reaching. But after 1600 it was not reprinted till 1928 when the Cresset Press published a finely illustrated *edition de luxe* of which it was my privilege to be the editor.

A writer with more original work to his credit than any hitherto mentioned entered the field of Ovid translation when Thomas Churchyard in 1572 published his version of the first three Books of the *Tristia*. He had made something of a mark with his contribution to *A Mirror for Magistrates* in 1563 of the 'tragedy' of *Shore's Wife*. He had served as a soldier in Scotland, Ireland and on the Continent, and had afterwards with little success sought to advance his fortunes as a hanger-on to the Court and the nobility. It may well have been the sense of frustration in his own career that prompted him to translate the most mournful of Ovid's works. But there is nothing to this effect in his curious dedication of his version to Sir Christopher Hatton. In it he makes no direct mention of Ovid but apologizes to Hatton for presenting him with 'another man's worke . . . sufficient to purchase good report', instead of his intended collection of *Churchyard's Chips*, a miscellaneous volume which saw the light in 1575. Like Golding, Churchyard used throughout the rhymed 'fourteener', though this is less suited to the elegiac metre of the *Tristia* than the hexameters of the *Metamorphoses*. As a specimen I quote his translation of the lines (II, 327 ff.) beginning:

Arguor immerito: tenuis mihi campus aratur;
    Illud erat magnae fertilitatis opus.

in which Ovid replies to the charge that he ought to have dealt in his verse with the war against Troy, or the victories of Rome or the exploits of Augustus himself:

As rightfully I am reprovde, in barren fielde I tilde,
That noble worke is far more large, with greater plenty fielde.
For though the slender boate is bould in smaller streame to play,
Yet like disport it dareth not in surging seas assay.
And doubtinge that for greater things my minde is farre unfit,
In dittyes small it may suffice that I do shew my wit.
But if thou should commaund to tell of Giantes grevous wounds,
Which they thrugh fyre of Jove did feele, the worke my wit
    confounds.
A fruitfull minde it doth requyre of Caesars actes to wright,
Least els perhappes with matter much the worke may want his
    right,
Which though I durst have take in hand, yet dreading much
    amonge,
Thy noble power I might abate, which were too great a wronge,
To lighter worke I therefore went, and youthfull verse addrest
With fayned love a care I had to feede my ficcle brest.

This is jog-trot verse, with a superfluity of monosyllables and in parts not lucid. Of the 1572 edition there is only one surviving copy in the British Museum, and this is imperfect, lacking the last pages, signature 'D'. But the translation found a public, for two more editions were issued in 1578 and 1580. The 1578 quarto is also extant in a single copy, formerly in Lord Spencer's Althorp library, from which it was reprinted in 1816 for the Roxburghe Club. It is now in the Manchester Rylands library, while the two surviving 1580 copies are in the Bodleian and the Huntington libraries.

To the translators already mentioned has now to be added an Elizabethan of the first rank, Christopher Marlowe. Four editions of his version of *Ovid's Elegies, three Books* and two of *Certain of Ovid's Elegies* were issued together, in every case, with *Epigrams* by Sir John Davies. All the editions were undated and the imprint on the title page of Middleburgh (in Holland) as the place of publication was almost certainly spurious. The so-called *Elegies* are the three Books of the *Amores*, and the presumption is that the translation dates from some time during Marlowe's Cambridge career, between 1581–87. A young scholar of his glowing temper would be attracted not only by the erotic elements in Ovid's poem but by its rich mythological lore. It is true, as I have said elsewhere, that Marlowe would not have got full marks in a scholarship examination. He made a number of 'howlers'. Thus the line 'Ipse locus nemorum canebat frugibus Ide', i.e. 'Ida the seat of groves was white with harvest', is rendered 'Ida the seat of groves did sing with corn', where Marlowe mistook 'cānebat' for 'cănebat'. Again the invocation 'linguis animisque favete', i.e. 'keep silence and attend', is turned into 'themselves let all men cheer'. On the other hand a number of apparent inaccuracies or obscurities are due either to changes in the meaning of words or to differences between the Elizabethan Latin texts of Ovid and those now in use. And it is to Marlowe's credit that he tried faithfully to render every Latin line into its English equivalent. This was all the more difficult because unlike the previous translators of Ovid he had not given himself additional elbow-room. His metre was the rhyming couplet of five-foot lines, where ten feet replaced the eleven feet of the Latin elegiac couplet. The compression sometimes led to awkwardness, but on the other hand it enabled Marlowe at times to reproduce the balance and terseness of the original as none of the previous translators had done, e.g.

Et celer admissus labitur annus equis.
And with swift horses the swift year soon leaves us.

and

Quo lapis exiguus par sibi carmen habet.
The little stones these little verses have.

Except for occasional colloquialisms which remind us of Turbervile, Marlowe's vocabulary is well-chosen and varied, and he avoids the excessive alliteration favoured by most Elizabethan translators. His versification is uneven and betrays something of the prentice hand, but at its best it foreshadows his later mastery of metre. Thus he translates in Book I, Elegy 13, Ovid's appeal to Aurora to delay her coming:

Whither runn'st thou that men and women love not?
Hold in thy rosy horses that they move not.
Ere thou rise, stars teach seamen where to sail,
But when thou comest, they of their courses fail.
Poor travellers, though tir'd, rise at thy sight,
And soldiers make them ready to the fight.
The painful hind by thee to field is sent;
Slow oxen early in the yoke are pent.
Thou cozen'st boys of sleep, and dost betray them
To pedants that with cruel lashes pay them.

It is, as will be remembered, a later line from the same elegy, slightly varied from its original form, 'O lente, lente currite noctis equi,' that bursts so movingly from Faustus's lips as his dread doom draws nigh.

And here is the version of some of the lines in Book I, Elegy 15, in which the poet prophesies his eternal fame:

Therefore when flint and iron wear away,
Verse is immortal and shall ne'er decay.
To verse let kings give place and kingly shows,
And banks o'er which gold-bearing Tagus flows. . . .
The living, not the dead, can envy bite,
For after death all men receive their right.

Then though death rakes my bones in funeral fire
I'll live, and as he pulls me down, mount higher.

If two highly placed prelates had fully had their way, Marlowe's translation of the *Amores* would not have contributed either to Ovid's immortality or his own. For by an order of the Archbishop of Canterbury and the Bishop of London the volumes containing the *Elegies* and Davies's *Epigrams* were publicly burnt with other books on 4th June 1599. But fortunately one or two copies of what appear to be the earliest editions escaped the flames, and their text is available to-day in the original spelling in Tucker Brooke's *Marlowe* and in modernized spelling in Bullen's *Marlowe* and L. C. Martin's edition of Marlowe's *Poems*.

It was not, however, through translations only that Ovid's influence was felt. His mastery of poetic narrative inspired a number of Elizabethan achievements in the same field. Thus Francis Meres testifies in 1598 'the sweet, witty soul of Ovid lives in mellifluous and honey-tongued Shakespeare, witness his *Venus and Adonis*, his *Lucrece*, his sugared sonnets'. Though Musaeus was the main source of Marlowe's *Hero and Leander* it is full of Ovidian echoes. And we have other echoes in such titles as Lodge's *Scilla's Metamorphosis* (1589), Marston's *The Metamorphosis of Pygmalion's Image* (1598), Harrington's unseemly *Metamorphosis of Ajax* (1599) and Tourneur's *The Transformed Metamorphosis* (1600).

But by far the most elaborate work with a *Metamorphosis* title still remains unpublished. It is *The Newe Metamorphosis* written by J. M., gent., and dated 1600. It is contained in three quarto volumes (B.M. Addit. MSS., 14,824–14,826) and includes twenty-four Books. A study of it by Dr. J. H. H. Lyon, with selections from the MS., was issued from the Columbia University Press in 1919. Lyon has shown, if internal evidence can be trusted, that J. M. was Jervis Markham, who thus in his Prologue describes his poetic miscellany and his Classical model:

Even as a Flemish Galleymaufrey made
Of flesh, herbes, onyons, both of roote and blade,
So shall you fynde them in this booke conteinde
For some strange things to write I onely ay'mde.
I ne're sawe any of our Nation yet

That me a patterne in this subiecte set,
Nor but one stranger, Ovid alone was he
That in this labour did incourage me.

There could be no more explicit acknowledgment of a debt,
and in a number of his tales, especially those relating the amours
of various classical gods and in the transformations with which
many of the stories close, the direct influence of Ovid is manifest.
But though the MS. is dated 1600 the allusions in it to Prince
Henry's death in 1612 and to Raleigh's *History of the World* published in 1614 prove that Markham must have been adding to it
for many years. Thus, though originally planned according to its
first sub-title as 'A Feaste of Fancie of Poeticall Legendes', it was
extended to include satirical, topical, and autobiographical features
which carry us very far from Augustan Rome.

But now let us return there under the guidance of two major
Elizabethans, George Chapman and Ben Jonson. To both of them
the tradition of Ovid's relations with an imperial Julia, in their
eyes the daughter, not the granddaughter, of Augustus, furnished
material upon which they worked in very different fashion.
Among Chapman's earlier writings is the curious poem *Ovid's
Banquet of Sence*, published in 1595. According to the 'argument'
which prefaces the poem, Ovid conceals himself in a garden of
the emperor's court where Julia, whom he calls Corinna, was
bathing. This gives him the opportunity of gratifying each of his
senses in turn. While bathing, Corinna plays upon her lute and
sings and thus enchants her lover's sense of hearing. Then the
odours or perfumes which she used in her bath satisfied his sense
of smell. Thereafter he ventured 'to see her in the pride of her
nakednesse' and 'discovered the comfort hee conceived in seeing,
and the glorie of her beautie'. He is then emboldened to ask for a
kiss to gratify his sense of taste, and after some demur she consents.

Ovid (sayd shee) I am well pleased to yield;
Beautie by vertue cannot be abusde;
    Nor will I coylie lyft Minervas shielde
Against Minerva, honor is not brusde
    With such a tender pressure as a kisse,
Nor yielding soone to words, though seldome vsde;

Nicenesse in civill favours folly is:
Long sutes make never good a bad detection,
Nor yielding soone makes bad a good affection.

Finally to crown the banquet Ovid begs that he may gratify the
'sences Emperor, Sweet Feeling'. But before this can be con-
summated they are interrupted and the poem comes to an abrupt
conclusion. As Miss Bartlett has suggested, Chapman probably
found it difficult to round off this paradoxical effort of 'an erotic
poem founded in the Neoplatonic doctrine of love. . . . The
doctrine is that man must partake to the full of sensual content-
ment in order that his mind may be excited to a higher love'.

Chapman had thus brought Ovid and Julia to life again in
amorous dialogue. There was only one further step to be taken, to
exhibit them in speech and motion on the Elizabethan stage. This
was the achievement of Ben Jonson in *The Poetaster* (1601). In the
opening scene Ovid is seen perusing the 15th *Elegy* of Book I of
the *Amores,* in which he predicts immortality for his poetry, and
of which Jonson gives an English version slightly different from
Marlowe's, part of which I have quoted. His father who has
destined him for the law bursts in furiously:

'Is this the scope and aim of thy studies? Are these the hopeful
courses wherewith I have so long flattered my expectations
from thee? Verses! poetry!'

Ovid in vain seeks to calm him, and his farewell injunction is,
'If thou wilt hold my favour abandon these idle studies that so
bewitch thee . . . and look only forward to the law'. As he goes
out fuming, a fellow poet of Ovid, Tibullus, enters with an
invitation to him from Princess Julia to meet her at the house of
Albius, a jeweller. Here there is a gay party in which only Pro-
pertius still mourning the loss of his Cynthia is a discordant som-
bre figure. This is a prelude to later more daring revels in which
the company headed by Ovid as Jupiter and Julia as Juno im-
personate the Roman deities. News of this is brought to Augustus,
who enters to stop the masquerade and to send Julia to prison and
Ovid to perpetual bansihment. Before they serve their sentences,
in a scene that irresistibly recalls the parting of Romeo and Juliet,

Julia appears at her chamber window to take a lingering farewell of her lover below:

> *Julia:* Ovid, my love, alas may we not stay
>   A little longer (think'st thou) undiscerned?
> *Ovid:* For thine own good, fair Goddess, do not stay.
>
> *   *   *
>
> *Julia:* I will be gone then and not heaven itself
>   Shall draw me back.
> *Ovid:*   Yet, Julia if thou wilt,
>   A little longer stay.
> *Julia:*   I am content.

But he remembers that 'if both stay, both die', and he flings away with Julia's image in his heart.

And I would ask you to note that this is not only the exit of Ovid from the Rome of Augustus but virtually from the London of Elizabeth. Except for a version of the episode of Salmacis and Hermaphroditus, assigned to Francis Beaumont in 1602, neither in translation nor otherwise did Ovid figure again before the Queen's death on 24th March 1603. For details of the further flow of translations before the Civil War, in which W. Saltonstall and George Sandys have conspicuous parts, I would refer you to the *Short-Title Catalogue*. The Elizabethan period, in its strict limits, has yielded material enough for an afternoon's survey. We have found fruitful contacts between Publius Ovidius Naso and Elizabethans of the front rank, Marlowe, Shakespeare, Chapman, Ben Jonson; also with reputable figures of lesser degree, Golding, Turbervile and Churchyard, as well as such minor personages as Howell, Hubbard and Peend. And behind these stand the great nameless company of readers who bought up so eagerly the editions that followed one another from the press.

Thus Ovid's influence was widespread and, I would claim, beneficial. Of course Howell was on the wrong tack when he exalted him as a moralist and still more Golding when he drew a parallel between him and the author of *Genesis*. At the opposite extreme were the prelates who consigned Marlowe's translation of the *Amores* to the flames. They on their part overestimated the demoralizing effect of a work of which so much was outside the ken of Elizabethan Londoners. And it is to be noted that while the *Metamorphoses*, the *Heroides* and the *Tristia* were turned into English there was no Elizabethan vernacular version of the *Ars Amatoria*.

But it is outside the sphere of morals that Ovid's really pervasive influence is to be traced. He spread before the eyes of the Elizabethans an enthralling wealth of mythological and legendary lore. It is true, as some American scholars have recently emphasized, that much of this is to be found in contemporary encyclopaedic dictionaries. But what they contained in dry outline was presented in glowing imaginative life in Ovid's pages. This made a direct appeal to the exuberant Elizabethan temper. At the same time Ovid's artistic, at times over-artificial, verse-technique had a valuable controlling and chastening influence. Redundancy and excess were constant temptations of the Elizabethans. We have seen how they affected Golding's and Turbervile's translations. Nevertheless they made conscious efforts to fall as little as might be below the linguistic and rhythmical standard set by their Latin model.

Marlowe by his natural instinct succeeded better, but even he profited by the discipline thereby involved. And Shakespeare himself echoed in one of his loftiest and latest utterances lines from the *Metamorphoses*. Does not our survey of Ovid and the Elizabethans go far to confirm Dr. Mackail's dictum, 'He was not a poet of the first order; yet few poets of the first order have done a work of such wide importance'?

SIX

SIR THOMAS BODLEY AND HIS LIBRARY

2ND MARCH 1945 marked the four hundredth anniversary of the birth of Thomas Bodley. Two other anniversaries connected with him have been fittingly commemorated. The Tercentenary of the opening of his Library on 8th November 1602 was celebrated by a great gathering in Oxford of Librarians and other representatives of the academic world, by a dinner in Christ Church Hall and by the publication of a splendidly illustrated volume, 'Pietas Oxoniensis' containing a life of Bodley and a sketch of the history of his Library. Another memorial volume, 'Trecentale Bodleianum', was issued on the 300th anniversary of his public funeral in Merton College Chapel 29th March 1613. This contained besides other matter a reprint of Bodley's autobiography and of the funeral orations in the Divinity School by the Deputy Public Orator and in the College Chapel by John Hales. The latter was included in an English version in an anniversary service.

For the main facts of Bodley's career we fortunately have the authority of an autobiographical sketch, written with his own hand, dated 15th December 1609. He was born at Exeter on 2nd March 1544-5 'descended both by father and mother, of worshipfull parentage'. His father, John Bodley, belonged to a family that had been long seated at Dunscombe, in the parish of Crediton; his mother to the family of Hone of Ottery St. Mary. John Bodley was a noted Protestant, and after the accession of Queen Mary he 'was so cruelly threatened' that he fled with his wife and family to Wesel in the duchy of Cleves, afterwards to Frankfort, and then in May 1557 to Geneva. Here Thomas, then aged twelve, was boarded with a physician, at whose house he read Homer with Robert Constantin, author of a Greek lexicon. He also attended at the College the lectures of Chevallier in Hebrew, in which he became specially proficient, of Beroaldus in Greek, and of Calvin and Beza in divinity.

Thus when his father returned to England after Elizabeth's

accession and sent Thomas to Magdalen College in 1559, he must have arrived in Oxford like Gibbon in the eighteenth century (according to the first half of his epigram) with 'a stock of erudition that would have puzzled a Doctor'. He remained at Magdalen till he took his B.A., 26th July 1563, but no mention of his name is found in the College records. After graduating he was elected a probationer-fellow of Merton College, and in 1564 was admitted a fellow. In the next year he began to give public lectures in Greek in the College Hall, without asking for a fee, but the College awarded him an annual stipend of four marks ($£2$ 13s. 4d.) and made this a permanent endowment of the lectureship.

After proceeding M.A. on 1st July 1566, he lectured on Natural Philosophy; in 1569 he was elected one of the Proctors, and afterwards for a long time acted as deputy Public Orator. It might well have seemed that he was committed for life to an academic career. But he had other plans in view. He was bent on travelling overseas, to become as proficient in modern languages as he was already in ancient, and to increase his experience in managing affairs, 'being wholly then addicted to employ myselfe and my cares, in the publick service of the State'. He left England in 1576 and spent four years in Italy, France and Germany. Some time after his return he was made in 1583 an esquire of the body to Queen Elizabeth. In 1585 he was employed on his first diplomatic mission, to the King of Denmark, the Duke of Brunswick, the Landgrave of Hesse and other German princes to induce them to help Henry of Navarre and the French Huguenots. He was next sent in May 1588 to Henry III of France, when he was being forced by the Duke of Guise to fly from Paris. Bodley speaks of himself as performing this mission 'with extraordinary secrecie, not being accompanyed with any one seruant (for so I was commanded) nor with any other Letters, than such as were written with the Queene's one hand to the Kinge, and sume selected persons about him'. The Queen's message, according to Bodley, proved of great advantage to Henry and to the French Protestants.

Meanwhile, apparently in 1587, he had married a rich widow, Anne Ball, daughter of a Bristol merchant, and in May 1589 a ship was requisitioned for her safe conduct to join him overseas. For in the latter part of 1588 Bodley had been appointed to the responsible post of English Resident at The Hague, taking the next place of precedence in the Council of State to Count Maurice and having a vote in all measures proposed. From Bodley's account it would appear that the good relations between the English and Dutch governments were imperilled by the insolent demeanour of some of Elizabeth's officials—probably Leicester is indicated— and it was only by his tact and conciliatory attitude that the situation was saved.

But after nearly five years' absence from England he was anxious to return, partly to look after his private affairs. Twice he obtained leave of absence from his post for limited periods. But it was not till the summer of 1596 that he succeeded in procuring what he calls his 'last revocation'. In his autobiography Bodley states that after he had made during his first leave of absence a highly confidential report in person to the Queen, 'all things were concluded, and browght to that issue, that was instantly desired'. But elsewhere it is recorded that she was not satisfied with some of his recommendations, and that he had heard that she had expressed the wish 'that he were hanged'.

But it was not only the wilful words of his royal mistress that disillusioned Bodley concerning the service of the State. In the most striking section of his autobiography he depicts himself as the victim of the mutual ill-will and jealousy of the Cecils and of Essex, both claiming to be his friends.

'From the very first day, I had no man more to friend, among the Lords of the Councell than was the Lord Threasurer Burleigh . . . he would always tell the Queene (which I receaved from herself and some other eare-witnesses) that there was not any man in England, so meete as my self, to vndergoe the Office of the Secretary: And sithence, his sonne the present Lord Treasurer hath signified vnto me in private conference, that when his father first intended to aduance him to that place, his purpose was with all to make me his colleague.'

On the other hand the Earl of Essex tried to make Bodley dependent upon him for advancement, and often took occasion 'to entertayne the Queene, with some prodigall speeches of my suffitiencie for a Secretarie', at the same time using 'words of disgrace' against the younger Cecil. The result was to prejudice Elizabeth against Bodley, and to sir up in Burleigh and his son the suspicion that he was privy to these odious comparisons. Robert Cecil, when he succeeded his father as Lord Treasurer, must have realized that, as Bodley protested, this suspicion was unfounded, for in January 1604-5, he pressed him to become Secretary of State. But though Bodley had received a token of the new sovereign's favour by being knighted on 18th April 1604 he held fast to his resolution formed in 1598 to retire from the Court, which till then had been 'the epilogue and end of all my actions', and 'to set up my staffe at the Librarie dore in Oxon'.

The carrying out of that resolution, with its far-reaching consequences, occupied completely the remaining years of Bodley's life. From 3rd July 1612 onwards till his penultimate letter on 29th October, to his Librarian, Thomas James, he spoke frequently of his ill health. He suffered from stone and other disorders, and after a lingering illness he died at his house in Little St. Bartholomew's, London, on 24th January 1613 in his 68th year. His wife had predeceased him by a year and a half, and he had no children. His brothers and other relatives and friends and Merton College were remembered in his will dated 2nd January. But the principal provision was for 'the perpetuall preservation support & maintenance of the Publique Librarie in the Vniversitie of Oxon' which 'dothe greatly surpasse all my other worldly cares'.

With his remarkable attention to details he also gave explicit directions for the ceremonial at his funeral. His body was to be brought for burial in Merton College Chapel, where he was to have a monument of plain marble with a suitable inscription. One hundred pounds were to be spent on a dinner at which the Warden and other members of Merton College, the Vice-Chancellor and Proctors, the Heads of Colleges and Halls with the Beadles, 'and as many as shall weare blackes being present at my funeralls shall be invited'. For as many poor scholars as there were years of his life black gowns were to be provided. The total expenses, including other gifts of mourning, were not to exceed £666 13s. 4d.

It took some time to carry out these elaborate instructions and the funeral did not take place till 29th March. The body was carried in state about 9 o'clock in the morning from Merton, through Christ Church to Carfax, and thence down the High ('the great street') to the Divinity Schools, where the Deputy orator, Richard Corbet, pronounced a Latin furneral sermon; afterwards in Merton, John Hales, a Fellow of the College, delivered another 'Oratio Funebris'. Two volumes of memorial verse commemorated his career and benefactions, one by 188 members of the University generally, the other by 52 members of his own College. The Merton collection was in Latin with a few items in Greek. The University volume was more polyglot. It was headed by some Latin verses by the Vice-Chancellor, followed by a tribute in Hebrew by the Rector of Lincoln, who was also Regius Professor of Hebrew. J. Wall of Christ Church, M.A., showed his versatility by contributing in Latin, Greek and Hebrew. An Italian nobleman, a member of Balliol, who called himself a humble and unworthy son of the University, wrote in his native tongue followed by a Latin translation. With less apparent reason Arthur Ducke of All Souls also used these two languages. Nearly all the other contributors wrote in Latin, except a few in Greek. But Peter Prideaux, of Exeter College, deserves special mention as the only one out of the multitude who dared to express himself in English. After noting that Ulysses was celebrated by Homer and Caesar by Lucan he continues:

> One volume was a monument to bound
> The large extent of their deserving paines.
> In learning's commonwealth was never found
> So large a decade to express thy straines
>   Which who desires to character aright
>   Must read more bookes than they had lines to write.

The monument for which Bodley had given directions was erected on the north wall of the choir in Merton College Chapel, executed in 1615 by Nicholas Stone. It represents him in half-length with books around, and a female figure beneath holding a library key.

Bodley was not the first Oxonian to cherish the idea of endowing his *alma mater* with a suitable library. Thomas de Cobham, Bishop of Worcester, determined about 1320 to leave his books to the University, and began to prepare for their accommodation a room above the Congregation House in the north-east corner of St. Mary's Church. Owing to a prolonged controversy with Oriel College, Cobham's design did not mature till about 1410, when the claim of the University to the books was confirmed by Henry IV, who gave also a small annual endowment. But a far more munificent benefactor was to appear in Henry's fourth son, Humphrey, Duke of Gloucester, who in 1439 sent his first gift of 129 MSS., followed in the next seven years by about 500 others. But Humphrey's generosity in a sense defeated itself. Cobham's library was quite unequal to housing all these 'preciose bokes'. On 14th July 1444 the University sent a letter to the Duke informing him that they intended to provide a more suitable building over the Divinity School then being erected, and begging him to accept the title of Founder. Humphrey replied to this hint of further favours expected from him by intimating that he proposed to bequeath £100 towards the cost of the building and 'all the Latyn bokes that he had'. He died intestate in 1447, and it was not without difficulty that the University obtained the benefit of his bounty.

Fortunately he did not live to see the outrageous activities of Edward VI's Commissioners for reformation of the University in 1550. As Andrew Clark has summed them up[1]: 'Publicly these Commissioners made a show of devout zeal by burning geometrical manuscripts because the diagrams were deemed magical signs, and manuscripts of the Gospels because the Greek letters were thought to belong to the black art. Privately they wrought even worse destruction. The parchment of manuscripts had a ready sale for mechanical uses to be cut up into measures and shapes for tailors, and guards and covers for bookbinders'. Thus it has come about that of Duke Humphrey's MSS. only three have survived at the Bodleian, though others have found their way elsewhere. Nor was this the end of the sabotage. In 1556 six 'venerabiles viri', including the Vice-Chancellor and Proctors, were commissioned to sell the shelves and benches of the now bookless library, 'ipsius Universitatis nomine'.

All this must have been fresh in the minds and on the lips of men when in 1559 Bodley entered at Magdalen. To so ardent a student the spectacle of this desecration was intolerable, and it

[1] *A Bodleian Guide* (1906), pp. 93–4.

continued to haunt him throughout his busy diplomatic career till on his retirement, in his own words, 'I concluded at the last, to set up my staffe at the Librarie dore in Oxon; being throwghly perswaded, that . . . I coulde not busie myselfe to better purpose then by redusing that place (which then in euery part laye ruined and wast) to the publique vse of Studients'.

In pursuance of this resolve he wrote to the Vice-Chancellor on 23rd February 1598, offering to undertake the 'cost and charge' of fitting up shelves and seats, of procuring benefactions of books, and of an annual endowment. The offer was gratefully accepted, and, as is always the case, the estimate for reconstruction was exceeded. From a contemporary letter of 3rd April 1599, we learn that Bodley's 'library costs him much more than he expected; because the timber-works of the house were rotten, and had to be new-made'. But who to-day would grudge the cost of such a noble shrine of learning as Duke Humphrey's restored library, with its glorious roof divided into squares each blazoned with the arms of the University, while the intervening bosses have Bodley's own arms?

On 25th June 1600, Bodley wrote to the Vice-Chancellor to the effect that he had begun to busy himself with the collection of books, and that he had provided a Register for enrolling the names of benefactors with their gifts. This Register consists of two large folio volumes in vellum. Among the earliest names are Thomas Sackville, Lord Buckhurst, the Earl of Essex, and a little later Sir Walter Raleigh, with a donation of £50. Bodley did not enter his own gifts, which included the MS. of the French 'Romance of Alexander', with paintings on a chequered background of gold and colour, and with quaint illustrations at the foot of many of the pages of trades, games, dress, etc.

In the first draft of the Statutes for the Library which Bodley drew up in his own hand, and which is preserved in MS. Bodl. 2867, he ordered that in the Register 'the munificence not onely of great and honorable personages, but of others of meane and vulgar calling must be respectiuely remembred. For in a case of shewing gratitude, it is meete in all congruitie, that no man be defrauded of that measure of thankes, that is due vnto his bountie'.

The Statutes provided for the appointment of a Keeper, 'a

graduat . . . and a Linguist, not encombred with mariage, nor with a benefice of Cure'. His times of attendance and his annual stipend were prescribed, together with pay for an assistant, and for 'some honest poore scholler', who was to wipe, sweep and keep clean all the Library books and anything else subject to the annoyance of dust. He was replaced in 1610 by a Janitor.

No kind of firelight was to be allowed in the building, the larger volumes were to be chained to the desks, and any smaller books of special value were to be studied only under the eye of the Keeper. No books were to be lent out on any pretext, but some might be exchanged for better editions, and some got rid of as being wholly superfluous or of no estimation. The privilege of using the library was not to be accorded to all and sundry, for that 'would but minister occasion of daily pestering all the rowme, with a troblesome haunt of the popular sort, which with their gazing, and babling, and trampling up and downe, may disturbe out of measure the endeuours of those that are studious'. Bodley then specified the various classes of graduates and some other groups who were to be admitted as Readers, but only after they had taken an oath to 'use both the bookes and everything els apperteining to their furniture, with a careful respect to their longest continuation.'

The Library, furnished with over 2000 volumes, was formally opened by the Vice-Chancellor on 8th November 1602 and in accordance with another prescription by Bodley on the anniversary of that day, or if it is a Sunday on the following Monday, the eight Curators pay their visit of inspection while the Library remains shut. On 20th June 1604 James I issued Letters Patent directing that the Library should be called by Bodley's name. On 28th August 1605, during a royal visit to Oxford, James spent a considerable time in the Library, and when looking at a bust of Bodley presented by the Chancellor, remarked that he should have been called Godly. He offered to present any rare books that Sir Thomas might like to choose from the royal collections, but characteristically failed to carry the promise into effect.

In the same year appeared the earliest Catalogue of the Library compiled by the first Keeper, Thomas James, who had already distinguished himself as a translator and editor, and who had

I

published a list of the MSS. in the Colleges of Oxford and Cambridge and in the Cambridge University Library. The Catalogue is a quarto of 425 pages with an appendix of 230 more. It includes both printed books and MSS. arranged under the four classes of Theology, Medicine, Law and Arts. It was dedicated to Henry, Prince of Wales.

How intimate were the relations of Bodley and the Keeper is apparent from the 231 letters from Sir Thomas to James which have been preserved in the Library. With two exceptions they were first printed by Thomas Hearne in 1703 in his 'Reliquiae Bodleianae', but they had to wait till 1926 to be admirably edited by G. W. Wheeler in their probable chronological order and in their original spelling and punctuation. They range over a period of just over thirteen years, from 24th December 1599 to 3rd January 1613. The first letter is signed 'your trewe affected frind', and the last 'your louing and very assured frind', and there are other equally whole-hearted signatures, as 'your affectionate euer' and 'your owne most affectionate'. In a letter written on 11th September 1601, Bodley tells him, 'I did euer from the time of our first acquaintance, affect yow from my hart: and they did me but right, that reported vnto yow, howe I thought my self happy in the choice of your person'. This choice was abundantly justified, yet Bodley did not hesitate to be critical of James in many respects. In particular he at first, in accordance with the terms of the draft statutes, in the letter of 11th September 1601, gave a point-blank refusal when James requested leave to take unto himself a wife. 'For the point of your mariage, I might by no meanes yelde vnto it; holding it absurd in yow or in any, for sundrie great respectes.' He also took ill the Librarian's request that his stipend of £20 p.a. should be increased. 'In good sooth I could expostulat very worthely with yow, for these your vnseasonable and vn-reasonable motions.' But Bodley soon relented. In the June of 1602 James's salary was raised to £26 13s. 4d., in 1613 to £33 6s. 8d., and on 11th August Bodley wrote to him in dignified and touching terms:

'I haue considered of your motion, about the mater of marriage, wherein I doe determine to give yow good satisfaction at my comming to Oxon, which shall be, God willing, on Thursday come seuenight. For although to tell yow truly I did neuer nothing more unwillingly, then myself to become the first breaker of my owne Institution, which I pvrpose heerafter shall stand inuio-lable, yet for the loue that I beare to yow in particular, I had rather incurre a publike note of defectiue proceeding, then that yow shuld falle, by my stifnesse, into termes of extremitie.'

Permission thus obtained James married Ann Underhill at St. Thomas's Church, Oxford, on 18th October 1602, and ten days later Bodley wrote 'wishing a great deale of happinesse to yow and yours'.

Another matter upon which Bodley held an 'inviolable' opinion was that 'riffe raffe bookes' should be excluded from the Library. He emphasizes this in his letters of 31st March 1602 and 17th December 1607 and reiterates it more explicitly in two of his latest letters to James. On 1st January 1612 he writes:

'Sir, I would yow had foreborne, to catalogue our London bookes, till I had bin priuie to your purpose. There are many idle bookes, & riffe raffes among them, which shall neuer com into the Librarie, & I feare me that litle, which yow haue done alreadie, will raise a scandal vpon it, when it shall be giuen out, by suche as would disagrace it, that I haue made vp a number, with Almanackes, plaies, & proclamacions; of which I will haue none, but suche as are singular.'

A fortnight later, perhaps in answer to representations by James, he delivered his ultimatum:

'I can see no good reason to alter my opinion, for excluding such bookes, as almanackes, plaies, & an infinit number, that are daily printed, of very vnworthy maters. . . . Happely some plaies may be worthy the keeping: but hardly one in fortie. For it is not alike in Englishe plaies, & others of other nations; because they are most esteemed, for learning the languages & many of them compiled, by men of great fame, for wisedome & learning, which is seldom or neuer seene among vs. Were it so againe, that some litle profit might be reaped (which God knows is very little) out of some of our play bookes, the benefit therof will nothing neere counteruaile, the harme that the scandal will bring vnto the Librarie, when it shal be giuen out, that we stuffe it full of baggage bookes'.

This was written a few years after the composition of 'The Tempest', 'Cymbeline' and 'The Winter's Tale', and in the year of the publication of Webster's 'The White Devil'.

Fortunately, however, Bodley had about a year previously taken an all important step which was destined to go far to nullify his resolution of banishing plays from the Library. At the suggestion of James he entered on 12th December 1610, into an agreement with the Stationers' Company under which they were to present a perfect copy of every book printed by them on condition that they might borrow these books if needed for reprinting and might examine and copy books presented by others.[1]

But even before the Company began to send books, though not as regularly as the contract warranted, the Library accommodation had proved insufficient.

Bodley therefore wrote to James on 16th May 1610: 'I haue now resolued upon the enlargement of the Librarie, & to sette it presently a foote.' For this he provided an annual endowment. On the following 16th July the first stone was laid of the eastern wing and of the Proscholium beneath it. The King made some atonement for his failure to give books by providing some timber from the royal wood of Shotover, and the building was finished in 1612.

Meanwhile Bodley had suggested taking down the Schools of Arts dating from 1439 and making the Bodley building one side of a quadrangular pile. He further urged that the work should be completed by a third story, the Picture Gallery. In his will he bequeathed the larger part of his property for this purpose, and the 'New Schools', as they were then called, were opened in 1619.

Amongst the volumes which were so rapidly overfilling the Library's shelves, a few of special interest may be mentioned. Ten Chinese works bought in 1606 and twenty Arabic, Persian and other MSS. presented in 1611 by the English Consul at Aleppo

---

[1] Dr. John Wallis, Keeper of the University Archives, writing to Dr. E. Bernard, Savilian Professor of Astronomy, on 23rd June 1691, states that 'Sir Thomas Bodley gave to the Company a piece of plate of 60^{li}'. See *Historical Introduction to First Minute Book of the Delegates of the Oxford University Press*, p. xxl. (Oxford Bibliographical Society, 1943.)

laid the foundation of the Oriental collections in which the Library is so rich. In 1615, three years after Prince Henry's death, his auditor gave his MS. Book of Hours which had formerly belonged to the Princess Mary. It has beautifully illuminated borders and exquisite drawings, and the donor in a note prefixed was careful to state that he gave it 'not for the religion it contains, but for the pictures and former royall owners' sake'. In the same year another donor gave a MS. on vellum containing three Miracle Plays in Cornish, the original speech of Cornwall. Even had Bodley still been alive 'the decent obscurity of a dead language' might have saved them from being rejected as 'riffe-raffes'.

In May, 1620, Thomas James resigned his office as Keeper of the Library, and was succeeded by John Rouse, Fellow of Oriel. Before his resignation James had virtually completed the second printed edition of the Catalogue, which was issued with a dedication to Prince Charles and a preface dated 30th June. It was arranged not under classes as its predecessor, but alphabetically, and included 16,000 books, of which between 3000 and 4000 were in French, Italian and Spanish. From the first qualified foreigners were admitted to the privileges of the Library and many of them took advantage of them.

In the same month of June King James presented the folio edition of his own Works. It was brought to Oxford by a special deputation, and a Convocation was held at St. Mary's Church for its reception. From there it was carried in a solemn procession, including the Vice-Chancellor and twenty-four Doctors in their robes, to the Library, where the new Keeper, Rouse, 'made a very prettie speech'. The King was all the more pleased at this tribute by Oxford because, as a contemporary letter-writer relates, 'Cambridge received them without extraordinary respect'.

The University would have done better to greet with all this ceremonial a volume received in sheets three years later from the Stationers' Company, the first Folio of Shakespeare's plays. The story of this copy is truly astonishing. Though Bodley had guarded against the loss of books from the library by borrowing he had allowed duplicates to be got rid of. Accordingly when the third Folio was published in 1664, with seven additional plays attributed to Shakespeare, the first Folio, which had been bound in Oxford

by William Wildgoose, was unchained and sold with other superfluous books by order of the Curators to a bookseller, who gave
£24 for the lot. About a century later, in 1759, it passed into the
library of Richard Tarbutt of Ogston Hall, Derbyshire. In
January, 1905, one of his descendants, ignorant of its original
ownership, brought it up to the Bodleian for inspection. One of
the Library staff, Mr. Strickland Gibson (later sub-librarian and
Keeper of the University Archives), recognized it in five minutes
(as he told me) by its Oxford binding as the Bodleian copy. For
£3000 it was redeemed and brought home again. I am glad to
remember to-day that I was among those who had the privilege
of making a modest contribution to that act of *pietas*.

William Herbert, Earl of Pembroke, was the elder of the
'incomparable pair of brethren' to whom the first Folio was dedicated in 1623. Six years later as Chancellor of the University he
presented a very valuable set of 242 Greek MSS. collected by
Barocci of Venice, which was deposited in the Bodleian. Another
large group of MSS. relating in part to the early history of science
in England came in 1634 from Sir Kenelm Digby. In 1635 Archbishop Laud, who had succeeded Pembroke as Chancellor, began
his munificent donations continued till 1640 of MSS. and other
treasures.   Among them is a MS. of the Acts of the Apostles
in Greek and Latin in parallel columns, with 74 special readings.
Another is the Peterborough version of the Anglo-Saxon Chronicle. In 1640 also a bequest of Robert Burton of Christ Church,
author of the 'Anatomy of Melancholy', enriched the Library with a
number of plays, almanacs and other types of the 'baggage books'
so obnoxious to Bodley. One wonders what he would have
thought of the singular gift in 1641 of the lantern caught in the
hand of Guy Fawkes presented by the son of the Justice of the
Peace who had arrested him.

The wealth of new accessions necessitated an Appendix to the
1620 Catalogue. This was compiled in 1635 by Rouse and contained about 1500 authors. Additional space was also urgently
needed. Bodley, in his will, had left property to provide for further extension, and the foundation stone of a west wing was laid
on 13th May 1634, and it was ready for use in 1640.

Hitherto all had gone prosperously with the Library, but the outbreak of the CivilWar and the setting up of the royalist head-quarters in Oxford brought changes in their train. Aubrey speaks of 'hurt donne by the Cavaliers (during their garrison) by way of embezzilling and cutting off chaines of bookes'. The King himself borrowed £500 of the Library's money, which was never repaid, but was entered as a debt owing by the Crown till 1782. But one incident stands to his moral credit. The Vice-Chancellor on 30th December 1645 gave an order that a book in the Library which Charles wished to read should be delivered to him. But when the Keeper showed him the Bodley statutes forbidding the loan of books, the King at once acquiesced, 'saying that it was fit that the will and statutes of the pious founder should be religiously ob-served'. Likewise Oliver Cromwell, when denied the loan of a manuscript in April, 1654, did not press his demand, 'commending the prudence of the Founder who had made the place so sacred'.

On the surrender of Oxford on 24th June 1646, Sir Thomas Fairfax, the Parliamentary commander, at once set a guard to protect the Library. He thereby amply earned the banquet with which he and Cromwell were entertained by the University on 19th May 1649, in the new west end of the building. In later years Charles II and James II were similarly feasted there, but at more than ten times the cost. From 1659 when about 8000 volumes bequeathed by John Selden, the antiquary, were placed there this part of the building has been known as the Selden end. The MSS. in Selden's bequest were chiefly Oriental or Greek, but among the printed books was a collection of early English black-letter tales and romances, unique or very rare.

Another very important bequest followed in 1671 when Thomas, Lord Fairfax (as he had now become), the preserver of the Library from violence in 1646, left a valuable collection of MSS., partly historical, together with a unique series of 161 vol-umes of genealogical MSS. compiled with his financial help by Roger Dodsworth.

In 1674 the third Catalogue of printed books was published in alphabetical order of authors' names. It was printed in the recently erected Sheldonian theatre, and was dedicated by Thomas Hyde the Librarian to Archbishop Gilbert Sheldon. Hyde in his dedi-cation speaks of the fatigue he had incurred in the compilation of the Catalogue, and of the sufferings he had endured in winter in the unheated premises. On the other hand Thomas Hearne declared, probably with exaggeration, that he had written only the dedication and preface and that the real work had been done by the Janitor.

No sooner had this Catalogue been completed than the flow of benefactions continued, though in the immediately following years they were chiefly of MSS. In 1675 Lord Hatton gave four volumes of Anglo-Saxon homilies, and in 1678 Frances Junius bequeathed a still more important collection of Anglo-Saxon and philological MSS. About the same time Colonel Edward Vernon presented a massive MS. of Middle-English verse and prose. In 1681 John Rushworth, who was a member of the Parliament held in that year at Oxford, gave a splendidly illuminated Latin MS. of the Gospels written by an Irish scribe Mac-Rigol, who died in A.D. 820, with an interlinear Anglo-Saxon version. In 1691 a valuable bequest of MSS. and printed books came from Thomas Barlow, Bishop of Lincoln, who had been Bodley's Librarian 1652-60. Among the folio volumes was a Roman Missal used in the private chapel of James II, with a printed Latin prayer pasted at the end for use when his Queen was with child in 1688.

The first decade of the eighteenth century was memorable in the history of the Library. Bodley's contract with the Stationers' Company had been replaced in 1662 by an Act imposing a statutory obligation on the Company to deliver a copy of each book printed by them to the Oxford, Cambridge and Royal Libraries. This Act, however, had been renewable every two years, and it was not till 1709 that the first permanent Copyright Act was passed ensuring to the Bodleian with certain other Libraries the delivery of a copy of every book entered at Stationers' Hall.

But other books and MSS. continued to pour in, chiefly by bequests, of which I can mention a few only of the most notable. In 1714 the Oriental collections were enriched by 744 MSS. left by Narcissus Marsh, Archbishop of Armagh. From another book-loving ecclesiastic, Thomas Tanner, Bishop of Asaph, came in 1736 about 600 volumes of MSS., many of them relating to the Civil War period as well as many valuable early printed English books.

Two years afterwards the fourth Catalogue of printed books appeared in two folio volumes. It purported to be the work in the main of two successive Librarians, but again Thomas Hearne challenged their claim. In this case he asserted that he himself, after being appointed Janitor in 1702 and Sub-Librarian in 1712-15, had compared every book in the Library with the 1674 Catalogue, correcting mistakes and adding notes. Much of the accuracy and fullness of the 1738 work is credited to him.

In 1753-4 Thomas Carte, the historian, forwarded many of his Ormonde and general Irish State papers, to which additions were later made. In the same year Henry Hyde, Lord Cornbury, great-grandson of Edward Hyde, Earl of Clarendon, left in his will Clarendon's MSS. to the University. The larger part of these were received in 1759. A MS. of the 'History of the Rebellion' in seven volumes was forwarded in 1785, and further additions have since been made. Simultaneously with the Carte and Clarendon collections the documents for seventeenth century history were further enriched by the Thurloe and Pepys State Papers, forming part of the immense bequest in 1756 by Richard Rawlinson, the non-juring Bishop. This included about 5000 MSS. and between 1800 and 1900 books. The Library staff were unable to cope with this overwhelming accession. W. D. Macray in his invaluable ' Annals' of the Bodleian states that they contented themselves with entering the printed books and ignoring the MSS. It was not till after H. A. Coxe became Librarian in 1860 that the full extent of Rawlinson's collections was ascertained. ' Cupboard after cupboard,' writes Macray, 'was found filled with MSS. and papers huddled together in confusion, while, last but not least, a dark hole under a staircase, explored by me on hands and knees, afforded a rich "take".'[1]

Another bequest almost rivalling that of Rawlinson in its varied wealth and interest was that of Richard Gough, formerly of Corpus Christi College, Cambridge. Under it the Library acquired in 1809 upwards of 3700 volumes of printed books and MSS. relating to the topographical history of Great Britain and Ireland and the Anglo-Saxon and Scandinavian literatures, together with a very valuable collection of Missals, Breviaries and

[1] 2nd edition (1890), p. 236.

other Pre-Reformation service-books. Additional magnificently illuminated Missals were received in 1834, the bequest of Francis Douce, formerly Keeper of MSS. in the British Museum, which also included over 300 specimens of fifteenth-century typography and many works of miscellaneous interest, besides prints, drawings and coins.

Contrasted with the vast composite collections of Rawlinson, Gough and Douce was the highly specialized Library of Edmond Malone of Trinity College, Dublin, which, after the completion of the Boswell-Malone edition of Shakespeare in 1821, was presented by his brother, Lord Sunderlin. Sir Thomas Bodley would doubtless have been horror-stricken by the arrival in his Library of these 800 or more 'riffe-raffe' books. For Malone's collection consisted almost entirely of Tudor and Stuart Literature, mainly dramatic, and it included the first and second Shakespeare folios, first quartos of many of his plays, a unique copy of the first edition of 'Venus and Adonis', and a volume of nine Beaumont and Fletcher plays which had belonged to Charles I and has a list of contents in his handwriting. Important additions to the Malone Shakespeareana were presented by Thomas Caldecott of New College in 1833, or bought at the Heber Library sale in 1834 or soon afterwards, at what now seems incredibly small prices. Thus by one of Time's strangest ironies the Bodleian, in defiance of its Founder's intentions, has become a magnet that draws students of English dramatic literature from all over the world.

While books and MSS. had thus for over two centuries been pouring into the Library in almost embarrassing profusion, it had received few monetary gifts. But in 1840 the munificent sum of £36,000 was bequeathed by Dr. Robert Mason of Queen's College. He might be saluted as the forerunner of the 'Friends of the Bodleian', the body first formed in 1925 of those who by an annual subscription have raised a fund which enables the Library to acquire volumes not covered by the Copyright Act, or not included in any of the benefactions already mentioned, or in those that have followed them, wherein special note may be made between 1888 and 1900 of Greek and Latin papyri discovered in Egypt, including the 'Logia Iesou' leaf.

The constant stream of accessions has raised ever-recurring

problems of accommodation. One after another since 1789 the rooms in the schools quadrangle have been taken over for the storage of books. Since 1860 the adjoining Radcliffe Camera has been allowed to be used as a receptacle for books and as an additional reading room. Quite recently its fine ground-floor story has been turned into a specialized English and Law Library and reading room. Part of the picture gallery has since 1907 been used as an upper reading-room containing many bound periodicals and the immense range of volumes of the Library Catalogue. The substructure of the Old Ashmolean and the cellarage of the Sheldonian Theatre have been pressed into the service, and there are now specialized offshoots—the Radcliffe Science Library in the Museum and the Library in Rhodes House.

But all this was not sufficient to save the Bodleian from what Dr. (now Sir William) Craster has called 'the creeping paralysis which had threatened it since infancy'.[1] More heroic measures were needed, and with the aid of a munificent grant from the Rockefeller Foundation, which undertook to provide three-fifths of the cost, a new Bodleian building has been erected in Broad Street, connected by an underground tunnel with the old, in which there will be room for about five million books, and which, if the present rate of increase holds good, will suffice for two centuries to come. This new building was officially opened by King George VI on 24 October 1946.

But amid all the transformations and enlargements the spirit of Bodley still broods over his great Foundation. We can still echo the lines of Henry Vaughan in the seventeenth century:

Most noble Bodley! we are bound to thee
For no small part of our eternity.

    ·   ·   ·   ·   ·

Th' hast made us all thine heirs; whatever we
Hereafter write, 'tis thy posterity.
This is they monument! Here thou shalt stand
Till the times fail in their last grain of sand.
And wheresoe'er thy silent reliques keep,
This tomb will never let thine honour sleep.

    ·   ·   ·   ·   ·

[1] *Oxford*, Special Number, February 1937, p. 25.

Thou can'st not die ! Here thou art more than safe,
Where every book is thy large epitaph.

We can still, like Charles Lamb visiting Oxford in vacation, take
shelter 'under the shadow of the mighty Bodley', and pace
reverentially with him beneath Duke Humphrey's roof. 'It seems
as if all the souls of all the writers, that have bequeathed theur
labours to these Bodleians were reposing here, as in some dormi-
tory or middle state. I do not want to handle, or profane the
leaves, their winding sheets. I could as soon dislodge a shade.'

SEVEN

CHARLES LAMB AND THE
ELIZABETHAN DRAMATISTS

THE story of how Lamb's *Specimens of English Dramatic Writers who lived about the Time of Shakespeare* originated was told by J. Dykes Campbell in the *Athenaeum*, 25th August, 1894, and was retold with slight additions by E. V. Lucas in volume IV of his edition of *The Works of Charles and Mary Lamb* (1904). As early as May, 1796, when Lamb was in his twenty-first year, he was transcribing in letters to Coleridge passages from a little extract book, full of quotations, from Beaumont and Fletcher in particular, to whom, as he puts it, 'all poets after Shakespeare yield in variety of genius. Massinger treads close on their heels.' In the following September, after the tragedy in which his sister, seized with sudden mania, killed their mother, he burnt both his own verses and the book of extracts. But by the spring of the next year he had begun to retranscribe the passages into a new note-book, and between 1798 and 1800 he was communicating his enthusiasm about some of the dramatists to Southey and Wordsworth.

It was after the failure of his farce *Mr. H*—in December, 1806— that Lamb, apparently under an arrangement with Longmans, took the *Specimens* in hand. As he tells in his preface, he made use of Dodsley's twelve-volume *Select Collections of Old Plays* (1744), 2nd edition by Isaac Reed (1780); Thomas Hawkins's *The Origin of the English Drama* (1773); D. E. Baker's *Biographia Dramatica* (1764, 2nd edition 1782); and the works, probably his own copies, of Jonson, Beaumont and Fletcher, and Massinger. But more than one-third of the *Specimens* were from plays which Lamb found only in the British Museum and in some scarce private libraries. His time for research among these was short, his two brief office holidays from the India House in 1807 and 1808. What he sought, as he tells, were 'scenes of passion, sometimes of the deepest quality, interesting situations, serious descriptions, that which is more nearly allied to poetry than to wit, and to tragic rather than to comic poetry . . . . My leading design has been to illustrate what may be called the moral sense of our ancestors.' The book was published probably towards the end of 1808. The *Monthly Review* gave it an unappreciative notice in April 1809. The *Annual Review* had a favourable article on it, possibly written by Coleridge.

In 1825 Lamb retired from the India Office, and next year, with all his time at his disposal, he returned to the Garrick collection in the Museum and 'discovered in it a treasure rich and exhaustless' beyond what he had previously imagined. By January 1827 he had filled two note-books with *Extracts* from the plays, supplementing the earlier *Specimens*. To his friend William Hone he offered these for publication in his weekly periodical, *Table-Book*, so arranged in articles as to run through the year. In 1835 the *Specimens* and the *Extracts* were printed together in a two-volume edition by Moxon, of which Lamb, as Lucas thinks, had seen the proof-sheets before his death on 27th December 1834. Lucas therefore took this 1835 reprint as the basis of his own admirable edition, to which he added some extracts from the note-books which Lamb did not send to Hone, and some passages in the articles which were not printed.

Lamb's treatment of Shakespeare's leading immediate predecessors presents some curious features. It may be set down to his credit that, at a time when the importance of Thomas Kyd's *The Spanish Tragedy* in the development of English drama was little recognized, he should have given a specimen from it. But unfortunately the specimen that he chose, though of the highest quality, is not from Kyd's pen. Horatio is murdered in the garden of his father Hieronimo, the Marshal of Spain, while he is making love to Belimperia. Her shrieks rouse the Marshal, and he comes forth in his shirt calling aloud:

What outcries pluck me from my naked bed,
And chill my throbbing heart with trembling fear?

He sees a body hanging on a tree.

But stay what murdrous spectacle is this?

Alas! it is Horatio, my sweet son.
O no! but he that whilome was my son.

Lamb ignores this passage, which was echoed for years in the Elizabethan theatre, and merely states, 'Upon this he goes distracted'. But it is in the gradual oncoming of Hieronimo's madness and in the delays and hesitations before he takes his revenge for his son's murder that Kyd shows his psychological insight and his dramatic skill. Indeed, the Marshal is never in the original play so completely distraught as in the scene quoted by Lamb which was one of the 'additions' in the 1602 quarto. Hieronimo is wandering at midnight in his garden, searching everywhere by torchlight for his murdered son, when a painter enters and the Marshal questions him.

Art a painter? Canst paint me a tear, or a wound?
A groan or a sigh? Canst paint me such a tree as this? . . . .
Canst paint a doleful cry?
Painter. Seemingly, sir.
Hier. Nay, it should cry; but all is one.
Well, sir, paint me a youth run thro' and thro' with villains' swords hanging upon this tree.

The whole scene is of supreme romantic quality, but from one point of view it is a major blunder of Lamb's to speak of it as 'the very salt of the old play' which otherwise is 'but a caput mortuum'. With his own lamentable family experience it is strange that he should have found merely 'flatness' in the delineation, apart from this 'addition', of Hieronimo's distracted grief, and that he should have found nothing but a 'caput mortuum' in the most dynamic in its influence of pre-Shakespearian plays. On the other hand he shows his discrimination in not accepting Henslowe's entry of two payments to Jonson for additions to *The Spanish Tragedy* as evidence that his hand is to be found there. 'I should suspect the agency of some "more potent spirit". Webster might have furnished them. They are full of the wild solemn preternatural cast of grief which bewilders us in *The Duchess of Malfy*.' The authorship of the Addition is still an enigma, but Lamb's description could not be bettered.

Lamb in his 1808 preface mentions Marlowe as one of the dramatists who have been 'slighted', and whose 'more impressive scenes' he intends to exhibit. Yet his treatment of the greatest of Shakespeare's predecessors is in the main curiously unsatisfactory. I do not lay stress on the fact that he begins his extracts from him with *Lust's Dominion*, which has now been rejected from the Marlovian canon. But what is truly astonishing is that he could find nothing better to quote from the two Parts of *Tamburlaine* than the description of his person and the account of his custom in war of pitching, as his fury mounts, symbolic tents of white, red, and black in turn. Of these quotations he remarks that he had difficulty in 'culling a few sane lines' from the play. 'The lunes of Tamburlaine are perfect "midsummer madness". Nebuchadnezzar's are mere modest pretensions compared with the thundering vaunts of the Scythian Shepherd.' Then he refers to the passage spouted by Pistol in 2 *Henry IV*, where Tamburlaine cries to the conquered kings yoked to his chariot,

Holla! ye pampered jades of Asia:
What, can ye draw but twenty miles a day?

'Till I saw this passage with mine own eyes I never believed that it was anything more than a pleasant burlesque of Mine Ancient's. But I assure my readers that it is soberly set down in a Play which their Ancestors took to be serious. I have subjoined the genuine speech for their amusement', and he proceeds to quote it at length in what we may call a derisory footnote. Of course the speech is superlative bombast, but it is strange that a man of Lamb's insight did not realize that it was dramatically appropriate to Tamburlaine and not merely material for amusement. It is still more surprising that a leader of the romantic critical movement should have been insensitive to the beauty and rapture of the lines beginning,

If all the pens that ever poets held
Had fed the feeling of their masters' thoughts:
or
Nature that formed us of four elements
Warring within our breasts for regiment
Doth teach us all to have aspiring minds.

Lamb is happier in his choice of extracts from *The Jew of Malta*, where he gives the opening scene of Barabas in his counting-house gloating with almost poetic fervour over his gold and jewels, followed by a passage in which he descants on the worldly prosperity of the Jews. Yet Barabas, even when contrasted with Shylock, is something more than the 'mere monster, brought in with a large painted nose, to please the rabble', as Lamb puts it.

From *Dr. Faustus* the selections are naturally the opening scene where the Doctor in his study 'runs through the circles of the sciences; and being satisfied with none of them, determines to addict himself to magic', and the tremendous climax when he awaits the midnight hour when Lucifer will claim his soul. Of this Lamb finely says, 'The growing horrors of Faustus are aw-fully marked by the hours and half-hours as they expire and bring him nearer and nearer to the enactment of his dire compact. It is indeed an agony and bloody sweat.' He then adds what strikes us to-day as rather a prim comment:

> Barabas the Jew, and Faustus the conjurer, are offsprings of a mind which at least delighted to dally with interdicted subjects. They both talk a language which a believer would have been tender of putting into the mouth of a character though but in fiction. But the holiest minds have sometimes not thought it blameable to counterfeit impiety in the person of another, to bring Vice upon the stage speaking her own dialect, and them-selves being armed with an Unction of self-confident impunity, have not scrupled to handle and touch that familiarly, which would be death to others.

He instances Milton speaking through Satan and the precise strait-laced Richardson through Lovelace. But while Lamb thus goes near to censuring Marlowe for dallying with interdicted subjects he is apparently unconscious that through the lips of Mephisto-philis the so-called atheist gives a spiritual interpretation of hell, which no 'believer' has ever bettered:

> Think'st thou that I who saw the face of God,
> And tasted the eternal joys of heaven,
> Am not tormented with ten thousand hells
> In being depriv'd of everlasting bliss?

K

It is with *Edward the Second* that Lamb is at his best in his dealing with Marlowe. The extracts are well chosen, including passages illustrating the barons' enmity towards the favourite Gaveston, the king's surrender of his crown, and his murder in the vaults of Berkeley Castle. Of the surrender scenes Lamb uses the unforgettable words, 'The reluctant pangs of abdicating Royalty in Edward furnished hints which Shakespeare scarcely improved in his *Richard the Second*.' And he declares that 'the death-scene of Marlowe's king moves pity and terror beyond any scene ancient or modern with which I am acquainted'. Whether any one scene in the whole range of drama from Aeschylus onward can thus be singled out as fulfilling beyond all others the Aristotelian view of the function of tragedy is disputable, but Lamb's arresting statement is proof that here at least he had come under the full spell of Marlowe's genius.

Of George Peele when he edited the *Specimens* Lamb does not appear to have had a high opinion. His only selection was from the opening episode in *David and Bethsabe* where David from above views Uriah's wife bathing and is inflamed by her beauty. While it is not of high poetic merit the passage has a Renaissance decorative charm, as in the lines:

Now comes my Lover tripping like the Roe,
And brings my longings tangled in her hair.

Yet Lamb has merely the acid comment, 'there is more of the same stuff, but I suppose the reader has a surfeit; especially as this Canticle of David has never been suspected to contain any pious sense couched underneath it, whatever his son's may'. When, however, in 1827 he published the *Extracts* he did more justice to Peele. He added further quotations from *David and Bethsabe* including the dialogue in which Nathan tells David 'thou art the man', and two speeches by rebellious Absalom.

He also gave extracts from *The Arraignment of Paris* where he was attracted more by the love of Paris for Oenone and her despair after his desertion than by the contest between the three goddesses for the golden apple and Paris' fine oration vindicating himself before the Olympian deities, from which he does not quote. What charmed him most was the roundelay sung by Paris and Oenone, 'Cupid's Curse', with the refrain,

> They that do change old love for new,
> Pray Gods they change for worse.

He wrote to his 'esteemed friend and excellent musician' Vincent Novello:

> I conjure you in the name of all the Sylvan Deities, and of the Muses, whom you honour, and they reciprocally love and honour you—rescue this old and passionate *Ditty*—the very flower of an old *forgotten Pastoral*, which had it been in all parts equal, *The Faithful Shepherdess* of Fletcher had been but a second name in this sort of writing—rescue if from the profane hands of every common Composer . . . . Oblige me; and all the more knowing Judges of Music and Poets; by the adaptation of fit muscial numbers, which it only wants to be the rarest Love Dialogue in our language. Your implorer. C.L.

Sad to say this typically Elian adjuration seems to have been fruitless.

Neither Greene not Lodge figured in the *Specimens*, but in the *Extracts* there is a passage from their joint-play *A Looking Glass for England and London*, where Alvida, the paramour to Rasni, the great king of Assyria, courts a petty king of Cilicia, and sings to him a 'passing passionate' song which doubtless attracted Lamb:

> Beauty, alas! where wast thou born,
> Thus to hold thyself in scorn,
> When, as Beauty kiss'd to woo thee,
> Thou by Beauty dost undo me?
>   Heigho, despise me not!

Lyly too makes an appearance in the *Extracts* with a short quotation from *Love's Metamorphosis* and five from *Sapho and Phao*, depicting the mutual love of the ferryman Phao and the high-born Sapho, in which there has been seen an allegory of the relations between Elizabeth and Leicester. (See pages 20*ff.*)

Passing from Shakespeare's predecessors to his contemporaries, let us turn first to Dekker. Lamb's longest excerpts in the *Speci-*

mens are from the loose-jointed comedy of *Old Fortunatus*, who is endowed with an exhaustible purse which allows him to travel where he will. The passages in which he chooses riches rather than wisdom, strength, health, beauty, or long life, and in which he recounts his travels to his sons are quoted. But Lamb's enthusiasm is chiefly reserved for the episode in which the French noble Orleans, a prisoner in the English king's court, is enamoured to frenzy of his daughter Agripyna, and bursts out to a friend:

> Ha, ha, when I behold a swarm of fools
> Crowding together to be counted wise
> I laugh because sweet Agripyne's not there,
> And weep because she is not anywhere;
> And weep because (whether she be or not)
> My love was ever and is still forgot: forgot, forgot, forgot.

On this Lamb somewhat surprisingly comments: 'The terror of a frantic lover is here done to the life. Orleans is as passionate an Inamorato as any which Shakespeare ever drew.' Then in his Elian reflective vein he adds:

> We have gone retrograde in the noble Heresy since the days when Sidney proselyted our nation to this mixed health and disease; the kindliest symptom yet the most alarming crisis in the ticklish state of youth; the nourisher and the destroyer of hopeful wits; the mother of twin-births, wisdom and folly, valour and weakness; the servitude above freedom; the gentle mind's religion; the liberal superstition.

From the much greater two-part play *The Honest Whore* Lamb's chief quotation is from the second Part where Bellafront, the reclaimed harlot, recounts some of the miseries of her former profession:

> when in the street
> A fair young modest damsel I did meet,
> She seem'd to all a Dove, when I pass'd by,
> And I to all a Raven; every eye
> That follow'd her went with a bashful glance;
> At me each bold and jeering countenance
> Darted forth scorn.

Upon this he comments in an unctuously moralizing vein akin to that which we have found in his footnote to *Dr. Faustus*:

> This simple picture of Honour and Shame, contrasted without violence and expressed without immodesty, is worth all the *strong lines* against the Harlot's Profession, with which both Parts of this Play are offensively crowded. A Satyrist is always to be suspected, who, to make vice odious, dwells upon all its acts and minutest circumstances with a sort of relish and retrospective gust.

Swinburne, as Lucas reminds us, has pointed out that Lamb has no word about the appealing figure of Bellafront's father, who in the disguise of a servant watches over the changes of her fortune: 'It is strange that Charles Lamb, to whom of all critics and all men the pathetic and humorous charm of the old man's personality might most confidently have been expected most cordially to appeal, should have left to Hazlitt and Leigh Hunt the honour of doing justice to so beautiful a creation.'

In *Satiromastix* I am glad that Lamb quoted a striking passage from the romantic plot of Sir Walter Terill and his bride Celestina, which more recent criticism has tended to overlook in dwelling upon the satirical attack by Dekker on Jonson as Horace. A short quotation from this attack was afterwards included in the *Extracts*, and Lucas prints (pp. 588-9) a number of notes and quotations relative to it found in Lamb's manuscript but which were not sent to Hone.

It is remarkable that Lamb makes no reference to the most delightful of all Dekker's plays, *The Shoemaker's Holiday*. To so devoted a Londoner this attractive picture of civic life in the capital, and the jovial figure of Simon Eyre among his craftsmen would, one thinks, have made an irresistible appeal.

If Lamb did not get the best out of Dekker, he, on the other hand, has the credit of doing justice to Marston, who until recently has been often underestimated partly owing to Jonson's burlesque of him in *Poetaster* and still more to his frequent lapses into rhodomontade. From *Antonio and Mellida* he detaches the episode in which Antonio's father, Andrugio, Duke of Genoa, banished from his own country, is cast up on the territory of his enemy, the Duke of Venice, with an attendant nobleman Lucio. He compares their situation with that of Lear in his distresses and the Duke of Kent, and in another of his exquisitely apt phrases says that 'Andrugio like Lear manifests a kind of royal impatience, a turbulent greatness, an affected resignation'. From the second Part, *Antonio's Revenge*, he first quotes the Prologue, beginning:

> The rawish dank of clumsy winter ramps
> The fluent summer's vein: and drizzling sleet
> Chilleth the wan bleak cheek of the numb'd earth,
> While snarling gusts nibble the juiceless leaves
> From the naked shuddering branch.

These lines contain some of Marston's outlandish terms, and while the prologue as a whole is impressive, Lamb goes too far when he claims that 'for its passionate earnestness and for the tragic note of preparation which it sounds [it] might have preceded one of those old tales of Thebes, or Pelops' line which Milton has so highly commended . . . . It is as solemn a preparative as the "warning voice which he who saw the Apocalypse heard cry" '.

Other passages from *Antonio's Revenge* are given, and are followed by citations from the tragedies *The Wonder of Women* and *Sophonisba*, from the tragi-comedy *The Malcontent* and the comedy *What you Will*. One of those from *What you Will* is a description of a gaily attired Venetian merchant in

> A Florentine cloth o' silver jerkin, sleeves
> White satin cut on tinsel, then long stock;
> French panes embroider'd, goldsmith's work.

On this Lamb's footnote has the flavour of an Elian essay:

> To judge of the liberality of these notions of dress we must advert to the days of Gresham [the great Elizabethan merchant who founded the Royal Exchange and Gresham College], and the consternation which a phenomenon habited like the Merchant here described, would have excited among the flat round caps and cloth stockings upon Change. . . . The blank uniformity to which all professional distinctions in apparel have been long hastening is one instance of the Decay of Symbols

among us, which whether it has contributed or not to make us
a more intellectual, has certainly made us a less imaginative
people.

From Dekker and Marston it is natural to turn to Ben Jonson,
concerning whom in the main Lamb displays fine taste and
judgement. An anthologist to-day would prefer to quote from
The Silent Woman and *Bartholomew Fair* than from Ben's earliest
extant play *The Case is Altered* or the incomplete pastoral *The Sad
Shepherd*. But the picture of a miser worshipping his gold from
The Case is Altered suggests another characteristically Elian
comment:

> The old poets when they introduce a miser, constantly make
> him address his gold as his mistress, as something to be seen, felt,
> and hugged; as capable of satisfying two of the senses at least.
> The substitution of a thin, unsatisfying medium for the good old
> tangible gold, has made avarice quite a Platonic affection in
> comparison with the seeing, touching, and handling pleasures of
> the old Chrysophilites. A bank-note can no more satisfy the
> touch of a true sensualist in this passion, than Creusa could
> return her husband's embrace in the shades.

There follow selections from *The Poetaster, Sejanus, Catiline,* and
The New Inn which, as Lamb puts it, 'may serve to show the
poetical fancy and elegance of mind of the supposed rugged old
Bard'. They are all well chosen, especially Lovel's discourse on
Love from *The New Inn,* the 'Romeo and Juliet' dialogue between
Ovid and Julia in *The Poetaster,* and the discussion on Poetry
between the emperor Augustus and his courtiers in the same piece.
This prompts Lamb to a defence of Ben against his enemies in
his own days and ours, who have said that he made a pedantic use
of his learning:

> He has here revived the whole court of Augustus, by a learned
> spell. . . . We are admitted to the Society of the illustrious dead.
> . . . Nothing can be imagined more elegant, refined and court-
> like than the scenes between this Lewis the Fourteenth of
> Antiquity and his Literati.

All this is admirable, but Lamb spoke unadvisedly when he

maintained that Virgil, Horace, Ovid, Tibullus, 'converse in our own tongue more finely and poetically than they expressed themselves in their native Latin'. Jonson's comic vein is illustrated by long selections from *The Alchemist* and *Volpone*. Of Sir Epicure Mammon's elaboration of the details of a sensualist paradise Lamb remarks with a spice of exaggeration, 'If there be no one image which rises to the height of the sublime, yet the confluence and assemblage of them all produces an effect equal to the grandest poetry.'

With Lamb's lack of appreciation of the *Tamburlaine* vein in Marlowe I should not have been surprised if he had been as critical as Dryden of the bombastic element in Chapmen's *Bussy D'Ambois*. But he quotes from it generously in the *Specimens*, including the account of the duel between Bussy and two friends against three adversaries in which Bussy is the sole survivor, and the contrast between the courts of Elizabeth and the French king Henry. Lamb also quotes at some length from *Byron's Conspiracy* and *Byron's Tragedy*, *The Tragedy of Chabot*, and from *Caesar and Pompey*. In the 1827 *Extracts* he adds to the *Bussy*, *Chabot*, and *Caesar and Pompey* quotations, and gives others from *The Revenge of Bussy D'Ambois*, and from three of the comedies. Had Lamb in 1808 devoted more attention to these comedies he might have modified part of his footnote in that year to the Chapman selections: 'Dramatic Imitation was not his talent. He could not go out of himself, as Shakespeare could shift at pleasure, to inform and animate other existences, but in himself he had an eye to perceive and embrace all forms.' In some of the figures in *The Gentleman Usher* and *All Fools* Chapman shows more powers of strictly dramatic creation than Lamb credits him with here. But in what follows he goes straight to the mark:

He would have made a great Epic Poet, if indeed he has not abundantly shown himself to be one; for his Homer is not so properly a translation as the Stories of Achilles and Ulysses rewritten. The earnestness and passion which he has put into every part of these poems would be incredible to a reader of more modern translations. His almost Greek zeal for the honour of his heroes is only paralleled by that fierce spirit of Hebrew

bigotry, with which Milton, as if personating one of the
Zealots of the old law, clothed himself when he sat down to
paint the acts of Sampson against the Uncircumcised.

Lamb then digresses into a passage of the finest critical quality
on the phraseology of Chapman's Homer.

Of all the Elizabethans Lamb's heart seems to have gone out
most fully to Thomas Heywood. In a footnote to an excerpt from
Fortune by Land and Sea, by Heywood and William Rowley, in
the 1827 *Extracts* he tells us, 'If I were to be consulted as to a
Reprint of old English Dramatists. I should advise to begin with
the Collected Plays of Heywood. He was a fellow Actor, and
fellow Dramatist, with Shakespeare.' This sentence is somewhat
misleading, as Heywood acted with the Lord Admiral's, not the
Lord Chamberlain's, Company, and he never, so far as we know,
collaborated with Shakespeare. Lamb continues:

> He possessed not the imagination of the latter, but in all those
> qualities which gained for Shakespeare the attribute of gentle, he
> was not inferior to him. Generosity, courtesy, temperance in the
> depth of passion; sweetness in a word and gentleness; Christian-
> ism; and true hearty Anglicism of feelings shaping that
> Christianism shine throughout his beautiful writings.

Of nothing in the Heywood canon are these words so true as of
the exquisite scene in *A Woman Killed with Kindness*, quoted in
the *Specimens*, where Frankford forgives the dying wife who has
sinned against him:

> Even as I hope for pardon at that day,
> When the great judge of heaven in scarlet sits,
> So be thou pardon'd. Though thy rash offence
> Divorc'd our bodies, thy repentant tears
> Unite our souls.

It is to this scene that Lamb appends the famous comment:
'Heywood is a sort of *prose* Shakespeare. His scenes are to the
full as natural and affecting. But we miss the *Poet*, that which
in Shakespeare always appears out and above the surface of the
nature.' While, of course, Heywood has not the Shakespearian
transfiguring quality, Lamb's definition suggests a more pedes-

trian element in him than he perhaps meant to imply. Lamb is also somewhat rash in asserting that his plots are almost invariably English. He himself quotes from the series of dramatized classical stories, *The Brazen, Silver,* and *Golden Age.* He attributes to Brome instead of Heywood the attractive two-part play, *The Fair Maid of the West,* which has indeed a Devon heroine, but which takes us in its course to Fayal in the Azores and to Morocco. And as Heywood tells in the introduction to his play *The English Traveller,* from which Lamb quotes, that he had a hand in 220 pieces of which only between 20 and 30 survive, any generalization about their plots must be speculative. And though Heywood was usually gentle, it has to be remembered that *The Late Lancashire Witches* (1634), by him and Brome, from which Lamb quotes both in the *Specimens* and the *Extracts,* was hastily written to stir up popular feeling against the unfortunate women who were in 1634 accused of witchcraft.

From *The Late Lancashire Witches* we may pass to *The Witch* of Middleton, from which Lamb quotes several scenes in which Hecate appears with her attendant spirits. If Middleton borrowed some of his witches' charms from *Macbeth,* on the other hand the figure of Hecate seems to have been imported into that play by the editors of the Folio from Middleton's piece. She is alien in speech and atmosphere from the midnight hags whom Macbeth meets on the blasted heath. Lamb in well-known words notes the difference between them and Middleton's witches: 'These are creatures to whom man or woman plotting some dire mischief might resort for occasional consultation. Those originate deeds of blood and begin bad impulses in men. . . . They are foul Anomalies of whom we know not whence they are sprung, nor whether they have beginning or ending.' The other Middleton selections in the *Specimens* are from *Women Beware Women, More Dissemblers besides Women,* and *No Wit like a Woman's.* In the *Extracts* he added quotations from other comedies including a short one from *A Game at Chess.* But Lamb does not seem to have realized the distinctive quality of this play as belonging to the Aristophanic tradition in that it was a merciless burlesque of the Spanish ambassador Gondomar as the Black Knight, and of Antonio de Dominis, as the Fat Bishop, and thus produced one of the greatest

Caroline theatrical sensations and had to be stopped by the Government.

Perhaps the most surprising omission from both the *Specimens* and the *Extracts,* as Swinburne has noted, is any quotation from Middleton and W. Rowley's *The Changeling.* The relation between Beatrice-Joanna and the saturnine De Flores, whom she employs to murder a detested wooer, and who exacts her person as his price, seems a theme ideally fitted for Lamb's penetrating diagnosis. On the other hand he has given a long selection from another play by these two dramatists, *A Fair Quarrel.* The title indicates the central situation. Captain Ager is called by a colonel in a dispute 'the son of a whore'. He challenges the colonel to a duel, but his mother to prevent risk to his life falsely accuses herself of unchastity. Thereupon Ager refuses to fight in what he thinks is a bad cause, but when the colonel charges him with cowardice, he considers that he has a fair quarrel and engages and defeats his adversary. It is an intriguing complication, but I confess that I am puzzled why it should have provoked from Lamb the long, remarkable footnote of which the earlier part runs:

> The insipid levelling morality to which the modern stage is tied down would not admit of such admirable passions as these scenes are filled with. A puritanical obtuseness of sentiment, a stupid infantile goodness, is creeping among us instead of the vigorous passions, and virtues clad in flesh and blood, with which the old dramatists present us. Those noble and liberal casuists could discern in the differences, the quarrels, the animosities of man, a beauty and truth of moral feeling, no less than in the iterately inculcated duties of forgiveness and atonement. With us all is hypocritical meekness. A reconciliation scene (let the occasion be never so absurd or unnatural) is always sure of applause. The audiences come to the theatre to be complimented on their goodness.

One would like to know if this singular outburst was prompted by any particular plays of the late eighteenth-century sentimental school of drama. I find it easier to appreciate Lamb's personal confession of the effect upon him of the scene in *The Revenger's Tragedy,* where the brothers Vindici and Hippolito denounce their mother who has urged their sister to become the paramour of the duke's son. 'I never read it but my ears tingle, and I feel a hot blush spread my cheeks, as if I were presently to proclaim such "malefactions" of myself, as the Brothers here rebuke in their un-natural parent; in words more keen and dagger-like than those which Hamlet speaks to his mother.' Lamb is naturally not troubled by the doubts of some modern students (including my-self) whether *The Revenger's Tragedy*, published anonymously, is by Cyril Tourneur, whose name is on the title-page of *The Atheist's Tragedy*, from which he gives some shorter quotations.

With Tourneur as a master of poetic tragedy Webster is naturally linked. Lamb gives a generous selection from his four chief plays, and of the two greatest he has written in his most exquisitely felicitous strain. He contrasts 'the dreadful apparatus' with which the Duchess of Malfi's death is ushered in with 'the conceptions of ordinary vengeance', such as Procrustes' bed and the like. 'To move a horror skilfully, to touch a soul to the quick, to lay upon fear as much as it can bear, to wear and weary a life till it is ready to drop, and then step in with mortal instruments to take its last forfeit—this only a Webster can do.' When Vittoria Corombona, the White Devil, has finished her specious defence of herself against the charges of murdering her husband and becoming the duke's mistress, 'we seem to see that matchless beauty of her face which inspires such gay confidence into her; and are ready to expect, when she has done her pleadings, that her very judges, her accusers, the grave ambassadors who sit as spectators, and all the court, will rise and make proffer to defend her in spite of the utmost conviction of her guilt'.

Of the dirge sung over Marcello by his mother—

> Call for the Robin-redbreast, and the Wren,
> Since o'er shady groves they hover,
> And with leaves and flowers do cover
> The friendless bodies of unburied men—

Lamb says, 'I never saw anything like this Dirge, except the Ditty which reminds Ferdinand of his drowned Father in *The Tempest*. As that is of the water, watery; so this is of the earth, earthy'.

The third of the group of masters of poetic tragedy is John Ford, of whom Lamb wrote to Wordsworth in October 1804 that he 'is the man after Shakespeare'. He gives selections from his chief plays, beginning with the beautiful description in *The Lover's Melancholy* of the contest for mastery between a youthful musician with a lute and a nightingale which became 'music's first martyr', and ending with scenes from *The Broken Heart*. Then follows the famous comment: 'Ford was of the first order of Poets. He sought for sublimity not by parcels in metaphors or visible images, but directly where she has her full residence in the heart of man; in the actions and sufferings of the greatest minds. There is a grandeur of the soul above mountains, seas, and the elements.' It was this eulogy that drew from Gifford in the *Quarterly Review*, December 1811, the denunciation of 'the blasphemies of a poor maniac who it seems once published some detached scenes from *The Broken Heart*'. When Gifford speaks of 'blasphemies' he is doubtless referring to Lamb's declaration that the transcendent scene of the spiritual martyrdom of the princess Calantha 'almost bears me in imagination to Calvary and the Cross'. Lamb did a notable service in gaining recognition for the genius of Ford, who had fallen into neglect, but he was asking for trouble in suggesting a comparison between the most sacred of all scenes and an episode in the work of a dramatist with whose finer qualities there mingles a tainted element.

The later figures of Shirley and Brome and relatively minor playwrights, Day, Glapthorne, Davenport, and others, who appear in the *Extracts* I must here pass over. But the wide range of Lamb's selections bears witness to his catholicity of taste and to his eagerness to rescue from neglect any dramatist, however obscure, or even anonymous, who was worth his salt. I turn lastly to the two whom Lamb in his preface to the *Specimens* had singled out as 'in the estimation of the world the only dramatic poets of the Elizabethan age who are entitled to be considered after Shakespeare', and in whose case he therefore looked upon himself as less of a pioneer—Fletcher and Massinger. With regard to Massinger neither Lamb's quotations nor comments would fully explain the exceptional rank accorded to him in 1808. He makes no mention of *The Roman Actor*, in Massinger's own opinion his best play, nor of *The Maid of Honour* so rated by some modern critics. From *A*

New Way to Pay Old Debts he gives one comparatively short scene. This play kept the stage for long more persistently than any Elizabethan piece outside the Shakespeare canon. When acted by Kean it had paralysing effects both upon his company and the audience. It is therefore surprising to hear Lamb's verdict on Massinger: 'He never shakes or disturbs the mind with grief. He is read with composure and placid delight. He wrote with that equability of all the passions, which made his English style the purest and most free from violent metaphors and harsh constructions of any of the dramatists who were his contemporaries.' No one would gather from this that Massinger is distinguished by his bold handling of religious and political themes, nor that his style, though pure and lucid, has less of poetic quality than that of any other major contemporary dramatist.

It is this poetic quality that so strongly marks the scenes that Lamb gives from the Beaumont and Fletcher plays, especially those relating to Aspatia in *The Maid's Tragedy* and to Euphrasia (Bellario) in *Philaster,* both of whom assume masculine disguise to serve their ends in love. From plays by Fletcher alone Lamb quotes from *Bonduca, Love's Pilgrimage, Wit without Money,* and the pastoral *The Faithful Shepherdess.* He has selected some of the most exquisite scenes from the pastoral and has appended a footnote declaring that Fletcher was infatuated in 'mixing up with this blessedness such an ugly deformity as Cloe, the wanton shepherdess'. As he sums it up in an expressive image, 'if Cloe was meant to set off Clorin by contrast, Fletcher should have known that such weeds by juxtaposition do not set off, but kill sweet flowers'. Lamb also shows himself a sound textual critic in assigning the first two scenes that he quotes from *The Two Noble Kinsmen* to Shakespeare, and the third to Fletcher. But two of the plays which he attributes to Fletcher only, *The False One* and *Thierry and Theodoret,* are now held to be in part from Massinger's pen. Yet there can be no doubt on metrical grounds that the scene in the latter which stirs Lamb to warmest enthusiasm is Fletcher's. Thierry, king of France, who is childless, is told by an astrologer that he shall have children if he sacrifices the first woman that he meets coming out of the Temple of Diana. This proves to be his wife Ordella veiled, and when she uncovers her face, he lets fall his sword. But she cries:

> Strike, sir, strike;
> And if in my poor death fair France may merit,
> Give me a thousand blows, be killing me
> A thousand days.

'I have always considered,' says Lamb, 'this to be the finest scene in Fletcher, and Ordella the most perfect idea of the female heroic character, next to Calantha, in *The Broken Heart* of Ford, that has been embodied in fiction. She is a piece of sainted nature.'

I wish Lamb had ended there. But he continues in a passage of which I quote parts:

> Yet noble as the whole scene is it must be confessed that the manner of it compared with Shakespeare's finest scenes is slow and languid. Its motion is circular, not progressive. . . . Another striking difference between Fletcher and Shakespeare is the fondness of the former for unnatural and violent situations, like that in the scene before us. . . . Shakespeare had nothing of this contortion in his mind, none of that craving after romantic incidents, and flights of strained and improbable virtue, which I think always betrays an imperfect molar sensibility.

Personally I cannot see why Fletcher's method in this affecting scene should be called 'circular'. There is more foundation for the reference to 'an unnatural and violent situation'. But the passage is a striking illustration of an attitude that tends to 'date' Lamb's criticism and that to some degree defeats his own splendid purpose. This purpose is most explicitly set forth in an unexpected place, in the footnote to his selections from Henry Porter's *The Two Angry Women of Abington* in the *Extracts*. Lamb there urges that the unexhausted treasures of the old dramatists should be revealed by their publication, and asks:

> Are we afraid that the genius of Shakespeare would suffer in our estimate by this disclosure? He would indeed be somewhat lessened as a miracle and a prodigy. But he would lose no height by the confession. When a Giant is shown to us, does it detract from the curiosity to be told that he has at home a gigantic

brood of brethren, less only than himself? Along *with* him, not *from* him, sprang up the race of mighty Dramatists.

Nothing could be truer, or more exactly expressed, than this and the rest of the passage. But what Lamb fails to see is that he himself tends to make of Shakespeare 'a miracle and a prodigy'. Indeed in his preface to the *Specimens* he speaks of his 'divine mind and manners'. He can scarcely ever refrain, after a panegyric on a scene from a contemporary play, from comparing it to its disadvantage with something similar in Shakespeare. This use of Shakespeare, whose genius, though it was transcendent, was not flawless, as a yardstick, becomes tiresome to us to-day and tends to degrade his contemporaries from the position of brethren to that of poor relations—the last thing that Lamb intended.

Nor in the light of our fuller knowledge to-day can all Lamb's estimates of the individual dramatists be fully accepted. He understood those of the Stuart age better than those of the Tudor, and some of his generalizations and his superlatives provoke resifting and retesting.

Moreover he was not so completely the first in the field as he believed. *Vixere fortes ante Agamemnona.* He had forerunners, unknown to him, who had sought to popularize the Elizabethan dramatists by means of anthologies. Dr. G. E. Bentley has recently called attention to a neglected work, John Cotgrave's *Treasury of Wit and Language* (1655).[1] Cotgrave might as well or even better have forestalled Lamb by calling his book *Specimens of English Dramatic Writers who lived about the Time of Shakespeare.* Indeed on the title-page he described his *Treasury* as 'Collected out of the most and best of our English Drammatick Poems', and in his preface he stated:

> The Drammatick Poem seems to me (and many of my friends better able to judge than I) to have beene lately too much slighted, not onely by such, whose Talent falls short in understanding, but by many that have had a tolerable portion of Wit, who through a stiffe and obstinate prejudice have (in neglecting things of this nature) lost the benefit of many rich

[1] See his informative article, 'John Cotgrave's "English Treasury of Wit and Language" and The Elizabethan Drama' (*Studies in Philology*, April 1943).

and usefull Observations, not duly considering, or believing, that the Framers of them, were the most fluent and redundant Wits that this age (or I thinke any other) ever knew.

Cotgrave can claim the distinction of being the first to compile an anthology entirely from English plays. But his selections are not considered in their dramatic relevance; they are arranged as 'rich and usefull Observations' under alphabetical subject-headings. In no case is the play or the author specified, but in a copy in the British Museum manuscript notes in several hands have identified nearly all these. As Dr. Bentley points out, they are predominantly Jacobean and Caroline; the predecessors of Shakespeare have virtually no place.

It was Cotgrave's deliberate omission to indicate the sources of his extracts that mainly led William Oldys to make a pre-judiced attack upon his anthology in his preface to Dr. Thomas Hayward's three-volume *The British Muse* (1738). It may have been on this account that Mr. R. D. Williams has ignored the *Treasury of Wit and Language* in his article, *Antiquarian Interest in Elizabethan Drama before Lamb*.[1] With him *The British Muse* serves as starting-point. It is true that Hayward had the advantage over Cotgrave in that in every case he gives the source of his quotations which on his title-page he describes as 'Thoughts, Moral, Natural and Sublime' from sixteenth- and seventeenth-century poets. His anthology, as this indicates, was of a general character and his extracts, grouped under subject-headings, are only in part taken from plays. Other works mentioned by Mr. Williams, such as the collections of Dodsley and Hawkins and the *Biographica Dramatica*, were, as Lamb himself has told us, used by him. They were not 'specimens' but included either whole plays or accounts of their authors and analyses of plot.

It is therefore no true service to Lamb to get his achievement out of focus, to assert with Swinburne that 'to him and to him alone it is that we owe the revelation and resurrection of our greatest dramatic poets after Shakespeare'. It is sufficient disproof of this to name Edmond Malone whose collection of plays, now in the Bodleian, rivals that Garrick collection in which Lamb found unending delight. Moreover, as I have tried to show, with in-

[1] In *Publications of the Modern Language Association of America* (June 1938).

creased knowledge, altered perspective, and varied taste, we may differ from some of his verdicts and ways of approach. But his is the unfading laurel of the poineer who first presented episodes from the Elizabethan playbooks not as 'beauties' or 'thoughts' but as specimens of dramatic quality. And the best of his accompanying notes, masterly in their content and form, combining clearest insight with delicacy of expression in prose of subtle and sensitive rhythm, raised criticism to the level of creation.

Finally, I would stress the fact that Lamb does not speak merely as a literary expositor. As some of my citations have shown, his comments spring not merely from his reading of the plays but from his experience of life. Here his footnotes seem to me to be akin to some of the observations in a work otherwise radically different in outlook—Dr. Johnson's *Lives of the Poets*. The spirit in fact in which Lamb worked was not that of an ordinary anthologist but of a crusader with a mission on behalf both of the dead and of the living. To the Elizabethan dramatists he felt that he owed the debt of rescuing them from undeserved neglect, of making reparation (to adopt Browning's words concerning the early Italian painters) to 'the wronged great soul of an ancient master'. For his contemporaries he was aflame to point them the way to share his enjoyment of the rich treasure that he had rediscovered. He would therefore have rejoiced in the activities of the Societies that have been founded in his name, and which, when they do homage to the Elizabethans, are following the trail that he has blazed.

EIGHT

THE SOLDIER IN ELIZABETHAN AND LATER
ENGLISH DRAMA

IN Tudor times there was no standing army. The idea still prevailed, coming down from the Anglo-Saxon era, that it was the duty of all citizens to serve the State in arms when occasion called. Hence Shakespeare and his contemporaries drew their chief impressions of military service from citizen armies recruited either by voluntary enlistment or by impressment. The professional soldier was an unfamiliar figure to them.

A Statute was enacted in 1557 in the reign of Philip and Mary for Taking of Musters. In the preamble it was stated that 'many of the most able and likely men have been through friendship or rewards released and discharged of the said service, and some other, not being able or meet, taken, appointed, or chosen thereunto'.

It was decreed that henceforth any man absenting himself from the Muster should go to prison for ten days, unless he paid a fine of forty shillings; and that any muster-master accepting money to discharge recruits should be fined ten times the sum that he had received.

It is plain, however, that the abuses continued. In the closing period of Elizabeth's reign there is documentary evidence to this effect from different parts of the country. Thus on 1st June 1602 it is reported:

The commissioners that were sent to view the 800 men sent of 12 shires to Bristol declare that intolerable hindrances are offered to the service; there was never man beheld such strange creatures brought to any muster. They were most of them either old, lame, diseased, boys or common rogues. Few of them had any clothes; small, weak, starved bodies taken up in fairs, markets and highways to supply the place of better men at home.

Hakluyt, in his account of 'The Voyage to Cadiz' (1597), relates that a certain lieutenant was degraded for the taking of money 'by the way of corruption of certain prest soldiers in the country and for placing others in their roomes, more unfit for service and of less sufficiency and abilitie'.

The words 'certain prest soldiers' are to be noted. In the absence of sufficient voluntary response to the country's military needs recourse was had by Elizabeth's government to the press-gang. A peculiarly unpleasant feature of its operations was to take advantage of the regulation by which everyone had to receive the Sacrament on Easter Day, and to seize every man in the congregation.

In the light of this contemporary evidence there would seem to be little exaggeration in the scenes in the two Parts of *King Henry IV*, dating from about 1597–98, in which Falstaff misuses the King's press damnably. In Act IV, ii, of Part I he makes his confession as he is on his way to Coventry to join the royal forces:

> I have got in exchange of a hundred and fifty soldiers three hundred and odd pounds. . . . And such have I, to fill up the rooms of them that have bought out their services, that you would think that I had a hundred and fifty tattered prodigals lately come from swine-keeping and from eating chaff and husks.

In Act III. ii. of the Second Part of *Henry IV* we come into still closer touch with Sir John's methods of recruiting, for we see him actually at work. He is in Gloucestershire at the house of Justice Shallow, whose duty it is to provide him with four 'sufficient' men from the district for the King's service. There are six ready for his inspection, of whom Ralph Mouldy and Peter Bullcalf are the best suited for soldiering. But after Falstaff has gone in to dinner with his host the pair offer a bribe to Bardolph, the knight's corporal, to be let off. On his return Bardolph whispers the news to Sir John, who thereupon releases the pair. Shallow remonstrates with him:

> Sir John, Sir John, do not yourself wrong: these are your likeliest men, and I would have you served with the best.

Fal: Will you tell me, Master Shallow, how to choose a man? Care I for the limb, the thewes, the stature, bulk, and big assemblance of a man? Give me the spirit, Master Shallow ... O give me the spare men, and spare me the great ones.

The only one of this awkward squad who shows up at all well is Francis Feeble, the woman's tailor. In spite of his name and occupation he is resigned to his fate:

By my troth, I care not; a man can die but once: we owe God a death: I'll ne'er bear a base mind: an't be my destiny, so; an't be not, so; no man's too good to serve's prince; and let it go which way it will, he that dies this year is quit for the next.

Feeble, reluctant to go fighting, yet prepared to answer his sovereign's call, and if need be, to die in his service, is more or less akin to the three soldiers over whom the dawn breaks on the day of Agincourt (*King Henry V*, IV. i.):

Court: Brother John Bates, is not that the morning which breaks yonder?
Bates: I think it be: but we have no great cause to desire the approach of day.
Williams: We see yonder the beginning of the day, but I think we shall never see the end of it.

They are joined by Henry V disguised, who tells them that 'no man should possess' the King 'with any appearance of fear lest he, by showing it, should dishearten his army'.

Bates: He may show what outward courage he will: but, I believe, as cold a night as 'tis, he could wish himself in the Thames up to the neck; and so I would he were, and I by him, at all adventures, so we were quit here.

Then follows the striking discussion on the king's responsibility for the souls of those who die when fighting at his command, and Henry's final pronouncement which has lost nothing of its force in our own day:

Every subject's duty is the king's; but every subject's soul is his own. Therefore should every soldier in the wars do as every sick man in his bed, wash every mote out of his conscience: and dying so, death is to him advantage; or not dying, the time was blessedly lost, wherein such preparation was gained.

Though the soldiers do not know that the King himself is speaking, they give their ready assent:

Williams: 'Tis certain, every man that dies ill, the ill is upon his own head, the King is not to answer for it.

Bates: I do not desire he should answer for me, and yet I determine to fight lustily for him.

It is the magnetic quality of their sovereign that inspires the English army recruited mainly from the common folk to over-throw the feudal array of France which far outnumbers them.

A very difficult problem was presented by the soldiers dis-banded after a campaign abroad who sought relief from public or private sources often by fraudulent methods. On 5th November 1591 when the Earl of Essex as Lord General was commanding the forces in Normandy sent by Elizabeth to help Henry IV of France in his struggle against the Catholic League, a Proclamation was issued by the Government against vagrant soldiers:

There is a common wandering abroad of a great multitude, of whom the most part pretend that they have served in the wars on the other side of the seas, though it is known that very many of them neither served at all, or else ran away from their service and are justly to be punished and not relieved; some indeed have served, and, falling with sickness, are licensed to depart; these deserve relief. . . .

Every soldier on landing, having the passport of the Lieutenant General or any special officer of commandment, to be paid five shillings for his conduct to the place where he was levied.[1]

The penalties threatened in the Proclamation of 5th November 1591 were not a sufficient deterrent, for on 13th May 1592, the Privy Council found it necessary to issue a further order:

It is credibly reported that, notwithstanding the Council's

[1] Quoted by G. B. Harrison in *An Elizabethan Journal,* i. 72–3 from Proclamations, 300 and A.P.C. xxii. 58.

orders for the restraint of such soldiers as without passport draw themselves from the service of the French King in Normandy, above two hundred men of strong and able bodies are landed at Dover and the places near without passport, in the company of some few sick men, and without stay. These men are allowed to beg in the county with the passport of the Mayor, using most slanderous speeches of the Queen's service and entertainment, tending to the great discouragement of such as be willing to serve.

A commission of three gentlemen was accordingly appointed to repair to Dover to inquire into the matter and take suitable steps.

It is in the light of such contemporary documents that we must interpret some of the figures in Elizabethan drama. Thus in Jonson's *Every Man in His Humour,* published in quarto in 1601 and in revised form in the folio of 1616, Brainworm, the servant of Knowell, assumes for his own ends the disguise of a soldier returned from the wars who has to scrape a livelihood by begging or by selling his now useless rapier for a song. He accosts Knowell's son Edward and his companion, the country gull Master Stephen (II. iv. 48 ff.):

Gentlemen, please you change a few crowns for a very excellent good blade here? I am a poor gentleman, a soldier, one that in the better state of my fortunes scorn'd so mean a refuge, but now it is the humour of necessity to have it so. You seem to be gentlemen well affected to martial men, else I should rather die with silence than live with shame: however vouchsafe to remember, it is my want speaks, not myself. This condition agrees not with my spirit.

Edward Knowell interrupts this whining tirade with the question: 'Where hast thou serv'd?' whereupon Brainworm rattles off a list of imaginary campaigns and sufferings:

May it please you, sir, in all the late wars of Bohemia, Hungaria, Dalmatia, Poland, where not, sir? I have been a poor servitor by sea and land, any time this fourteen years, and followed the fortunes of the best Commanders in Christendom. I was twice

shot at the taking of Aleppo, once at the relief of Vienna; I
have been at Marseilles, Naples, and the Adriatic Gulf, a
gentleman-slave in the galleys; thrice where I was most danger-
ously shot in the head, through both the thighs, and yet, being
thus maimed, I am void of maintenance, nothing left me but
my scars, the noted marks of my resolution.

In spite of Edward Knowell's protests, the gull Stephen insists
on buying the rapier. Encouraged by this success Brainworm then
tries his tricks on his own master, Knowell (II. v. 78):

Good sir, by that hand, you may do the part of a kind gentleman in lending a poor soldier the price of two cans of beer (a
matter of small value); the King of Heaven shall pay you, and I
shall rest thankful. It's hard when a man hath served in his
Prince's cause and be thus.—Honourable worship, let me derive
a small piece of silver from you!

Knowell turns upon him in words which doubtless echo the
indignant reproaches hurled at some of the begging fraternity of
discharged soldiers to which Brainworm was merely pretending
to belong:

Believe me, I am taken with some wonder
To think a fellow of thy outward presence
Should in the frame and fashion of his mind
Be so degenerate and sordid base!
Art thou a man, and sham'st thou not to beg?
To practise such a servile kind of life?

Another character who assumes the disguise of a begging
soldier, with a list of imaginary campaigns to his credit, is young
Lord Nonsuch in Edward Sharpham's *Cupid's Whirligig* (1607).
    In the winter months of 1607–8 (31st October to 13th February)
the members of St. John's College, Oxford, held an elaborate
series of revels, recorded in an extant MS. in the College library,
which has been entitled *The Christmas Prince*. A number of plays
and shows were performed in honour of Thomas Tucker, a
Bachelor of Arts, who was elected a Christmas Lord or Prince.
Among the shorter plays was one called *Time's Complaint* which
introduces two soldiers. One is Manco, who counterfeits lameness

and has turned to beggary for a livelihood. He is one of the very type that the Privy Council threatened with severe penalties. He is complaining that things are not going well with him:

> O what a vile hard-hearted Time is this.
> Now no dissembling practice, no lame shifts
> Will serve the turn to pick a living out.
> I fear me I will trot on both my legs,
> Forget (though loth) halting before my friends,
> And from this easy trade of beggary
> Betake me to some honest drudgery.
> O what a blessed time hath Manco seen
> When in the summer at some hill's descent,
> Or at a church porch in the winter time,
> I could have begged five shillings every day.

But 'ale-houses have now all the custom got'. Yet he makes one more attempt to extort charity by an appeal to a stranger who now enters:

> Good pitiful gentleman, one penny or halfpenny for the lame and maimed. I beseech your good worship to consider the necessity of the poor.

But the stranger is a justice of the peace, and a burgess of Parliament who indignantly refuses to go counter to the statutes against martial rogues, and sends Manco packing after a good drubbing.

The other soldier in *Time's Complaint* is Bellicoso, a cashiered corporal who lays the blame of his discharge on his commanding officer:

> Myself when I first went to serve the wars
> Had money in my purse, clothes on my back,
> And hoping to receive my monthly pay,
> Spent freely. But my captain, Prodigo,
> Makes but one throw at dice of ten men's pay,
> Which being lost for wages gives us oaths.
> And when we farther urge him, pays us blows.

So he left the army, and on his return home, 'needy and ragged', was put out of doors by his elder brother as a sturdy vagabond.

Bellicoso may have been one of the returned soldiers who in abusing his captain was, in the words of the Privy Council, 'using most slanderous speeches of the Queen's service', though there is no doubt that there were instances of officers wrongfully withholding their soldiers' pay.

Thus Sir Thomas Knyvett, in his treatise *The Defence of the Realme* (1596), writes:

> The corruption of our wars springeth only from the rash and evil choice which hath been most commonly made of needy, riotous, licentious, ignorant and base colonels, captains, lieutenants, sergeants, and such like officers, who have made merchandise of their places, and without regard of their duty or respect of conscience have made . . . sale of their soldiers' blood and lives to maintain their unthriftiness and disorders.

But for genuine casualties, as has been seen, the government attempted to make provision on their return. There is a striking entry in D'Ewes' *Journals of Parliament* under the date 5th April 1593[1]:

> It is agreed in the House of Lords that there shall be a charitable contribution made towards the relief and help of soldiers maimed and hurt in the wars of France, the Low Countries and on the seas. To this end every Archbishop, Marquis, Earl and Viscount shall pay 40s., every Bishop 30s., and every Baron 20s. . . . These sums are willingly being paid by all who attend the Parliament. Further, it is agreed that those who have saved their charges by not attending the Parliament shall pay double, that is the Archbishop of York and every Earl £4, Bishops £3, and Barons 40s.; and those who have been present but seldom shall pay a third part more than those who have attended regularly. And if any Lord Spiritual or Temporal should refuse or forbear to pay (which it is hoped in honour none will) the ordinary means will be used to levy the money.

It is to be hoped that the expectations were not too sanguine and that the members of the Upper House all paid their quota.

---

[1] Quoted by Harrison, *op cit.*, i, 221–2.

But it puts a strain upon the imagination to think of the hat being passed round in the House of Lords to-day for the benefit of those who have suffered on land or sea or in the air.

A distinction should be drawn between the 'prest' and the discharged soldiers in Elizabethan drama, who had their prototypes in actual contemporary figures and the extensive group of military braggarts who had their origin in the *miles gloriosus* of Roman comedy. As they thus have their roots in literary tradition and not in historical reality, and are essentially un-English in their blending of boastfulness and cowardice, we can pass them quickly in review and give them short shrift.

First comes Basilisco in *Soliman and Perseda*, written by Kyd or one of his school about 1592. He is pedant and braggart combined, whose sword is his 'oratrix', but who flies from the battlefield because he is 'valiant but mortal'. He was known to Shakespeare in *King John* and may have given a hint for Falstaff's soliloquy in *Henry IV*, Part I, at Shrewsbury fight, though Sir John is far too complex and dazzling a creation to be ranked with the braggart soldier type. Its main Shakespearian representatives are Pistol, with his fire-eating rhodomontade in *Henry IV*, Part II, and *Henry V*; and Parolles, the 'window of lattice', the 'Jack-an-apes with scarves' in *All's Well that Ends Well*. Ben Jonson's Bobadill in *Every Man in his Humour* is a variant of the type, with his strange oaths—'by the foot of Pharaoh', 'by the body of Caesar'— his devotion to the newly found herb 'Trinidado' or tobacco, and his pride in the esoteric lore of the fencing-school which was anathema to Mercutio. Jonson presents yet another variant in Captain Tucca, in *Poetaster* who uses his copious vocabulary of slang to pour contempt upon civilians and to belittle the arts. And bringing up the rear of this outlandish procession is Bessus in Beaumont and Fletcher's *A King and No King*, who wins a battle, and gains a reputation for valour, by taking flight with his company so precipitately that he charges into the enemy.

While the dramatists may in the above examples have tricked out the general type of braggart soldier from some degree of personal observation, it is definitely of traditional, not of contemporary origin. But one wonders if there were any living models for the couple of pacifists whom we encounter, of all unexpected places, in the two Parts of Marlowe's *Tamburlaine*. In Part I, Act II. iv. the Persian king Mycetes, while a battle rages, goes into hiding, with the crown in his hand, and soliloquises:

> Accursed be he that first invented war,
> They knew not, ah, they knew not simple men,
> How those were hit by pelting cannon shot
> Stand staggering like a quivering aspen leaf,
> Fearing the force of Boreas' boisterous blasts.
> In what a lamentable case were I,
> If Nature had not given me wisdom's lore.

Is there not a touch here of the 'superior' attitude which the pacifist is apt to assume at all periods?

A yet more striking example of the pacifist temper is exhibited in Part II by Tamburlaine's eldest son, Calyphas. When the Scythian conqueror gives his three boys a lecture on 'the rudiments of war' (III. ii. 53 ff.) Calyphas murmurs:

> My Lord, but this is dangerous to be done,
> We may be slain or wounded ere we learn.

When battle is joined with the enemy he turns a deaf ear to his brother's call to him to take his part (IV. i. 27 ff.):

> I know, sir, what it is to kill a man:
> It works remorse of conscience in me,
> I take no pleasure to be murderous.

It might be the plea of a conscientious objector to-day, but Tamburlaine gives it short shrift, for on his return as victor from the field he at once executes martial justice on Calyphas by stabbing him to death.

As compared with some of the country districts London has an honourable place in Tudor military annals. The citizens of the capital enrolled in their thousands in the train-bands that exercised at Mile End. Sir John Fortescue suggests that Shakespeare's knowledge of military formations and drill was largely derived from observation of these train-bands. Justice Shallow in Part II of *Henry IV* (III. ii. 301 ff.) remembers how in his Clement's Inn days a 'little quiver fellow' would manage his piece at Mile End green.

In *All's Well that Ends Well* (IV. iii. 303 ff.) Parolles says that Dumain 'had the honour to be an officer at a place called Mile-End'.

In the last Act of Beaumont and Fletcher's *Knight of the Burning Pestle* there is a lively picture of a Mile End review which even through the burlesque gives us the sense of the Londoner's martial spirit (i. 61 ff.). The grocer's wife bids their apprentice, Ralph—

> call all the youths together in battle-ray, with drums and guns and flags to march to Mile-End in pompous fashion, and there exhort your soldiers to be merry and wise, and to keep their beards from burning, Ralph; and then skirmish and let your flags fly, and cry 'Kill, kill, kill'.

Ralph holds an inspection of the persons and munitions of his company, and then bids them stand and give ear (ii. 61 ff.):

> Gentlemen, countrymen, friends, and my fellow-soldiers, I have brought you this day from the shops of security and the counters of content to measure out in these famous fields honour by the ell and prowess by the pound. Let it not, oh, let it not, I say, be told hereafter that the noblest issue of this City fainted; but bear yourselves in this fair action like men, valiant men and freemen!

Ralph is the captain of his company and he gives commands in turn to his lieutenant, the ancient and the sergeant, the last being a non-commissioned officer. These are the four officers of a company, which normally consisted of one hundred men in square formation. Except for General, loosely applied, these are the only military titles used by Shakespeare, apart from corporal, which, as a rule, he substitutes for sergeant. From this Fortescue infers that he had no knowledge of larger bodies of troops than companies. He never mentions a colonel, the commander of a regiment which included a number of companies, nor his next in rank, a sergeant-major, the equivalent of a major to-day. What is still more remarkable is that the words cavalry and infantry are both missing from his wide vocabulary.

Shakespeare's Bardolph and Nym, both hanged for theft in the Agincourt campaign, disgrace the rank of corporal. Nor is the next grade in seniority, that of ancient, the ensign or standard bearer, fortunate in two such different representatives as Pistol and Iago.

A singular representative of his rank is the Humorous Lieutenant in Fletcher's play of that name (1619). 'Humorous' is used in its Elizabethan sense of temperamental. It is the lieutenant's peculiarity that, when he is diseased owing to his loose habits of life, he bears himself bravely in battle. But when he has been paradoxically cured by a slicing wound received in the fray, he finds his constitution mightily altered and has no longer any mind to fight. His colleagues have to trick him into the belief that he is again suffering from mortal illness to rouse him to a pitch of over-impetuous martial valour.

Proceeding to one rank higher, to the captains we find a foil to Jonson's blustering Tucca in *Poetaster* in Shakespeare's Fluellen. Tucca, though nominally in the service of the Emperor Augustus, has not a word to say about Roman military matters. Fluellen, though in the service of Henry V of England, keeps always before his eyes 'the true and ancient prerogatifes and laws of the wars' to be found above all in 'the disciplines of the pristine wars of the Romans'. Had he lived in later days he would have needed none of Fougasse's cartoons to warn him against indiscreet speech, likely to be of value to the enemy. As he tells his colleague, Captain Gower, who has hailed him too loudly, 'if you would take the pains but to examine the wars of Pompey the Great, you shall find, I warrant you, that there is no tiddle taddle or pibble pabble in Pompey's camp'.

It would have been a shock to Fluellen to hear of the breach of discipline by one Roman captain, Poenius, in Fletcher's *Bonduca* (c. 1619). During five years he had distinguished himself in the varying fortunes of the conflict between the imperial forces and the British warrior-queen, more familiar to us as Boadicea. A new general, Suetonius, has recently arrived from Rome to force the issue to a victorious conclusion. He sends an order to Poenius that he must bring up his regiment for an encounter with the enemy. The captain is convinced that it is madness to attack the over-whelmingly superior British force. He refuses to obey the general's command and orders his soldiers to retire. But when the battle is joined, the Romans aided by Boadicea's mistaken tactics are victorious. Poenius is overcome with shame and, though Suetonius magnanimously forgives him, he falls upon his sword just as his own infuriated men rush in crying: 'Kill him, kill him, kill him!'

Another captain who is presented in an unusual situation is Ager in Middleton and Rowley's play *A Fair Quarrel*. Captain Ager has been insulted by a military friend of higher rank, a Colonel, who in a fit of passion has called him 'son of a whore', which kills—

> At one report two reputations,
> A mother's and a son's.

After challenging the Colonel to a duel Ager seeks to make certain of his mother's honour, and in her anxiety to save his life she falsely accuses herself of unchastity. Ager therefore declines to fight in what he thinks is an unjust cause in spite of the reproaches of the friends who are acting as his seconds (III. i. 22-5):

> Bid farewell to th'integrity of arms,
> And let that honourable name of soldier
> Fall from you like a shivered wreath of laurel
> By thunder struck from a desertless forehead.

He speaks words of pardon and peace to the Colonel who thereupon proclaims him 'a base submissive coward', but at the word 'coward' Ager cries, 'Now I have a cause', crosses swords with the Colonel and gives him a wound that disables him. In the end the two are reconciled and Lady Ager's honour cleared, but the capital interest is in the situation of a soldier whose honour is too sensitive to draw a sword until he has a fair quarrel.

The Colonel in *A Fair Quarrel*, who is not given a name, is one of the few characters in Elizabethan drama who are expressly assigned that rank. For the most part officers above the rank of captain are somewhat loosely called General or are left without exact definition of their status. Even *Henry V* in the prologue to Act IV is called 'the royal captain of this ruin'd band'. In the first line of *Antony and Cleopatra* Philo speaks of 'this dotage of our general's', and a few lines below of 'his captain's heart'.

Antony however is among the warrior-kings and leaders in the

Shakespearian tragedies—Caesar, Cassius, Coriolanus, Macbeth and Othello—who fall outside the limits of my survey. It is true that they are soldiers, but it is not in their military capacity that we think of them. It is their conflicts in the soul, not their deeds of arms, that are of account, so here it does not behove us to linger beside their mighty figures.

Non ragionam di lor, ma guarda e passa.

But there is one resplendent warrior who catches the eye and must have his salute before we pass—the Harry Hotspur of *Henry IV*, Part I, 'the king of honour', as his foeman Douglas calls him. He is ready to 'pluck bright honour from the pale-faced moon', or dive for her to the bottom of the deep—

So he, that doth redeem her thence, might wear,
Without corrival, all her dignities:

Without corrival! For all his dazzling gallantry his conception of honour is at heart egotistical—or at best it is a romantic survival from the age of the tournament into the more realistic Renaissance world.

As a foil to Hotspur stands Bussy d'Ambois, the French soldier of fortune in Chapman's play called after him. They have in common a reckless gallantry and a passion for flamboyant utterance. The exploit in which Bussy with two of his friends has an encounter with three hostile courtiers and is the sole survivor of the fray would have been exactly to the Percy's liking. But there is a coarser, more purely self-seeking strain in Bussy than in Hotspur. His very first words might be intended as a mocking comment on Percy's idolatry of honour:

Fortune, not Reason, rules the state of things,
Reward goes backward, Honour on his head.

Cast in similar mould to Bussy is another of Chapman's protagonists, the Duke of Byron, as described by a courtier:

he is a man
Of matchless valour, and was ever happy
In all encounters, which were still made good

With an unwearied sense of any toil,
Having continued fourteen days together
Upon his horse.

Intoxicated by victory he turns traitor to his sovereign, Henry
IV of France, and playing for the highest stakes loses all. Like the
Duke of Guise in Marlowe's *Massacre at Paris*, he has sought in
vain to scale the 'high pyramides' to find thereon the diadem of
France.

But the ambitions of a Byron or a Guise grow pale beside the
totalitarian aspirations of Marlowe's Scythian conqueror, Tamburlaine, who achieves his aim of being—

a terror to the world.
Measuring the limits of his empery
By east and west, as Phoebus doth his course.

For the most attractive pictures in Elizabethan drama of soldiers
of the highest ranks we must go to Beaumont and Fletcher.
Themselves men of good social standing they may have had more
opportunities than some of their fellow-playwrights of coming
into contact with them. I have already dealt with the curious
figure of Captain Poenius in Fletcher's *Bonduca* whose mutiny is
forgiven by his general Suetonius, magnanimous both to his
Roman subordinates and his British foes. He has a worthy counterpart in the British general Caratach, who rebukes his queen and
sister-in-law, Bonduca, for charging the Romans who have been
twice defeated with cowardice. He might be speaking our own
convictions in the world wars in his answer to the question:
'Is not peace the end of arms?'

Not where the cause implies a general conquest.
Had we a difference with some petty isle,
Or with our neighbours, lady, for our landmarks. . . . .
After a day of blood, peace might be argued,
But where we grapple for the ground we live on,
The liberty we hold as dear as life,
The gods we worship and, next those, our honours,
And with these swords that know no end of battle,
Those men beside themselves allow no neighbour, ...

And where they march but measure out more ground
To add to Rome, and here i' the bowels on us;
It must not be.

The magnanimity shown by the two generals in *Bonduca* is
stretched almost to the limit of the incredible by Archas, the hero
of Fletcher's *The Loyal Subject*. The new young Duke of Muscovy
owes a spite against this aged general who in his father's reign
had been called upon to chide him for a display of incompetence
as an officer. With bitter words he discharges him from his service,
banishes him to his country house, and appoints the evil-hearted
Borosky in his place. But at the news of a Tartar invasion Borosky
feigns illness and the Duke has to recall Archas, whom the soldiers
demand as their leader. But when he has won the day the Duke
shows himself ungrateful and bids him to return to his country
house. Yet once again he summons him to the court to a banquet
where he is treacherously seized and put in the hands of Borosky,
who carries out what the Duke had intended to be merely a
threat, and subjects Archas to the torture of the rack on the hypo-
critical charge that he has committed sacrilege by using again the
arms that on his retirement he had dedicated on the altar. In vain
is the old general's indignant cry (IV. v. 138 ff.):

I confess I took 'em,
The vow not yet absolved I hung 'em up with;
Wore 'em, fought in 'em, gilded 'em again
In the fierce Tartars' blood, for you I took 'em,
For your peculiar safety, lord, for all;
I wore 'em for my country's health, that groan'd then;
Took from the temple, to preserve the temple.

Enraged by the ill-treatment of their general, the soldiers
mutiny and, headed by his son, Colonel Theodore, they threaten
to burn down the palace and afterwards to desert to the Tartars.
It is only the voice of Archas himself after his release from torture
that can appease the rebels and bring about a general reconcilia-
tion.

Such a picture of loyalty, extravagant in its self-renunciation,
could, I think, have been drawn only when under the influence

of the Stuart doctrine of the divine right of kings. *The Maid's Tragedy* by Beaumont and Fletcher shows more explicitly how potent that doctrine was and yet that in the eyes of another loyal subject it had its limit. The King of Rhodes has forced Amintor into a marriage that is to be only one in name, with Evadne, who is his mistress. On their wedding night she tells him the secret, and he feels paralysed (III. i):

> In that sacred word
> 'The King' there lies a terror: what frail man
> Dares lift his hand against it?

And to the King himself he afterwards avows (III. i):

> there is
> Divinity about you that strikes dead
> My rising passions.

But to the soldier-brother of Evadne, Melantius, even a royal adulterer is not sacrosanct. His rank is never mentioned, but he is evidently a victorious leader in many campaigns. These are the thanks for his services. The family honour must be avenged and at the bidding of Melantius, Evadne herself stabs her paramour to death. It is not surprising that in the reign of Charles II the Lord Chamberlain prohibited the performance of what had been a very popular play.

It was in this 'good King Charles's golden days' that, except for Cromwell's 'New Model', the standing army first came into existence in England. There were then established or put on a new footing the Coldstream, Grenadier and Life Guards, the Blues, two regiments of Dragoons, one of them the Scots Greys, and four regiments of infantry, among them the Royals and the Buffs. It was not till 1740 that Lieutenant Edmonds' regiment, the 42nd Highlanders, called the Black Watch from its dark tartan, came into regular being.

But neither in the Restoration heroic tragedy, with its fantastic ideals of love and honour, nor in the artificial comedy of manners shall we find reflections of the contemporary new military types. In the early eighteenth century, however, there arose a more naturalistic type of comedy, and in some of the plays of Richard Steele and George Farquhar, who had both held commissions, we are introduced to representatives of the standing army of their period. In Steele's play, *The Funeral*, or *Grief à-la-Mode* (1701), Lord Hardy and his friend Campley are captain and ensign in a regiment of Guards which had taken part in the Battle of Steenkirk, August 1692, where the regiment had suffered severe loss. Hardy is reviewing a number of recruits with odd names 'Alexander Cowitch, Humphrey Mundungus, William Faggot, Nicholas Scab, Timothy Megrim, Philip Scratch, Nehemiah Dust, Humphrey Garbage, Nathaniel Matchlock'. They recall Falstaff's ragged regiment, but they include some old soldiers, who are re-enlisting. Matchlock had saved his captain's life at Steenkirk, but this had profited him little. Ensign Campley asks him:

> How far out of the country did you come to 'list? Don't you come from Cornwall? How did you bear your charges?
> *Match.*: I was whipped from constable to constable.
> *Cam.*:   But what pretence had they for using you so ill? You did not pilfer.
> *Match.*: I was found guilty of being poor.

Well may Hardy give him money and bestow upon him a sergeant's halberd. He then turns to another old soldier, Timothy Ragg:

> I thought when I gave you your discharge, just afore the peace (of Ryswick, 1697), we should never have had you again. How came you to enlist now?
> *Ragg:*   To pull down the French King.
> *Lord Hardy:* Bravely resolved! But pull your shirt into your breeches in the meantime.

And so Hardy good-humouredly deals with the rest, Tatter, Clump and Bumpkin.

A few months after the production of Steele's play the short peace was broken, and English troops under Marlborough set out for the Continent 'to pull down the French King'.

There is an echo of the War of the Spanish Succession in Farquhar's *The Recruiting Officer* (1706). The title part is that of Captain Plume of the Grenadiers who has just arrived in Shropshire from the 1704 campaign of Blenheim. His sergeant, Kite, has been enlisting two country bumpkins, who accept from him the Queen's shilling in the shape of the Carolus, a golden broad-piece, which they take to be merely a picture of Queen Anne. When they learn the truth they protest vigorously, but Plume cajoles them by promises of wealth and advancement to remain in the ranks. This pair are nominally volunteers, but there is a later scene, when men are being recruited under the impressment Acts which recalls how Falstaff misuses the King's press damnably.

The Acts are being administered by a bench of three justices, but it is Plume and Kite, corresponding to Sir John and Bardolph, who have the decisive word. When the bench are about to dis-charge a fellow who has a wife and five children, Plume inter-jects that 'the husband keeps a gun and kills all the hares and part-ridges within five mile round', whereupon one of the justices cries: 'A gun, nay, if he be so good at gunning, he shall have enough on 't.' Another of those brought before the bench is a collier who works in the coal-pits. One of the justices thereupon declares, 'This fellow has a trade and the Act of Parliament here expresses that we are to impress no man that has any visible means of livelihood.' But Kite is equal to the occasion: 'May it please your worships, this man has no visible means of livelihood, for he works underground.'

Though Plume has a clever tongue and wins the hand of an heiress he is a disreputable rake who does little credit to his office. Yet he shines beside his colleague, Captain Brazen, who by his boasts of imaginary exploits in love and war carries on the role of the braggart soldier.

Seventy years later, in Sheridan's *The Rivals* (1775), Captain Absolute had also come to Bath to recruit, according to the testi-mony of his servant, Fag, but whether for 'men, money, or constitution' mattered to no one. And we might almost think that Fag was drawing on Shakespeare or Farquhar rather than his own imagination when he declares that his master has enlisted five disabled chair-men, seven minority waiters and thirteen billiard-markers. But Jack Absolute, though he has a commission in a marching regiment and an allowance from his father of fifty pounds a year besides his pay, is, as far as we see in the play, a carpet-knight. His only military manoeuvre is to pose as Ensign Beverley, in a lower rank than his own, to win the hand of a romantic heiress who is bent on marrying a poor suitor. But he shines by comparison with the countrified militiaman, Bob Acres, an eighteenth century variant of the braggart soldier. And Captain Absolute and his friends are representatives of a more elegant and fastidious society than Farquhar's Captain Plume and his associates.

For nearly a century after the Sheridan and Goldsmith era English drama suffered a long period of decline. As our document, therefore, for the soldier of the Napoleonic war years I will not take a contemporary play, but Thomas Hardy's epic-drama *The Dynasts*, which justly claims 'a tolerable fidelity to the facts of its date'. In a few of the episodes relating to the English army we find under changed conditions features recurring similar to those made familiar in Elizabethan and eighteenth century drama. In Part I, Act I, iii, the recruiting problem is again urgent, and early in 1805 Sheridan, not as a playwright but as a parliamentarian, with Fox, Windham and others, is attacking in the House of Commons an Act for the Defence of the Realm passed by Pitt's government, which one of its opponents describes as an Act—

> that studies to create
> A standing army, large and permanent;
> Which kind of force has ever been beheld
> With jealous-eyed disfavour in this House.

Falstaff's ragged regiment and Captain Plume's rustic recruits have a descendant in Private Cantle of the Wessex Locals, the whole eighty of whose company ran away, 'though we be the bravest of the brave in natural jeopardies', when they heard that Boney 'lives upon human flesh, and has rashers of baby every morning for breakfast' (Part I. II. v). But like the men who fought at Agincourt, the Private Cantles when led and disciplined can do great deeds.

In Part II. III. i, there enter some three hundred of the Forty-third Regiment on their way to Coruña, 'about half of whom are crippled invalids, the other half being presentable and armed soldiery'. They are rallied by a sergeant who, though wasting away from a hacking cough, gives the command:

'Now, show yer nerve and be men. If you die to-day, you won't have to die to-morrow. Fall in! All invalids and men without arms march ahead as well as they can. Quick—mar-r-r-ch (*exeunt* invalids, etc.). Now! 'Tention! Shoulder-r-r-r firelocks!'

At the order they seem preternaturally changed into alert soldiers, and march on to take part in the battle where Sir John Moore meets his heroic end.

Then pass from the Peninsula to the final scenes in and near Brussels in July, 1814. Might not the Captain Absolute of a later generation be the young officer who has lost a dance with his partner at the Duchess of Richmond's ball before setting out for Quatre-Bras, and might not Miss Lydia Languish be that partner who on the following morning after seeing him go by doesn't care about having a view of the Duke of Wellington: 'I don't want to see him. I don't want to see anything any more!'

But unlike the young lady we do want to see him as he rides along the field of Waterloo in the crisis of the battle, with a shell bursting near him, and General Hill warning him:

> I strongly feel you stand too much exposed.
> *Well.:* I know, I know. It matters not one damn!
> I may as well be shot as not perceive
> What ills are raging here.
> *Hill:* . . . what commands
> Have you to leave me, should fate shape it so?
> *Well.:* These simply: to hold out unto the last,
> As long as a man stands on one lame leg
> With one ball in his pouch!—Then end as I.

Then he turns to some of the men near him:

> At Talavera, Salamanca, boys,
> And at Vitoria we saw smoke together:
> And though the day seems wearing doubtfully,
> Beaten we must not be: What would they say
> Of us at home, if so?

From Waterloo turn to the Crimea, where T. W. Robertson

lays the scene of Act III of his play, *Ours*. In this indefinite way he designates the regiment to which most of the male characters belong. Robertson made his fame in 1865 as a theatrical realist with *Society*, followed by *Ours* (1866), and by *Caste* (1867). But there is not much realism in *Ours* except in the episode of an officer who has a leg wound acting as cook and roasting the mutton for the mess. And though ladies were in their place at the Duchess of Richmond's ball before Waterloo, we are not prepared for their arriving, a trio of them, in the officers' hut of Ours in the Crimea. Well may a sergeant, who enters with an order book, express surprise, as the stage direction has it, at seeing ladies. And he is to be no less surprised by their questions:

> *Blanche:*   Has the regiment far to go?
> *Sergeant:*   Ours, mum?
> *Blanche:*   Yes.
> *Sergeant:*   We're going to the front into . . .

But before he can add 'action', the wounded officer interjects 'to parade'. And to relieve them from all anxiety he adds later, 'They never do get killed in Ours.' Nor does anyone get killed in the play. Yet the honour of the British Army is preserved in other ways. The Captain of Ours gains possession of a Russian 'colour', and shows himself worthy of the hand of an heiress previously wooed by a Russian prince, and the Colonel proves himself under severe domestic provocation a true officer and gentleman.

This may also be said of George D'Alroy and Captain Hawtree in *Caste*, but the fact that they are soldiers is only incidental to the main theme of the play, more challenging then than now, that character can defy social barriers.

The Balkans are not far removed, as the crow flies, from the Crimea, and there is only a generation between 1866, the date of *Ours*, and 1894, that of George Bernard Shaw's *Arms and the Man*. But into what a different world we are transported. Mr. Shaw's aim was to strip away the false romance attaching to the Stage-soldier. He shows on the one hand the veteran professional Captain Bluntschli confessing that his nerves go to pieces after three days under fire, climbing up a water pipe to escape his pursuers, and finding chocolate more useful on the field of battle than cartridges. As a foil to the chocolate-cream soldier there is the Don Quixote Saranoff, leading a cavalry charge against machine guns, which would have meant suicide for him and his men had not the wrong cartridges been sent for the guns. He thus becomes a hero by winning a battle the wrong way.

Thus twenty years before the outbreak of the world-conflagration in 1914 Mr. Shaw had made a characteristic assault upon the romance of war. And the strange conditions of the four years' conflict, in which the individual soldier was dwarfed by novel mechanized forces and unprecedented mass-formations, intensified the 'debunking' attitude to the glorification of the military career. Outside the drama this is illustrated in the change of tone from Hardy's *Men that March Away*, written in August, 1914, to the bitter realism of the war-poems of Robert Nichols and Siegfried Sassoon composed in the later stages of the struggle. And a similar temper is displayed in the most successful play inspired by the four years' war, R. C. Sherriff's *Journey's End*, first presented in December, 1928. The scene is laid in a dug-out in the British trenches before St. Quentin, and the action of the play lasts from the evening of Monday 18th March 1918 till the following Thursday towards dawn. We soon learn that Bluntschli was not so far out in his rating of commissariat over cartridges. The officer who is handing over the dug-out to Osborne of the incoming company tells him that they had three 'Minnies' bang in the trench yesterday:

Osborne: Do much damage?
Hardy: Awful. A dug-out got blown up and came down in the men's tea. They were frightfully annoyed.
Osborne: I know. There's nothing worse than dirt in your tea.

Mason, the officer's cook, is all of a flurry because the tin of pineapple chunks that he got from the canteen has turned out to be apricots, which the Captain can't stand. And Trotter, another officer, can't stand soup without the pepper, which has been forgotten. 'War's bad enough *with* pepper, but war without pepper —it's—it's bloody awful.'

The principal figures are thus, so to speak, gastronomically introduced. They are representatives of the British unprofessional army called into being by the world-war. Osborne, the oldest and most level-headed of the group, is a schoolmaster and an athlete who had played 'Rugger' for England. Trotter is a typical Cockney who feels quite braced up in the trench when he hears a 'bloomin' little bird' singing: 'Sort of made me think about my garden of an evening—walking round in me slippers after supper, smokin' me pipe', and growing the hollyhock eight feet high of which he carries about a 'photer'.

The central and most complex character is Captain Stanhope, who had come out straight from school when he was eighteen and has now been in command of the company for a year. As Osborne tells, 'He's never had a rest. Other men come over here and go home again ill, and young Stanhope goes on sticking it, month in, month out.' He has paid the cost in shattered nerves and has taken to heavy drinking. So it is a shock to him to find that a young officer who has just come out to join the company is no other than Raleigh, his hero-worshipper at school and the brother of a girl with whom he is in love. Won't Raleigh see and tell her the idol is breaking before his eyes?

Yet through all Stanhope proves himself the born leader. Osborne, his senior in age, declares: 'There isn't a man to touch him as commander of men. . . . I love that fellow. I'd go to hell with him.' He shows his *flair* in his handling of Hibbert, who is shamming neuralgia to avoid going back into the trenches. By making him stand the test, to the last five seconds, of death from his captain's revolver, and then telling him that they all at times share his feelings, Stanhope gets Hibbert to be like the others who 'just go on sticking it because they know it's—it's the only thing a decent man can do'. And when Raleigh writes his only letter home before a bit of shell puts a stop to his soldiering for ever, it is not to give Dennis, as he still calls Stanhope, away, but to report what he has heard from a sergeant that 'he is the finest officer in the battalion, and the men simply love him. He hardly ever sleeps in the dug-out; he is always up in the front line with the men, cheering them on with jokes, and making them keen about things, like he did the kids at school.' Were not these words almost echoed in the official announcement of the award of the Military Cross to a captain in the Royal Warwickshire Regiment? 'He has high powers of leadership, particularly when on patrol, and is unruffled when under fire. He has set an excellent example throughout, has the complete confidence of his men.'

Is it not in 1918, and in 1940, the same spirit and the same relation between leader and men as in Shakespeare's play when Henry V, on the field of Agincourt before the day of battle breaks, wanders through the camp in disguise, jesting with a pair of privates and heartening them out of their despondent mood? And, indeed, as I have tried to recall some of these pictures of the soldier in British drama from the later sixteenth to the earlier twentieth century, I have been struck by the fundamental similarity that has persisted throughout all changes of period and conditions.

Whether before or after the establishment of standing regiments the British army has been essentially a citizen force. The Britisher, however adventurous and courageous, has never, as represented in drama, been fond of fighting for its own sake. A Hotspur is the exception that proves the rule. And I would suggest that neither Mr. Shaw nor any other modern playwright has exposed more devastatingly the meretricious element in martial glory than has Shakespeare in his portrayal of Harry Percy for ever chasing the will o' the wisp 'honour' till he meets his fate on Shrewsbury field at the hands of the seemingly madcap Prince of Wales. Yet Hotspur is a gallant gentleman, not to be classed with the braggart-soldiers who form an exotic group of alien literary origin.

The spirit in which the Englishman takes up arms has been the same from century to century. Feeble enlists under Falstaff, with the words: 'A man can die but once . . . . I'll ne'er bear a base mind—he that dies this year is quit for the next.' It is with similar words that the sergeant rallies his straggling company on the retreat to Coruña: 'Now show yer nerve and be men. If you die to-day you won't have to die to-morrow.' The London Jacobean train-bands left their shops of security and their counters of content to bear themselves in action like valiant men and freemen. They have their worthy descendant in the Cockney Trotter, who in the trenches never loses his cool nerve and his shrewd mother-wit.

A gallant fatalism, a sense of duty, a patriotism that has in it nothing flamboyant but is closely linked with prosaic home and

local ties—these have always been strong motives with the
English soldier. But as he appears in English drama, he is influenced most of all by the magnetic quality of his leaders. It is the
contagious example of King Henry at Agincourt that transforms
the outnumbered English troops into a victorious array. And the
other military protagonists whom we meet in Elizabethan plays,
whatever their presumed nationality, have all been drawn from
native models. The noble British Caratach, the magnanimous
Roman Suetonius, the devotedly loyal subject Archas, the scrupulously conscientious Colonal Ager, and Melantius acutely sensitive
to his family honour—all have the qualities of leaders of men. And
so throughout the centuries. Steele's Lord Hardy, addressing his
recruits as gentlemen soldiers and promising that if they do their
business nothing will be too good for them, is greeted with cries
of 'Bless your honour.' Farquhar's Captain Plume can soothe the
feelings of the bumpkins tricked into enlisting by his sergeant,
and win the declaration: 'Give me a shilling; I'll follow you to the
end of the world.'

So the British private follows his leader, wherever it may be—
Sir John Moore leading the Forty-second Regiment in person
before Coruña till a cannon-ball shatters his shoulder; Wellington
exposing himself to the bursting shells at Waterloo; the Colonel
of *Ours* in the Crimea, and Captain Stanhope in the trenches at
St. Quentin. There is no sound of heroics, nothing of 'the pride,
pomp and circumstance of glorious war'. But we hear the calm
voice of Wellington:

Beaten we must not be: what would they say
Of us at home, if so?

Or that of Stanhope in the more colloquial idiom of to-day:
'We must just go on sticking it because it's the only decent thing
a man can do.'

It was only after I had planned this survey that I came across
the statement by Sir John Fortescue that it is in Shakespeare's
pages that the military student must read the history of the
Elizabethan soldier. I have tried to show that this history is to be
traced not only in Shakespeare but in his dramatic contemporaries;
and that in some of his theatrical successors we can follow the

thread up to our own day. Will the second world war be mirrored in plays yet to be written? If so, modern conditions may help to throw the sailor and airman into bolder individual relief. But the British soldier of all ranks, from commanding officer to private, will continue, I believe, to play his part unchanged in essentials, as he has been shown to us in our play-books from the Tudor age till to-day. . . . The ink was scarcely dry on these last words when they had their immediate confirmation in the marvellous drama enacted on the beaches of Dunkirk.

NINE

AMERICAN SCENES, TUDOR TO GEORGIAN, IN THE ENGLISH LITERARY MIRROR

IT is a singular piece of good fortune that America makes its entry by name into the earliest phase of Tudor drama. Columbus in search, as he thought, of the fabled empire of Cathay landed in the Bahamas in October, 1492. In June, 1497, John Cabot, sailing from Bristol with letters patent from Henry VII, discovered the coast of Labrador. According to his own untrustworthy account, the Florentine Amerigo Vespucci had reached the mainland shortly before Cabot. Two of his later voyages in 1499 and 1501 are better authenticated and he succeeded in having the western continent named after him. The great Lorraine cartographer Martin Waldseemuller published in 1507 the first edition of his *Cosmographiea Introductio*, with an accompanying map and globe. He there stated that the newly found 'quarta orbis pars' had the right to be called America because Americus had first discovered it, and he so marked it on his map and globe. In the earlier part of 1517 the first entirely English band of 'venturers' set out on a voyage of discovery to the western lands, but a mutinous outbreak brought the enterprise to an ignominious close. Among the venturers was the printer and playwright, John Rastell, who, as Dr. A. W. Reed has shown, referred to this disastrous happening in his interlude *The Nature of the Four Elements* (1519). In the course of this didactic piece Experience gives Studious Desire a geographical lecture in which, as has recently been proved, Rastell follows Waldseemuller closely.[1] Thus Experience declares:

These new lands found lately
Been called America by cause only
Americus did first them find.

He follows Vespucci's account, included in Waldseemuller's

---

[1] See 'Sources of Rastell's "Four Elements" ', by Elizabeth M. Nugent, in *P.M.L.A.,* March 1942. The spelling in my quotations is modernized.

volume, of the conditions in which the inhabitants of these remote
districts live:

> Building nor house they have none at all,
> But woods, cots, and caves small;
> No marvel though it be so,
> For they use no manner of iron
> Neither in tool nor other weapon
> That should help them thereto.

How far these and other details are founded on observation it is
not possible to say, but they furnish a picture of the life of the
Western natives in its most primitive phase. For the rest Rastell
voices the sentiments of a patriotic Tudor Englishman:

> Oh, what a thing had been then
> If they that be Englishmen
> Might have been the first of all
> That there should have taken possession,
> And made first building and habitation,
> A memory perpetual!
> And also what an honourable thing,
> Both to the realm and to the King,
> To have had his dominion extending
> There into so far a ground,
> Which the noble King of late memory,
> The most wise prince, the seventh Henry,
> Caused first for to be found.

Here Rastell alludes indirectly to Cabot's expedition, but he makes
no mention of Columbus. He then strikes an evangelizing note:

> And what a great meritorious deed
> It were to have the people instructed
> To live more virtuously,
> And to learn to know of men the manner,
> And also to know God their Maker,
> Which as yet live all beastly,
> For they neither know God nor the Devil,
> Nor never heard tell of heaven or hell.

These two strains, the imperialist and the missionary, thus struck at the outset, were to be often repeated.

Rastell was the brother-in-law of Sir Thomas More, who in *Utopia*, first published in Latin at Louvain in 1516, makes it clear that he too had been influenced by Vespucci's narratives. More tells Peter Giles that the seaman Raphael Hythloday, who gave him the account of Utopia, had been a follower of the Florentine adventurer, to whose widespread reputation Sir Thomas bears emphatic witness: 'He joined himself in company with Amerike Vespuce, and in the iij last voyages of those iiij that be now in print and abroad in every man's hands, he continued still in his company, saving that in the last voyage he came not home again with him.' Hythloday had stayed behind and had travelled through many lands, including the strange country of Utopia, of which on his return he gives More the detailed description.

Then we pass over some sixty or more years till we come, in Richard Hakluyt's prose epic, *The Principal Navigations, Voyages, Traffics and Discoveries of the English Nation*, to the first accounts of the attempted colonization of the district that was to bear the name of Virginia in honour of the Queen. She had granted letters patent to Sir Walter Raleigh for the discovering and planting of new lands and he sent out an expedition in April, 1584, a report of which was made to Sir Walter by one of the captains, Arthur Barlow. He draws an idyllic picture of the land and of its people. There are 'many goodly woods full of deer, conies, hares and fowl, even in the midst of summer in incredible abundance'. In these woods are the highest and reddest cedars of the world, pines, cypresses, sassafras, and other trees. Grapes grow in such abundance that they climb towards the tops of high cedars. The king's brother came to meet them 'and made all signs of joy and welcome, striking on his head and his breast and afterwards on ours to show we were all one. . . . We were entertained with all love and kindness, and with as much bounty (after their manner) as they could possibly devise. We found the people most gentle, loving and faithful, void of all guile and treason and such as live after the manner of the golden age.'

Of the later expeditions to Virginia sent out by Raleigh in 1585, 1586, and 1587 the most notable report is that by the famous mathematician Thomas Harriot, 'servant' to Sir Walter and friend of Marlowe. His account, as might be expected, is of a more realistic and practical type than Barlow's, dealing in turn with 'merchantable commodities', 'commodities for the sustenance of man's life', and 'commodities for building and other necessary uses'. The most signal item is the first mention by an Englishman of a herb which is called by the inhabitants 'Uppowoc' and by the Spaniards 'Tabacco'.

> The leaves thereof being dried and brought into powder, they use to take the fume or smoke thereof, by sucking it through pipes made of clay, into their stomach and head . . . whereby their bodies are notably preserved in health, and know not many grievous diseases, wherewithal we in England are often times afflicted. This Uppowoc is of so precious estimation amongst them that they think their gods are marvellously delighted therewith; whereupon sometime they make hallowed fires and cast some of the powder therein for sacrifice.

The reports by the voyagers fired the imagination of contemporary poets. Spenser doubtless heard of them first-hand from Raleigh when they met at Kilcolman. In justifying to sceptics the existence of his land of 'faerie' he cites the many great regions lately discovered.

> Who ever heard of the Indian Peru?
> Or who in venturous vessel measured
> The Amazon huge river now found true?
> Or fruitfullest Virginia who did ever view?

Without a knowledge of Barlow's and Harriot's reports one cannot appreciate the full significance of Spenser's choice of the epithet 'fruitfullest'. More explicit and detailed are Drayton's allusions in his ode *To the Virginian Voyage*, published in 1605. In the last stanza he apostrophizes 'industrious Hackluit', the reading of whose voyages will inflame men to seek fame. In words that directly echo Barlow's report Drayton urges his countrymen to hold

> Earth's only paradise, VIRGINIA,
> Where Nature hath in store

Fowl, venison and fish,
    And the fruitfull'st soil,
    Without your toil,
Three harvests more
All greater than your wish.
And the ambitious vine
Crowns with his purple mass
    The cedar reaching high
    To kiss the sky,
The cypress, pine,
And useful sassafras.

After bidding the voyagers bring forth heroes in those far regions
and plant the English name Drayton gives his outlook an ingenious turn:

And as there plenty grows
Of laurel everywhere,
    Apollo's sacred tree,
    You may it see
A poet's brows
To crown, that may sing there.

This conception of the newly discovered regions as a future
home not only of English statesmanship and piety but of English
song and eloquence finds fuller and more striking utterance
through the lips of Samuel Daniel. Had he been reading the
recently published final edition of Hakluyt's *Voyages* just before
he wrote his poetic dialogue *Musophilus* (1599), between a courtier
and a man of letters? The latter upholds 'heavenly eloquence' as
the 'pow'r above pow'rs', and makes an impassioned plea to his
countrymen to realize the full value of their precious possession
of their native speech. But even more pertinent to our subject
is the prophetic stanza:

And who (in time) knows whither we may vent
The treasure of our tongue? To what strange shores
This gain of our best glory shall be sent,
T' enrich unknowing nations with our stores?
What worlds in th' yet unformed occident
May come refin'd with th' accents that are ours?

What is specially striking here is Daniel's use of the word 'occi-dent', and his vision of a great sphere for English speech in the West, for the idea still lingered that voyages to America had the East Indies as their ultimate bourne.

When we turn to the dramatists there is, I think, more of a problem. Sir Walter Raleigh the second, the Oxford Professor, has said that 'without the voyagers Marlowe is inconceivable. His imagination is wholly preoccupied with the new marvels of the world and his heart possessed by the new-found lust of power'.[1] With all respect to the twentieth-century bearer of a great name I query this description. It was with the marvels of classical antiquity rather than those of the new world that Mar-lowe's imagination was primarily 'preoccupied'. If Tamburlaine dies gazing upon a map and bidding his sons conquer the lands outside of his triumphant grasp, it is the map of the continental cosmographer Ortelius which is his inspiration. It was not till a year after the Second Part of *Tamburlaine* that Hakluyt's first edition of *The Principal Navigations* was published, in 1589. In his later association with Harriot and Raleigh Marlowe must have heard details at first hand of their overseas enterprises. But he never mentions Virginia by name, though Faustus may have it in mind when he declares that he will order his attendant spirits to

Search all corners of the new-found world
For pleasant fruits and princely delicates.

Nor does Shakespeare mention Virgina, though he brings us closer to it than Marlowe. As readers of *The Tempest* know, the opening scene of the play was suggested by the shipwreck, in 1609, on the Bermudas of the ship, the *Sea-Venture*, in which Sir George Somers, Deputy Governor, was sailing to the colony now at last firmly settled. An account of the catastrophe by Sylvester Jour-dain, one of the ship's company, was published in 1610, entitled *The Discovery of the Barmudas, otherwise called the Ile of Divels*. The reference in the play to the 'still-vexed' or tempestuous 'Ber-moothes', and Stephano's exclamation, on the first sight of Cali-ban, 'Have we devils here?' are echoes of Jourdain's tract. Caliban

---

[1] Richard Hakluyt's *The Principal Navigations*, vol. xii, p. 104 (1905).

can scarcely be other than an anagram of cannibal, and his dam's god Setebos is a deity of Patagonian origin. But I fell less confident than many that in the relations of the servant-monster with Prospero, and afterwards with the drunken sailors, Shakespeare was depicting the effects of the contact between the primitive savage and higher and lower types of civilization. Perhaps we read more than was intended into what was and is primarily 'good theatre'.

Among the company in the *Sea-Venture* was John Strachey, who had been appointed secretary to the colony of Virginia. During the period of nine months when the whole company was supposed to be lost, John Donne made an application to be preferred to the supposed vacant post in February 1610. The news of the preservation of Somers and his associates which reached England four months later disappointed Donne's hopes. Had they been realized, Drayton's vision of Virginia as a fruitful poetic ground might have been fulfilled in unexpected wise.

The first mention of Virginia by name in a play is in *Eastward Hoe* by Chapman, Jonson, and Marston (1605). The needy knight, Sir Petronel Flash, is seeking to mend his fortunes by sailing thither, and one of his associates, Captain Seagull, describes the country in glowing phrases which lay less stress on its natural beauties, as Barlow and Drayton had done, than on its (largely imaginary) wealth in precious metals and in succulent viands.

> Gold is more plentiful there than copper is with us . . . all the chains with which they chain up their streets are pure gold; all the prisoners they take are fettered in gold: and for rubies and diamonds, they go forth on holidays and gather 'hem by the sea-shore, to hang on their children's coats, and stick in their caps . . . [it is] temperate and full of all sorts of excellent viands; wild boar is as common there as our tamest bacon is here: venison as mutton.

There is reason for believing that the scenes in *Eastward Hoe* dealing with the projected voyage to Virginia, which ends disastrously with a shipwreck in the Thames, are from the pen of Chapman. In any case he was associated with Inigo Jones in devising *The Mask of the Middle Temple and Lincoln's Inn* presented by members of the two Inns on 15th February 1613 in honour of the marriage of Princess Elizabeth and the Elector Palatine. Here Virginian princes are introduced who have crossed 'the Britain ocean'

> To do due homage to the sacred nupitals
> Of Love and Beauty, celebrated here.

They are followed by the Virginian priests of the Sun who salute their deity as he sets with hymns. Thereupon Eunomia, representing truly civilized order, cries:

> Virginian princes, you must now renounce
> Your superstitious worship of these Suns,
> Subject to cloudy darkenings and descents,
> And of your fit devotions turn the event
> To this our British Phoebus, whose bright sky
> (Enlighten'd with a Christian piety)
> Is never subject to black error's night,
> And hath already offer'd heaven's true light
> To your dark region.

Of all the inducements that have been offered to forsake paganism for true religion none can have been stranger than this presentation of James I in the role of the British Phoebus, the earthly representative of the Godhead.

In contrast with such home-bred fancies is the informative account based on long and varied personal experience by Captain John Smith in *The General History of Virginia, Summer Isles and New England* (1624). After a romantic career in southern and eastern Europe Smith became the leading spirit in the expedition which at last in 1606–8 established a settled colony in Virginia. Later in 1614 he explored the coastline of the territory to the north to which he first gave the name of New England. In his *General History* Smith reports in detail on the natural characteristics of Virginia and on the manners, occupations, and religious beliefs of the natives, whose chief god is the devil. Though he notes the climatic variations, he is as enthusiastic as his predecessors about its attractions. In an eloquent flight he presents it as 'a nurse for soldiers, a practice for mariners, a trade for merchants, a reward for the good, and that which is most of all a business (most acceptable to God) to bring such poor infidels to the knowledge of God and his gospel'. Thus the evengelizing note first sounded by Rastell is again predominant.

In the fifth book of the *History* Smith describes the Bermudas and pictures vividly the astonishment of the company of the *Sea-Venture* when they landed in a region which was 'to all sea-men no less terrible than an enchanted den of Furies and Devils, the most dangerous, unfortunate, and forlorn place in the world, but they found it the richest, healthfulest and pleasantest they ever saw'. Instead of a succession of seasons 'there seems to be a continual Spring . . . there is no one day throughout the 12 months but that in some hour thereof the sun looks singularly and clear upon them; for the temperature it is beyond all others admirable'. It is a caprice of nomenclature that in tribute to Sir George Somers the land of perpetual Spring should have been called *The Summer Islands,* as in Edmund Waller's poem published in 1645 celebrating a battle between the settlers and two stranded whales. There are clear echoes of Smith's phrases in the lines:

> For the kind Spring which but salutes us here
> Inhabits there, and courts them all the year.
> Ripe fruits and blossoms on the same trees live:
> At once they promise what at once they give.
> So sweet the air, so moderate the clime,
> None sickly lives or dies before his time.

More distinctively Waller's own is the epigrammatic touch in:

> Tobacco is the worst of things which they
> To English landlords, as their tribute, pay.
> Such is the mould that the bless'd tenant feeds
> On precious fruits, and pays his rent in weeds.

Andrew Marvell had certainly read Waller's poem when in his verses on the Bermudas he makes the singers in an English boat speak of 'the huge sea-monsters', and thank God for

> this eternal Spring,
> Which here enamels everything.

But Marvell had also received first-hand reports about the Bermudas when lodging at Eton in 1653 with John Oxenbridge, a Fellow of the College, who had previously been a tutor of Magdalen Hall, Oxford, till dispossessed by Laud in 1634. He had then voyaged twice to the Bermudas but had returned in 1641. It was of him and similar refugees from religious persecution that Marvell was thinking in the lines:

> He lands us on a grassy stage,
> Safe from the storms, and prelate's rage.
> He cast (of which we rather boast)
> The Gospel's pearl upon our coast,
> And in these rocks for us did frame
> A temple where to sound his name.

A traveller of a very different type soon afterwards was the girl, later to be known as Mrs. Aphra Behn, who voyaged to the West Indies and to the neighbouring town of Surinam, then in English possession but after the Restoration to become part of Dutch Guiana. Surinam lies just outside the territorial confines of my survey, but in her novel, *Oroonoko* (1688), Mrs. Behn gives, as far as I know, the first picture (if she is to be believed) from personal observation of an aspect of colonial life far removed from the idyllic presentations of the early voyagers and the poets. We are introduced to the life of the plantations where the negro slaves rise in revolt against their tyrannical masters. Their leader is the African prince, Oroonoko, who had been trapped and sold into slavery where he meets again his lovely bride, Imoinda, sharer of the same fate. Mrs. Behn purports to tell their story from first-hand knowledge, culminating in Imoinda's death at her husband's hand and his own stoical fortitude amid tortures at the stake. Whatever element of fact there may be in the narrative, Oroonoko and Imoinda are idealized portraits of the 'noble savage' contrasted with the debased representatives of civilization. The novel at once became popular and was the source of Thomas Southerne's play, similarly named, which when revived at the Malvern Theatrical Festival in the 1930's proved still to have a moving power.

With the native Indians, as distinguished from the negroes,

Mrs. Behn describes the planters as living on the friendliest terms, and she pictures them as unspoilt children of nature. 'These people represented to me an absolute idea of the first state of innocence before man knew how to sin.' More than a trace of this idealizing vein enters, whether seriously meant or not, into Steele and Addison's references to a visit to London in the spring of 1710 of four Iroquois chiefs, known as the Emperor of the Mohocks and three Indian kings. They were received in audience by Queen Anne on 19th April and were afterwards entertained by leading dignitaries before leaving this country on 8th May. Three days later in No. 171 of the *Tatler* Steele dilated upon their lofty behaviour towards their landlord, an upholsterer, probably the father of Thomas Arne, the muscian:

> These just and generous princes, who act according to the dictates of natural justice, thought it proper to confer some dignity upon their landlord before they left the house. One of them had been sick during his residence there, and having never before been in a bed, had a very great veneration for him who made that engine of repose so useful and so necessary in his distress. It was consulted among the four princes by what name to dignify his great merits and services.

They thereupon decided to call him 'Caradoque, which is the name of the strongest fort in their part of the world', and sending for him each of them in turn took him by the hand and saluted him by this name. How the worthy upholsterer received this singular form of recompense is not recorded.

Nearly a year later, in No. 50 of the *Spectator*, 27th April 1711, Addison, declaring that he had followed the Indian kings during their visit 'a whole day together', published an abstract of a journal which he pretends one of them had written and left behind by mistake. In this he represents how various features of English religious, political, and social life would strike a child of nature. It anticipates on a slighter scale Goldsmith's method in *The Citizen of the World*.

Steele and Addison were here almost as far divorced from reality as Chapman with his Virginian kings and priests in the 1613 Inns of Court *Mask*. Very different was to be the case, some twenty years later, of George Berkeley. The idealist philosopher had in 1722, according to his own account, determined to pass the rest of his days in Bermuda. Probably the descriptions by Waller and Marvell had led him to conceive of the islands as an earthly paradise. But it was not this fair prospect that mainly lured him on. It was the evangelizing zeal which since Rastell's first reference to America had been so dominant a note. And this with Berkeley had a double object:

> The reformation of manners among the English in our Western plantations, and the propagation of the Gospel among the American savages, are two points of high moment. The natural way of doing this is by founding a college or seminary in some convenient part of the West Indies, where the English youth of our plantations may be educated in such sort as to supply their churches with pastors of good morals and good learning —a thing (God knows) much wanted. In the same seminary a number of young American savages may also be educated till they have taken the degree of Master of Arts.

In September 1728 he set sail, with the promise of a parliamentary grant of £20,000 for the establishment of the college which Walpole was determined to frustrate.

In January 1729 he arrived at Newport in Rhode Island and in that colony he remained three years. The vision of the Bermuda College gradually faded, but it was on Rhode Island that Berkeley wrote the most attractive of his works, the seven dialogues entitled *Alciphron*. With their philosophic significance we are not now concerned. But in their setting they bear marks of the neighbourhood in which they were composed. Thus at the beginning of the second dialogue 'we went down to a beach about half a mile off; where we walked on the smooth sand, with the ocean on one hand, and on the other wild broken rocks intermixed with shady trees and springs of water, till the sun began to be weary'. And the opening of the fifth dialogue is delayed by the incursion of half a dozen fox-hunting country squires, who after the fashion of their English prototypes 'passed the afternoon in a loud rustic mirth, gave proof of their religion and loyalty by the healths they drank, talked of hounds and horses, elections and country fairs'.

With Berkeley a prolonged phase of the American scene in English eyes comes to a close. Henceforward the native Indians in their state of nature and their atmosphere of perpetual spring pass into the background. And the evangelizing note which had been dominant since it had been first sounded by Rastell two centuries ago became muted in an age which frowned upon 'enthusiasm'. Political and commercial causes of friction were rapidly coming to the forefront between the home government and the colonies. When George III came to the throne they numbered thirteen. In the south to Virginia there had been added the two Carolinas and Georgia; in the north New England included Massachusetts, Rhode Island, Connecticut, and New Hampshire; between lay the middle States, New York, Pennsylvania, New Jersey, Delaware, and Maryland.

The rights and wrongs of the measures that led to the Revolutionary War and to the Declaration of Independence on 4th July 1776 belong to the historian's province. My concern now is with their impact on our literature. Has there ever been a more striking and abrupt transition from the voyagers' narratives, the poems, plays, and romances, linked together almost like a chain, in which America had hitherto been reflected in this country, to the stately oratory and political philosophy of Burke and Chatham?

I am aware that some shadows have fallen over the figure of Burke. A distinguished member of The English Association, Sir Philip Magnus, has exhibited some of his financial transactions in a dubious light. An eminent man of letters, Mr. G. M. Young, lecturing on him as 'a master mind', made one wonder how far he could claim such a title. 'Who now reads Bolingbroke?' asked Burke. Will some future critic's question be, 'Who now reads Burke?' It is true, of course, also that the distinction between taxation of the colonies for revenue and the levying of commercial duties which was fundamental in his and Chatham's eyes has lost its significance to-day. But to me at any rate Burke's two speeches on America in their maxims of general and permanent application enshrine the quintessence of political wisdom.

If intemperately, unwisely, fatally you sophisticate and poison the very source of government, by urging subtle deductions

and consequences, odious to those you govern, from the un-
limited and illimitable nature of supreme sovereignty, you will
teach them by these means to call the sovereignty itself in
question. When you drive him hard, the boar will surely turn
upon the hunters.

My hold of the colonies is in the close affection which grows
from common names, from kindred blood, from similar privileges, and equal protection. These are ties which, though light
as air, are as strong as links of iron.

Do not dream that your letters of office, and your instructions,
and your suspending clauses, are the things that hold together
the great contexture of the mysterious whole. . . . It is the spirit
of the English Constitution which, infused through the mighty
mass, pervades, feeds, unites, invigorates, vivifies every part of
the empire, even down to the minutest member.

'The great contexture of the mysterious whole.' Those are the
keywords to Burke's conception of a State, an Empire, as a
spiritual, mystical body, not a mechanical conglomeration of its
individual units but an organic, vitalizing whole.

If there are any who distrust political philosophers they may give
more willing ear to the 'elder statesman', Lord Chatham. On
30th May 1777, moving an address to the Crown to stop hostilities
in America, he spoke in what now seems a prophetic strain, an
anticipation of General Eisenhower's role in the second world war:

You have been three years teaching them the art of war; they
are apt scholars, and I will venture to tell your Lordships that
the American gentry will make officers enough, fit to command
the troops of all the European powers. What you have sent
there are too many to make peace, too few to make war. If
you conquer them, what then? You cannot make them respect
you; you cannot make them wear your cloth; you will plant an
invincible hatred in their breasts against you.

Six months after this speech of Chatham the surrender of
General Burgoyne on 19th October at Saratoga was the turning-
point of the war, though it dragged on till the capitulation of

Lord Cornwallis at Yorktown on 19th October 1781.

In his play *The Devil's Disciple* Bernard Shaw has given a vivid apologetic delineation of Burgoyne, soldier and dramatist, with his 'fastidious delicacy of sentiment, his fine spirit and humanity', contrasted with the eighteenth-century 'Colonel Blimp', Major Swindon, who asks Richard Dudgeon, posing as the Presbyterian minister, Anderson, 'Do you mean to deny that you are a rebel?'

Richard: I am an American, sir.

Swindon: What do you expect me to think of that speech, Mr. Anderson?

Richard: I never expect a soldier to think.

Burgoyne is boundlessly delighted by this speech, which almost reconciles him to the loss of America.

I heard this typically Shavian quip for the first time not in London but in New York, where the play was presented by the American Theatre Guild to an appreciative audience.

The ratification of the Federal Constitution in 1789 and the election of Washington as the first President were the prelude to that astonishingly rapid spread of the new republic to the west and to the south, by which the thirteen States were multiplied to forty-eight. But for half a century, though Washington Irving and Fenimore Cooper became popular on this side of the Atlantic, our own literature bore little direct impress of the American scene.

In 1794 Coleridge and Southey, with the two Fricker sisters to whom they were engaged, cherished for a time the visionary scheme of 'Pantisocracy', a settlement on the banks of the Susquehanna river in Pennsylvania, where their days were to be divided between labour to provide food and intellectual intercourse. It was a socialist dream, without anything of the missionary fervour which had inspired Berkeley's project of a Bermudas college. And frankly material were some of the motives which drew to the United States from the 1830's onwards the visiting men of letters to whom we mainly owe our Victorian pictures of American scenes.

When Captain Marryat left Liverpool for New York on 3rd April 1837, his professed, and in part true, object was to ascertain what might be the effects produced upon the English character and temperament by differences of climate, circumstances, and form of government. But he also hoped to further the establishment in the U.S.A. of international copyright, and he made literary capital out of his tour soon after his return to England by publishing in 1839 his *Diary in America* in two parts, each in three volumes. He began by stressing the fact that the Americans were not yet 'in the true sense of the word a nation. Not only are the populations of the various States distinct but those of the cities'. He shows keen if somewhat acid gifts of observation in distinguishing the characteristics of New York and Boston, Philadelphia and Washington. The descriptive passages of the *Diary*, as might be expected from the author of *Peter Simple* and *Midshipman Easy*, have verve and colour and even after a century of momentous changes are well worth reading. It is noteworthy that Marryat found the same difference in the attitude of the whites to the native Indians and the negroes that Mrs. Behn had recorded in *Oroonoko*. 'It is remarkable, that although the Americans treat the negro with contumely they have a respect for the red Indian: a well-educated half-bred Indian is not debarred from entering into Society, indeed they are generally received with great attention.' Marryat was astonished to find that the free negroes, however intelligent and well behaved, were even worse off in the northern and eastern than in the Slave States.

> They are deprived of their rights as citizens. . . . In fact in the United States, a negro, from his colour, and I believe his colour alone, is a degraded being. Is not this extraordinary, in a land which professes universal liberty, equality, and the rights of man? In England this is not the case. Nor indeed is it the case in the Slave States, where I have frequently seen a lady in a public conveyance with her negress sitting by her and no objection has been raised by the other parties in the coach; but in the Free States a man of colour is not admitted into a stage coach.

Such a passage cannot have found favour, especially in the New England States. But still greater resentment was aroused by some of Marryat's political observations. He acknowledged that democracy was the form of government *best suited to the present conditions of America,* but contrasted a democracy, the rule of 'the majority, who are as often wrong as right', with 'a republic ruled by the most enlightened and capable', and claimed that monarchical England was much more republican in her institutions than America.

And wounding to American susceptibilities in perhaps their tenderest spot was the mockery of his account of the New York celebrations on 4th July 1837 of the sixty-first anniversary of the Declaration of Independence. He represents it as a drunken saturnalia. 'There is something grand in the idea of a national intoxication. . . . A staggering individual is a laughable and sometimes, a disgusting spectacle; but the whole of a vast continent reeling, offering a holocaust of its brains for mercies vouchsafed, is an appropriate tribute of gratitude for the rights of equality and the *levelling spirit* of their institutions.'

On 3rd January 1842 a greater novelist than Marryat set sail for America and was enthusiastically welcomed. It was characteristic of Charles Dickens that soon after his arrival, at banquets held in his honour in Boston, Hartford, and New York, he inveighed with increasing bitterness against the abuses due to the lack of international copyright. Though his diatribes fanned rather than cooled the popular fervour concerning his visit, they led to outrageous attacks upon him, especially in disreputable newspapers, which help to account for the pungent and provocative tone of his *American Notes* published soon after his return to England on 1st July. It is true that Dickens in his concluding remarks stated that the Americans 'are by nature frank, brave, cordial, hospitable, and affectionate', but he added that these qualities are sadly sapped and blighted in their growth among the mass. He is eloquent on the charms of Cincinnati and Westpoint and rises to lyrical ecstasy over 'the tremendous spectacle' of Niagara. But he made mock of the sermons and lectures to which the ladies of Boston, the hub of American culture, flocked in crowds. 'The peculiar province of the Pulpit in New England . . . would appear to be the denouncement of all innocent and rational amusements. . . . With regard to the other means of excitement, the Lecture, it has at least the merit of being always new. One lecture treads so quickly on the heels of another, that none are remembered.'

In his description of New York he enlarges on the misery of the wretches confined in the Tombs prison. But this pales beside the harrowing picture of the horrors of lifelong solitary confinement in the Philadelphia Penitentiary. The Federal Capital Washington is introduced as 'the headquarters of tobacco-tinctured saliva'. Instead of the City of Magnificent Distances Dickens dubs it the City of Magnificent Intentions.

> Spacious avenues that begin in nothing and lead nowhere: streets mile-long that only want houses, roads and inhabitants; public buildings that need but a public to be complete; and ornaments of great thoroughfares, which only lack great thoroughfares to ornament—are the leading features. . . . Such as it is, it is likely to remain.

If only Dickens could revisit it to-day and see its thronged avenues and the sunlit beauty of its classic white marble buildings! During his stay in Washington he visited the two Houses of Congress almost every day, with the result that he drew up a virulent indictment of the members, especially of the Lower House, which was quite unjustifiable from his imperfect knowledge. No less unbalanced was his attack on the American 'licentious Press'. On the other hand it was all to the good that the humanitarian fervour of Dickens should be roused to white heat by the spectacle of the brutalities of negro slavery. In striking contrast is his picture of an Indian chief whom he met on a steamboat on the way to Louisville. Far from having an 'untutored mind' he spoke English perfectly well and was an enthusiast for Scott's poetry. He was, says Dickens, 'as stately and complete a gentleman of Nature's making as ever I beheld; and moved among the people in the boat, another kind of being'. Here once more in an unexpected connexion the noble savage reappears, and the emphasis on his superiority to his fellow passengers must have been an additional irritant to American readers of the *Notes*.

Nor was this all. Dickens went out of his way to introduce into his next novel, *Martin Chuzzlewit* (1840), a number of episodes based on all that he had seen or imagined of the worst sides of American life. In particular he sought to expose their vaunted 'moral sense' as merely a cloak for hypocrisy and double-dealing.

It is highly to the credit of what he himself called 'the national generosity and magnanimity' that on his second visit to the United States twenty-five years afterwards he received the warmest of welcomes. And on his part he publicly testified to the amazing changes, moral, physical, and social, that had taken place in the interval. The greatest of these, and the one that must have gone most deeply home to Dickens, was the abolition of slavery after the victory of the North in the Civil War early in 1865.

Meanwhile the other chief Victorian novelist had in 1853-4 and 1855-6 during two lecture-tours seen many both of the Free and Slave States during what were to be the last years of the old regime. When Thackeray as a sequel to his visits laid the scene of his next novel, *The Virginians*, for the most part in America, he was personally better advised than Dickens when he chose the Revolutionary period rather than the contemporary epoch as his background. And the fortunes of the descendants of Colonel Esmond and George Warrington will always be of interest, even though Thackeray's pen could not recapture the full brilliance of his greatest historical novel. But for our present purpose, which is concerned only with the results of first-hand contemporary observation, *The Virginians*, without disrespect to its author, may be left out of account.

G. S. Gordon has noted that these Victorian visitors failed to re-cognize America's 'vast and proper task, which was the taming of a continent'. I would add that they had also shown little appreci-ation of the great American achievement, in the sphere of govern-ment, by devising a novel form of constitution. It was static where the English was flexible; it separated rigidly the executive, legislative, and judicial functions; it reserved for the individual States all powers not specifically allocated to the Federal Govern-ment. Whatever its drawbacks it has proved equal to the task of bringing the vast territories between the Atlantic and the Pacific into a political unit and of commanding devoted allegiance. It is remarkable that the first Englishman, so far as I know, to re-cognize this explicitly was not a politician or a lawyer but a poet and man of letters—Matthew Arnold. Before visiting the States in 1885 Arnold had written what he called 'A Word about America'. To this he afterwards added 'A Word More', which contains the following candid admission:

> The more I saw of America, the more I found myself led to
> treat 'institutions' with increased respect. When I went to the
> United States I had never seen a people with institutions which
> seemed expressly and thoroughly suited to it. I had not properly
> appreciated the benefits proceeding from this cause. . . . As
> one watches the play of their institutions, the image suggests
> itself to one's mind of a man in a suit of clothes which fits him
> to perfection, leaving all his movements unimpeded and easy.
> It is loose where it ought to be loose, and it sits close where its
> sitting close is an advantage.

This passage seems to me of greater significance than the
criticism of various aspects of 'Civilization in the United States'
which followed in a later essay.

The institutions which had won the appreciation of Arnold were
a few years later, in 1888, to be analysed and expounded in detail
by James Bryce in his classic work, *The American Commonwealth*.
It is an inspiring thought that the man who in his younger days
had traced the growth and fall of the Holy Roman Empire should,
as the fruit of three visits to the United States, have been able to
bring his exceptional historical powers to the illumination of the
workings of the democratic scheme of government in the New
World.

If Rupert Brooke had read his Bryce before he visited the
United States in 1913, he could have stood up to the youth whom
he met on the liner, and who after telling him, 'You'll never
understand America', asked, 'Would you like to hear me recite
to you the Declaration of Independence?', and did. But the letters
which Brooke wrote from New York and Boston, before going
on to Canada, for publication in *The Westminster Gazette*, showed
little interest in American institutions. They are first-rate journal-
ism, hitting off American personal and social characteristics
somewhat after the fashion of Marryat's *Diary*, though with a
keener epigrammatic edge. Thus he observes that 'the American
by race walks better than we; more freely, with a taking swing
and almost with grace. How much of this is due to living in a
democracy, and how much to wearing no braces, it is very

difficult to determine.' He describes the 'drummers' or commercial travellers by whom he was fascinated in his hotel.

These people are for ever sending off and receiving telegrams, messages and cablegrams; they are continually telephoning; stenographers are in waiting to record their inspirations. In the intervals of activity they relapse into a curious trance, husbanding their vitality for the next crisis. . . . All day there are numbers of them sitting, immote and vacant, in rows and circles on the hard chairs in the hall. They are never smoking, never reading a paper, never even chewing. The expressions of their faces never change.

Brooke's insight goes deeper when he crosses the border into Canada, but there I cannot follow him now.

I return to New York, where in the autumn of 1935 I heard Mr. J. B. Priestley give a talk to a class of Columbia University students. He was on his way to the ranch in Arizona, last of the forty-eight States to be incorporated, where he spent some winters with his family and which forms the background to his remarkable work, *Midnight in the Desert* (1937). In it he presents views of an America older than was discovered by the Tudors and more modern than was visited by the Victorians. On the one hand, there is the remote, self-centred, artificial life of Hollywood:

In Europe when you have agreed to work in films, you merely take a certain route every morning from your own front door. But in America, you cross the continent and go to Hollywood. . . . Once there, after crossing mountains and deserts, you must get into films, stay in films, or perish. You are, as it were, wrecked on an island that does nothing but make films.

Contrast with this feverish existence the primeval, eternal realities of the Arizona country:

The New World! It seemed to me the oldest country I had ever seen, the real antique land, first cousin to the moon. Man had been here such a little time that his arrival had not yet been acknowledged. . . . There is no history here because history is too recent. This country is geology by day and astronomy at night. It offers a broad view of what is happening generally in the solar system, with no particular reference to Man.

Of all the marvels in the Arizona landscape it is the Grand Canyon, the chasm 280 miles long and in parts a mile deep, that rouses Mr. Priestley to an ecstasy that outdoes that of Dickens at Niagara.

It is not a show place, a beauty spot, but a revelation. . . . The Colorado River made it, but you feel when you are there that God gave the Colorado River its instructions. It is all Beethoven's nine symphonies in stone and magic light. . . . If I were an American, I should make my remembrance of it the final test of men, art and policies. I should ask myself: Is this good enough to exist in the same country as the Canyon?

The answer to that question is to-day being worked out in conditions which could not have been foreseen when the words were written. As Mr. Churchill said when receiving his honorary degree at Harvard on 6th September 1942, 'You cannot stop. . . . We have now reached a point in the journey where there can be no pause. We must go on.' I venture to think that in envisaging the future it is not without advantage and inspiration to look back, as we have been doing, upon the American scenes reflected in the English mirror through four centuries. In the earliest mention of the new-found lands in our literature Rastell's aspiration was for Henry VIII's dominion to be extended there. How this was realized under his successors, and in what glowing pages the epic process was chronicled, we have seen. Even in the discontents that arose between the mother country and the eighteenth-century colonies and their disastrous sequel English oratory found its most potent source. Then during periods of political alienation our Victorian novelists and essayists visited the States and drew material thence for their pens. In the last half-century, with closer social relations, there has been a more understanding interpretation by English visitors of what the Americans like to call their 'way of life'. Thus by that 'power of words' of which Daniel had sung England and America have remained linked across three thousand miles of ocean, and in despite of repeated excursions and alarums on the international stage. It was on this foundation that in another striking passage of his Harvard speech Mr. Churchill foresaw a renewal of political union after a different pattern from the single sovereignty, the only formula envisaged by Burke and Chatham. 'This gift of a common tongue is a priceless inheritance and it may well some day become the foundation of a common citizenship. I like to think of British and Americans moving about freely over each other's wide estates with hardly a sense of being foreigners to one another.'

This (as it may prove) prophetic utterance of the then British Prime Minister before the University of Emerson, Longfellow, and Lowell, and of which President Roosevelt was a graduate, may well serve to close this series of American scenes in the English literary mirror and keep us expectantly keyed up to watch for those to be reflected there in the days to come.